Bilingual Education of Children

NEWBURY HOUSE SERIES:

STUDIES IN BILINGUAL EDUCATION

*Sponsored
by
The International Center
for Research on Bilingualism
Laval University*

Published:

BILINGUAL EDUCATION IN A BINATIONAL SCHOOL
By W. F. MACKEY

THE LANGUAGE EDUCATION OF MINORITY CHILDREN:Selected Readings
BERNARD SPOLSKY, Editor

BILINGUAL EDUCATION OF CHILDREN: The St. Lambert Experiment
WALLACE E. LAMBERT and G. R. TUCKER

Forthcoming:

THE AMERICAN BILINGUAL TRADITION
HEINZ KLOSS

A SOCIOLINGUISTIC APPROACH TO BILINGUAL EDUCATION
ANDREW COHEN

ESSAYS ON BILINGUAL SCHOOLING IN THE UNITED STATES
A. BRUCE GAARDER

BILINGUALISM IN EARLY CHILDHOOD
(Conference on Child Language)
THEODORE ANDERSSON and W. F. MACKEY, Editors

Bilingual Education of Children

The St. Lambert Experiment

WALLACE E. LAMBERT
McGill University

G. RICHARD TUCKER
McGill University

NEWBURY HOUSE PUBLISHERS, INC.

NEWBURY HOUSE PUBLISHERS, INC.

Language Science
Language Teaching
Language Learning

68 Middle Road, Rowley, Massachusetts 01969

Library of Congress Card Number: 76-131121
ISBN: 912066-08-3

Cover arrangement: Holly Nichols

Printed in the U.S.A.   First printing: August, 1972

In memory of
George A. Moore

Acknowledgements

The long-term program of research represented in this book has been supported over a period of years by grants to W. E. Lambert and G. R. Tucker from the Canada Council, the Defence Research Board, and the Ministry of Education of the Province of Quebec, and to each of these institutions we express our gratitude. We are grateful also to administrators, principals, and teachers of the South Shore Protestant Regional School Board, the Municipalité Scolaire Catholique de St. Lambert, the Protestant School Board of Greater Montreal, and the Commission des Ecoles Catholiques de Montréal for their continual encouragement and assistance. We wish also to thank our colleagues—Alison d'Anglejan, Marcel Just, John Macnamara, Norman Segalowitz, Sidney Segalowitz, and Fred Silny—who collaborated with us during various phases of this study, and a large number of undergraduate and graduate students at McGill and the University of Montreal who conducted the interviewing and testing. See Lambert and Macnamara (1969), Lambert, Just, and Segalowitz (1970), Lambert, Tucker, d'Anglejan, and Segalowitz (1970), Tucker, Lambert, d'Anglejan, and Silny (1971), and Lambert, Tucker, d'Anglejan, Silny (1972).

We are grateful and indebted in many ways to the members of the St. Lambert Bilingual School Study Group, particularly Mrs. Olga Melikoff, Valerie Neale, and Murielle Parkes, who have befriended and helped us on numerous occasions during the past six years. Finally, we want to say "Thank you!" as warmly as we know how to the children in the experimental and control classes who, over the years, have become very special friends.

We dedicate this work to the memory of George A. Moore, a graduate student of ours who died in an accident in the summer of 1971. He was a very close friend of ours and a source of inspiration during this investigation not only because of his own extraordinary language-learning abilities, but also because of his wisdom and knowledge about the bilingual process that he so willingly shared with us.

Acknowledgments

Contents

Tables

Chapter One

Introduction

The research described in this book started about seven years ago when a group of parents asked themselves a simple but somewhat odd question: What would happen if children were to attend kindergarten and elementary school where a foreign or second language was used as the major medium of instruction? We will set aside for the time being the practical question of why anyone would want to try out such a scheme and the linguistic question of what languages would be involved, and concentrate first on the broader issue of how language affects thinking and learning, since this is the issue that takes priority whenever one discusses the idea.

The typical reactions of most North American, monolingual parents with whom we have discussed the idea run something like this: "How would that possibly work? A child wouldn't understand a word spoken to him. You don't mean you'd do this at age four or five when he's just getting his own language rolling, learning new words, and beginning to understand his parents and other children? Even if he got to follow a bit, he'd spend all his time just learning the new names for things. How would he ever learn anything in school other than the language? Anyway, he'd never get to know the language as well as youngsters who speak it naturally, and even if he developed some skill in that language, he could never think in it or become creative in it. What's more, he'd get hopelessly behind in his own language!"

When we put the same question to people from Central and Eastern Europe, from the Middle East, the Mediterranean area, and from Scandinavia, they, in sharp contrast, were neither surprised nor puzzled by the idea. Their point of view runs something like this: "Why not? Sounds like a good way to promote bilingualism. Many of us followed just such a program and now we can handle two and sometimes three languages equally well. It never bothered me or held me back in any way. Quite to the contrary."

Many immigrants to North America or to major European centers approach the idea with still another point of view: "That's what most of us have had to do. Why not? It's the best way to master the language of the new country and forget about the old one."

When we discussed the issue with those from developing nations where one of the more prestigious world languages has been imported, we find that either they see no problem in the scheme or they show a sensitivity to a totally different aspect, with a point of view that seems to be as follows: "They might learn the language all right, but maybe they'd learn it too well. The danger in the plan lies in a hidden form of linguistic colonialism. What would happen to the home language? Educators might never get back to it, and then the children run the risk of losing their own cultural roots."

In Switzerland, we frequently encountered another type of reaction: "Why switch languages? You'd be tampering with the child's allegiances as well as his thinking processes. Our system of cantons serves a quite different purpose—to assure members of each ethnolinguistic group the right to be educated in their own language."

These reactions reflect fundamentally different views of bilingualism, each one based on different degrees and types of experiences with more than one language. For someone who knows one language only, bilingualism or multilingualism may well seem like a mysterious, strange, and essentially foreign process. Because of his own limited linguistic experience, the monolingual person is prone to link language inseparably with both thinking and learning. He is more likely than a bilingual to wonder whether a person can really "think" equally well in two languages. Most bilinguals in fact are usually perplexed when asked which language they "think in." Generally they try to explain the phenomenon by saying that they listen and respond through one language or the other, but when required to concentrate on a problem, they have no clear notion of language playing an important role. Through their own experiences they are more likely than the monolingual to be aware of the symbolic nature of language and the arbitrariness of symbol-referent relationships. They also are more likely to separate language from thinking and from learning.

Others tend to link language with culture or with allegiances, and, in particular settings, with survival, achievement, and status. The fully bilingual and bicultural individual is well aware of these important relationships, but at the same time is able to adjust his language usage to social settings, thereby demonstrating that he belongs in more than one cultural or status category. Languages need not stigmatize or limit him in any way.

This book tells the story of a community-based Canadian project aimed at developing nativelike skills in a second language by having that language used as the main medium of instruction during the elementary school years. As we have already suggested, most monolingual parents in North America would consider this a radical and worrisome educational undertaking. Their worries would not likely be allayed by a reminder that this switch of home and school languages is the everyday experience of many North American children—for example, those from immigrant families attending public schools, and those from American Indian or Eskimo families who attend federally-sponsored schools. The trouble is that these youngsters are more likely than most to have a bleak future both academically and occupationally, and any attempt to explain their plight in terms of ethnic minority status or loss of cultural ties would not likely be all that reassuring for parents preoccupied with the welfare of their own young children.

What then prompted a group of Canadian parents to offer their children as guinea pigs? Although they had many reservations at the start, they were nonetheless concerned about the apparent ineffectiveness of current methods of teaching foreign languages, not only at the high school level, but also in the elementary schools where FLES (Foreign Languages in the Elementary Schools) programs and half-hearted attempts at bilingual training seemed to promise much more than was ever actually realized. They were impressed with recent educational research which showed what could be accomplished in teaching science and mathematics in the kindergarten and elementary grades, and they realized how valuable early experience with a foreign language can be, since in bilingual settings young children become bilingual as a matter of course when given the opportunity to interact regularly with those who speak the other language.

As residents of Quebec, they were also concerned that political movements were under way to make French the "working language" of the province, meaning that their children would likely encounter strong pressures to learn the language when they finished their schooling. In this sense, these representatives of Canada's majority group were looking a generation ahead with the hope that they could provide their children with a thorough mastery of the present minority group's language. But more than this, these parents and the school authorities who became involved in the project realized that, as residents of a bicultural and bilingual society, they are part of a much larger experiment in democratic coexistence that requires people of different cultures and languages to develop mutual understanding and respect. They believed that learning the other group's language fully was an essential first step.

The study had its start when a group of these parents from the community of St. Lambert, a suburb of Montreal, got in touch with several of us at McGill University who were interested in developing full-fledged bilingualism in the Quebec social setting. Over the years we had encouraged many parents, both English-speaking and French-speaking, to place their children in the other language school system for the elementary grades. To try it for a whole group of children, however, was easier said than done. There are two public school systems in Montreal, one Catholic and one Protestant (actually, non-Catholic), each with a number of French- and English-language schools under its jurisdiction. The idea of switching home and school languages generated no enthusiasm among school administrators or teachers, not even in the larger Catholic school system where there should be relatively few difficulties in shifting French- and English-speaking teachers.

The French-Canadian educators and school administrators who were initially approached worried about having too many English-speaking children introduced into their system, because they knew from experience that English (the language of greater utility and prestige in the community) spreads rapidly among French-speaking children, somewhat like a contagious disease, as is the case with higher prestige languages in most bicultural settings. In fact at the same time as these English-Canadian parents were thinking of ways of surrounding their children with the French language as early as possible, French-Canadian educators and politicians were trying to stop the spread of English by postponing its introduction into the school system until grade V or later. The thought of introducing a group of English monolingual children into a French class also worried teachers, who felt it would be difficult to create an appropriate atmosphere and to work effectively with a mixed group of French- and English-speaking children. A 50-50 proportion might be particularly disruptive, and it would be very difficult to judge what would be the optimal "colony" size so as not to disrupt the education of the French-speaking youngsters.

The St. Lambert parents had their own types of reservations. They were especially concerned about placing one or two of their children into a totally French-Canadian kindergarten class, even if that could be arranged from an administrative point of view. The alternative they favored would allow them to oversee and monitor the content of the educational program. They were willing to place their children in experimental French classes within the English-language section of the Protestant school system, meaning that groups of English-speaking children would enter the new linguistic world of French together, all children starting essentially at the same point. After a series of discussions among parents, school administrators, and representatives of McGill's Language Research Group the South Shore Protestant Regional School Board authorized such a program to begin on an experimental basis in September 1965. The purpose of the program was to promote functional bilingualism by using French as the language of instruction. A fascinating account of these deliberations and their repercussions in the community has been written by a member of the parent committee, Mrs. Olga Melikoff, and is presented as Appendix 1. It was decided to follow two classes of children, all from English-speaking homes, through kindergarten and at least grade I. Decisions about subsequent grades would depend on the results of careful examination of the progress made by the children after the first grade. The first would be called the Pilot Class, entering kindergarten in September of 1965, and a second group, the Follow-up Class, would start kindergarten in September of 1966. The setting would be an English-language, Protestant elementary school in St. Lambert, and enrollment would be entirely voluntary.

Although a number of parents became interested immediately, this does not mean that it was a simple matter to start the program. In the Montreal community there were extreme and conflicting opinions about any type of program designed to promote bilingualism and biculturalism. One gets some appreciation of the range of feelings by studying the briefs submitted to the Commission of Inquiry on the Position of the French Language Rights in Quebec by the principals of French and English Catholic schools. The principals of French Canadian Schools (L'Association des Principaux de Montréal) strongly endorsed French language priority in Quebec. They argued that "modern means of communication have defeated the resistance to foreign influences that [the former cultural] isolation offered. The frontiers are abolished and everyone comes together on the same public square. Children, in general, are incapable of improving their language because they are continually under the influence of a language often neglected in the family . . . and bastardized in the society. The government is the only means capable of advancing French-Canadian people lost in the middle of an Anglophone ocean" (1969). This attitude led to the following requests for governmental support: (1) "that new immigrants be integrated into the French milieu by an appropriate law; (2) that French be the normal language of work in industry, commerce, business; (3) that French be given priority in social contexts, publicity and posters," and so forth. What is of interest is that no mention at all is made of any plan to learn about the English-Canadian culture or language.

The brief from the Association of (English-speaking) Catholic Principals of Montreal (1969) is just about as protective and guarded in outlook. Its first two recommendations set the tone: "(1) We recommend that the acquired rights of English-speaking parents to have their children's education in the official language of their choice be enshrined in law. (2) We recommend that the above rights be extended to all immigrants who have chosen or will choose to reside in Quebec" (p. 14). Their approach to learning the second language is basically conservative: "While we favor bilingualism and the effective teaching of the French language from kindergarten to grade XI, we reject the so-called bilingual school which attempts to give equal or nearly equal importance to two languages as media of instruction. We are of the opinion that the average child cannot cope with two languages of instruction and to try to do so leads to insecurity, language interference, and academic retardation . . . We have all met people who in adult life suffer from chronic linguistic confusion. We advocate the use of only one language as a medium of instruction so that the student will master the language skills of his mother tongue or of the primary language of instruction. We advocate the use of the second language from kindergarten to grade III through songs, dialogue, etc. This incidental presentation of the second language is to be followed in grades IV to XI by a systematic study of the second language through audio-lingual methodology based on a structure-global approach" (p. 32 ff).

These views, we believe, are manifestations of a philosophy of fear that jeopardized the opportunities available in Canada to develop a new Canadian way of life by drawing on the best of the many traditions already in North America or still coming from abroad. Fortunately, there were certain school principals and administrators courageous and forward-looking enough to let the experiment get started. But even so, in many ways it was to be an experiment within an experiment, that is, an educational investigation within the context of a community-based struggle to change established ways of education and bringing up English-speaking youngsters in Quebec (see Appendix 1).

At the request of the School Board and the Provincial Ministry of Education, we were asked to formally evaluate and assess the program. As researchers and evaluators, we had our own concerns about the possible consequences this type of educational program might have on the cognitive development and academic standing of pupils taught in other than their home language. The research literature on the topic is not altogether encouraging. For example, Michael West (1926) reported a large academic handicap for children trained through a foreign language. Cheeseman (quoted in Isidro, 1949) also found that Malay children who enter schools taught in English fall far behind those taught in the home language. And Prator (1950) carefully describes the important Iloilo experiment conducted in the Philippines in which one group of pupils took their first year of schooling in the home language and a matched group studied through English. The achievement standings at the end of grade I clearly favored those instructed in their home languages. Even though the message of these studies is clear, certain questions arise about the reliability and generalizability of the conclusions. As to reliability, a more recent study conducted in the Philippines, designed as a replication of the Iloilo experiment, had a quite different outcome (Davis, 1967). In this case, Filipino pupils instructed entirely through English performed as well as carefully matched counterparts instructed through Tagalog. Furthermore on careful reading of the earlier studies one has the impression that the children learning through English may have had to neglect educational content and focus instead on the mastery of a second language apparently taught in a mechanical, routinized manner by nonnative speakers of the language. One also wonders about the relevance and interest of English for Indian, Malaysian, or Filipino children who generally leave school and return to rural communities after three or so years. In planning the St. Lambert experiment, we tried to take these factors into consideration by making the development of language skills incidental to educational content. In other words, the children were enticed into the mastery of the new language in a natural manner in their daily interaction with teachers who were native speakers.

Although we began the study with certain worries, these were more than balanced by our overall confidence in the basic idea underlying the project. One source of confidence was the earlier McGill research on the intellectual and academic performance of bilingual in contrast to monolingual youngsters (Peal and Lambert, 1962; Lambert and Anisfeld, 1969). These studies compared the abilities of ten-year-old French-Canadian monolinguals and bilinguals from comparable socioeconomic and home background. The bilinguals had opportunities to develop nativelike skill in English in natural ways at home or in the neighborhood that the monolinguals did not have. The analyses showed the bilinguals to be much superior on measures of intelligence, reliably further ahead in school grade, significantly better than the monolinguals in school work in general, and more sympathetic in their attitudes toward English-speaking Canadians. Developing bilingual abilities, then, seems worthwhile for many reasons.

A similar trend is noticeable in an Irish study of the effects of bilingualism on schooling (Macnamara, 1966). In that social setting, groups of children from English-speaking districts, and presumably English-speaking homes, who take all of their schooling through the medium of Irish (Macnamara's group 5, p. 48 ff. and p. 101 ff.) apparently fare very well in comparison to those taught exclusively in the home language, be it English (group 1) or Irish (group 6). For instance, group 5 had the highest nonverbal IQ and the highest mean score in English, was essentially tied with the all-Irish group in Irish, and had the best mean score in computational arithmetic.* In this case, the bilingual children switched home and school languages and appeared to progress with no difficulties.

One other source of confidence came from the theoretical and experimental work of the Russian psychologist Vygotsky (1962). His brilliant analysis of the benefits derived from studying a foreign language, especially the transfer of conceptual development from the foreign to the native language, was particularly encouraging to us as the project started. We will have occasions to discuss Vygotsky's views in detail in chapters to follow.

---

*The fact that they were somewhat behind the other English-background children on a test of arithmetic problems may well be due to the fact that, because of school requirements, group 5 had an Irish translation of the Problem Arithmetic test rather than the English version given groups 1-4. Since group 5 scored highest in the English tests, they very likely would have done as well or better on the English version especially because concepts of buying, selling, dividing, etc. would be all the more vivid in their home language.

Chapter Two

The Research Plan and Procedures

Our major purpose was to assess and evaluate the impact of elementary schooling conducted primarily in a second language on the linguistic, intellectual, and attitudinal development of children. It was, then, to be a longitudinal, continuing study. We were interested not only in how the children following this type of experimental program would fare in comparison with conventionally trained French-speaking children following a standard program in French, but also how they would compare with English-speaking children following the standard academic program in English. In other words, we wanted to determine how the home-school language switch would affect their progress in French as well as their standing in English. We wondered, too, if this experience might have a beneficial effect on language-learning capacity in general. At the same time, we were interested in how children trained in this manner would do in a nonlanguage subject matter such as mathematics, and more generally, whether the experience would have a beneficial or harmful effect on their intellectual growth.

As we describe the investigation, some readers may feel we give too many details. Perhaps then it will be helpful to explain in advance that our purpose is to tell the story to many different readers; some will be experts in the fields of education and psychology who will want the details in order to evaluate and criticize our interpretations and conclusions; some will be undergraduate and graduate students who may appreciate the introduction to research planning that is provided; some will be teachers who may skip over technicalities on first reading, but, let us hope, will come back to them later in order to see what the results actually mean; and some will be interested nonspecialists who may want to follow the project closely because of its potential social importance.

Various innovative approaches to bilingual education have been tried in many settings around the world, but very few have been systematically evaluated. Important exceptions are the studies conducted in the Union of South Africa by Malherbe (1946), in Ireland by Macnamara (1966), in the Philippines by Davis (1967), and in the United States by Richardson (1968). Still, longitudinal evaluations are rare, and experienced school administrators now realize that they need accurate descriptions of the characteristics and objectives of educational programs as well as long-term evaluations. Parents and funding agencies are also beginning to insist on long-range accountability of this type. It may be useful therefore to illustrate how we feel educational programs of this sort should be evaluated before describing what we were finally able to do in the actual situation.

A Suggested Model for Evaluating Bilingual Programs

The research and evaluation component of a project typically includes diverse types of pretesting and posttesting, a description of the actual program, and a factual reporting of findings. Consider, for example, the case of a bilingual program designed for English-Canadian children. Ideally, one would like to be able to make statements at the end of the year about the progress of the "experimental" class relative to that of "controls," e.g., groups of English-Canadian children following a traditional program of English instruction; French-Canadian children following a similar bilingual program; and French-Canadian children following a traditional program of French instruction. If possible, all students would be selected from similar socioeconomic backgrounds.

The first stage of the research program would involve a small-scale sociolinguistic survey of the communities involved, such as that proposed by Fishman, Cooper, Ma et al. (1968). Information would be gathered about the family's socioeconomic status, parents' aspirations for their children's educational and occupational future (cf., Bloom, 1964), and their attitudes toward the ethnolinguistic group whose language their children are to learn. With this information, one could describe more fully the parental and home backgrounds of the program participants and establish a basis for equating and comparing experimental and control classes from the start.

As for the children themselves, it is valuable to assess their performance on nonverbal IQ tests (such as Raven's Progressive Matrices test, 1956; 1958), a picture-vocabulary test, and various readiness tests to establish base lines for equating groups and making comparisons at a later time. The general idea is to collect objective information about the community, the parents, and the children who are to participate in the experimental program *before* examining the program itself and the children's performance in the course of the program.

Posttesting involves the administration of a battery of tests—group or individual, standardized or homemade—that have good promise as barometers of the cognitive and linguistic performance of the children involved. If care has been taken to select reasonably comparable control groups, one can then make meaningful conclusions about the *relative* progress of the children in the experimental classes. If possible, data can be collected from the children themselves, their parents, and other members of the community about the subjective opinions each of these groups have about the program after it is under way.

The Actual Plan

This, of course, is a model, and as is typical in everyday affairs, we were not able to follow it in every respect even though it did serve as an important guide. First we had to select what we thought would be appropriate English and French comparison groups. These were chosen from middle-class neighborhoods, generally comparable to those in which the children in the Experimental Class lived: one English Control group (Control I) of twenty-two children was a companion first-grade class located in the same school as the Experimental Class in the suburb of St. Lambert, and the second (English Control II) comprising twenty-six children was chosen from a residential neighborhood in Montreal. The French Control Class of twenty-two children was chosen from a French-Catholic school also situated in St. Lambert in a middle-class neighborhood. Since kindergarten training is available to all children in the Montreal area without cost, we saw to it that all those involved in the experiment had attended kindergarten for two hours a day. Those in the Control groups, of course, had kindergarten instruction in their native languages, while the twenty-six children Experimental Class had a monolingual French-speaking teacher who stressed the development of French language skills through story telling, vocabulary buildup, songs, and group projects in plastic arts.

The number of children in each class needs some explanation. The total number of pupils per class is fixed in the Quebec school systems to be between twenty-seven to thirty-three. The actual numbers mentioned for the various groups are generally lower because we include in our analyses only those children who were present for both the fall and spring testings, and, in the case of the Experimental Classes, only those who came from exclusively English-speaking homes and who had attended the French kindergarten program. In all cases, though, each teacher had approximately thirty children in her charge.

Intelligence and home background. The similarity of neighborhoods was only a first step in equating the groups. In light of the well-documented influence that social class has on language and intellectual development, it was necessary in light of the limited number of students involved in the study to equate the Experimental and Control Classes as carefully as possible in terms of intelligence and various socioeconomic indices.

The Progressive Matrices test of general intelligence, developed by Raven (1956), was used to gauge the intellectual levels of the children. The Raven test has proven to be one of the most reliable and valid measures of general intelligence, and since it is nonverbal in form, it is especially useful for comparing children from different ethnic and linguistic backgrounds (although, interestingly enough, it does have substantial intercorrelations with standard verbal measures of intelligence). All children were tested within the first month of schooling in September 1966. The standings of the four classes at the start are presented in Tables 1 and 2. Note the similarity of mean IQ scores, the fact that there are no statistically reliable differences among them, and the similarity of distributions of scores, as presented in Table 2.

It should be apparent that no attempt was made to preselect or screen children for the Experimental Classes on the basis of IQ or other variables; thus both the Pilot and the Follow-up Classes included children with a wide range of IQ, and a few of the children even had recognized perceptual-motor deficits.

We also used the home-background schedules of Bloom (1964), Davé (1963), and Wolf (1963) which constitute a very comprehensive method for assessing a family's socioeconomic status, particularly those aspects of home background that affect academic progress. The interview schedules developed by Davé (1963) and Wolf (1963) were adapted for our purposes. The procedure involves an hour-long interview with parents, usually conducted in the home, where one can assess the size and style of living quarters, the amount and diversity of reading material available, the parents' style of speech, and so forth. In certain cases where visits could not be arranged, extensive telephone interviews were conducted. The six major themes touched on in the interviews are listed below.

1. *Emphasis placed on education by influential figures in the child's environment*

    (a)   Parental aspirations for the child's education
    (b)   Parent's own aspirations
    (c)   Parent's interest in academic achievement
    (d)   Social pressure for academic achievement
    (e)   Standards of reward for educational attainment
    (f)   Knowledge of the child's educational progress
    (g)   Preparation and planning for the attainment of educational goals

2. *Quality of the child's linguistic environment*

    (a)   Quality of the language used by the parents
    (b)   Opportunities for the enlargement and use of vocabulary and sentence patterns
    (c)   Keenness of the parents for correct and effective language usage

Table 1

Pilot Class Comparisons on Measures of Intelligence and Components of Socioeconomic Status at the Start of Grade I, September 1966

	Experimental Class (N=26)	English Control I (N=22)	English Control II (N=26)	French Control (N=26)	F-ratio
Intelligence					
Raven Scores: Sept. 1966	18.73	18.42	18.72	18.53	n.s.
Socioeconomic Indices					
1. Emphasis on Education	6.53	6.49	7.46	6.19	4.75 df 3,97,p<.01
2. Quality of Linguistic Environment	6.97	7.13	6.85	6.11	2.70 df 3,97,p<.05
3. Guidance in School Work	6.44	6.11	5.77	6.81	n.s.
4. Enrichment of Home Environment	6.69	6.13	6.92	7.00	n.s.
5. Family-wide Activities	5.98	6.07	6.38	5.93	n.s.
6. Educational Facilities	6.69	6.64	7.08	6.59	n.s.

Table 2

Pilot Class Comparisons of Raven's Intelligence Scores at the Start of Grade I, September 1966

Percentiles	Scores of the Standardization Group*	*Percentage of Students Falling in Percentile Groups:*			
		Experimental Class	English Control I Class	English Control II Class	French Class
95	23 or over	14	11	24	8
90	21-22	27	32	8	13
75	17-20	32	11	40	63
50	14-16	18	11	20	8
25	11-13	9	32	8	8
10	10 or less	0	5	0	0
		N = 22	N = 19	N = 25	N = 24

*A sample of 300 Dumfries (Scotland) children, six years of age, at start of grade 1.

3. *Availability and quality of guidance on matters related to school work*

4. *Enrichment of the child's home environment*

    (a)   Availability and use of materials related to school learning

    (b)   Nature and quality of toys, games, and hobbies made available to the child

    (c)   Opportunities for thinking and imagination in daily activities

5. *Extent and nature of extracurricular activities undertaken by the family*

    (a)   Extent and content of indoor activities of the family

    (b)   Extent and content of outdoor activities during weekends and vacations

6. *Use of educational facilities: Books, periodical literature, library, etc.*

    (a)   Variety of material used by the family members (e.g., books, magazines, newspapers)

    (b)   Encouragement given child in the use of such material (e.g., helping him to obtain library permission, suggesting that he trade reading material with friends)

After the scores for each theme had been tabulated, data were statistically analyzed. There were two home-background features that reliably differentiated the groups: *the emphasis placed on education*, with the English Control II Class scoring highest and the French Control lowest, and *the quality of the linguistic environment*, with the English Control I Class scoring highest and the French Control lowest.

From Tables 1 and 2 it is evident that the groups were comparable with regard to intelligence, as indexed by the Raven measure, and most of the components of socioeconomic status. Thus, our attempts to choose comparable groups of children seem to have been largely successful. But because the groups did differ in two respects, the question arose as to which procedures should be used for equating or statistically controlling these differences as well as other less obvious ones that might exist among the four groups of children. We decided to use an analysis of covariance procedure described by Snedecor (1956; pp. 421-423 and 440-445) to adjust each of the end-of-year test scores for any initial differences among children in IQ or socioeconomic status. The adjusted mean scores were tested by analysis of variance and when significant variations among means occurred, these were tested further with the Newman-Keuls technique described by Winer (1962, p. 86). We are fully aware of the problems associated with the use of analysis of covariance (cf. Elashoff, 1969); Fennessey, 1968). Our general strategy was to equate the groups as well as possible in advance, without making the choice of control classes artificial in any way, and to consider the covariance analysis as a final safety adjustment, that is, as one additional mode of equating the comparison classes from the start.

Parental attitudes. In a bicultural setting like Montreal, it is particularly important that parental attitudes be as comparable as possible from group to group at the start, especially attitudes toward the other ethnolinguistic group whose language is to be learned. The role played by attitudes of this sort in the language-learning process has been fully documented by Lambert and Gardner (1972), and the value of taking account of attitudes in educational research has been discussed by Hayes, Lambert, and Tucker (1967). Our plan was to select pupils for the English Canadian Control Classes who would very likely have been part of the Experimental Class if given the opportunity. In other words, we wanted the English-speaking control children to serve as a type of holdout comparison group.

To assess attitudes, we interviewed each child's mother, reasoning that children at five or six years of age would not be able to express such views reliably whereas the family-wide feelings would likely be represented by the mother. With this idea in mind, mothers were asked to give their views of the value, if any, of having their children learn the other group's language. Here we wanted to see if the parental groups differed in terms of the "instrumentality" or the "integrativeness" of their orientations. *Instrumental* orientations emphasize the practical or economic advantages of learning a second language whereas *integrative* orientations stress the gratifications of an interpersonal sort that might follow from having skill in a second language (cf. Lambert and Gardner, 1972). A copy of the questionnaire and a summary of the comparisons among the parental groups are presented in Tables 3 and 4. Table 4 also shows the extent of social and institutional contact English and French-Canadian families have with one another.

Several summary statements can be made about these results. The major finding is that there are no statistically significant differences between the parents of the Experimental and English Control groups on any of the questions: both have resided in Quebec for long periods, mainly lifetime residents; both have the same proportion of family members who use the two languages to "some" extent in the home (about 15 to 23 percent); both have the same degree of fluency in English, and the same level of competence in French, mainly a "little only" for mothers and a "little" to "fairly well" for the fathers.

As to the importance of learning a second language, several interesting similarities among the groups come to light. In general, all parents agree about the most and least important reasons for learning the other group's language. The most important reasons are: (1) to meet and converse with more and varied people; (2) to understand members of the other group and their way of life; (3) to develop friendships with members of the other group; and (4) to get a good job. Note that all reasons except (4) are integrative in content, meaning that all the parents, English and French-Canadian alike, value most the interpersonal and social aspects of second-language competence.

Table 3

Parent Questionnaire and Coding System

Pupils's Name _____

School _____

TO THE PARENTS:

1. How long has the mother lived in the Province of Quebec? _____
2. How long has the father lived in the Province of Quebec?   _____
   Coded as: 0=less than 1 year; 1=1-2 years; 2=2-5 years; 3=5-10 years;
   4=over 10 years.
3. At home, does the *mother* speak to the children in English or French?
   (a) English only (*coded* as 0)
   (b) both English and French (*coded* as 1)
   (c) French only (*coded* as 0)
4. At home, does the *father* speak to the children in English or French?
   (a) English only ___0___
   (b) both English and French ___1___
   (c) French only ___0___
5. At home, do the *brothers and sisters* speak to each other in English or
   French?
   (a) English only ___0___
   (b) both English and French ___1___
   (c) French only ___0___

6. Does the *mother* coded as:

		not at all	a little	fairly well	fluently
(a)	speak English:	0	1	2	3
(b)	read English:	0	1	2	3
(c)	understand English:	0	1	2	3

7. Does the *father*

(a)	speak English:	0	1	2	3
(b)	read English:	0	1	2	3
(c)	understand English:	0	1	2	3

8. Does the *mother*

(a)	speak French:	0	1	2	3
(b)	read French:	0	1	2	3
(c)	understand French:	0	1	2	3

9. Does the *father*

(a)	speak French:	0	1	2	3
(b)	read French:	0	1	2	3
(c)	understand French:	0	1	2	3

The study of French could be important to me because:

It would help me better understand the French people and their way of life.

    Coded as:

    Not my feeling   1 : 2 : 3 : 4 : 5 : 6 : 7   Definitely my
       at all   feeling

I think it would some day be useful in getting a good job.

    Not my feeling ___ : ___ : ___ : ___ : ___ : ___ : ___   Definitely my
       at all   feeling

It would enable me to gain good friends more easily among French-speaking people.

    Not my feeling ___ : ___ : ___ : ___ : ___ : ___ : ___   Definitely my
       at all   feeling

One needs a good knowledge of at least one foreign language to merit social recognition.

    Not my feeling ___ : ___ : ___ : ___ : ___ : ___ : ___   Definitely my
       at all   feeling

It would enable me to begin to think and behave as the French do.

    Not my feeling ___ : ___ : ___ : ___ : ___ : ___ : ___   Definitely my
       at all   feeling

I feel that no one is really educated unless he is fluent in the French language.

    Not my feeling ___ : ___ : ___ : ___ : ___ : ___ : ___   Definitely my
       at all   feeling

It would allow me to meet and converse with more and varied people.

    Not my feeling ___ : ___ : ___ : ___ : ___ : ___ : ___   Definitely my
       at all   feeling

I need it for some specific education or business goal.

    Not my feeling ___ : ___ : ___ : ___ : ___ : ___ : ___   Definitely my
       at all   feeling

Answer the following questions by placing a check mark (X) to the left of the statement which appears most applicable to you. Try at all times to answer as *accurately* as possible.

Remember that this questionnaire will not be seen by anyone in the School System. Only members of our research team will have access to your answers.

1.   I try to speak French.

    coded as: 3   a. every opportunity I get
               2   b. now and then
               1   c. only when I absolutely have to
               0   d. never

2. We read French newspapers (e.g., La Presse, Le Devoir).
    - _3_ a. very often
    - _2_ b. regularly
    - _1_ c. seldom
    - _0_ d. never

3. We read French magazines.
    - _3_ a. very often
    - _2_ b. regularly
    - _1_ c. seldom
    - _0_ d. never

4. We listen to French radio broadcasts.
    - _3_ a. very often
    - _2_ b. regularly
    - _1_ c. seldom
    - _0_ d. never

5. French Canadians are invited to our house.
    - _3_ a. very often
    - _2_ b. regularly
    - _1_ c. seldom
    - _0_ d. never

6. We attend French plays and theater.
    - _3_ a. very often
    - _2_ b. regularly
    - _1_ c. seldom
    - _0_ d. never

Table 4

Pilot Group Comparisons on Parent Questionnaire

	Experimental Class (N = 22)	English Controls (N = 38)	French Controls (N = 22)
Mother's residence in Quebec	3.82	3.70	3.95
Father's residence in Quebec	3.82	3.68	4.00
Mother speaks to children in: one language only (0) both English & French (1)	0.18	0.13	0.18
Father speaks to children in: one language only (0) both English & French (1)	0.23	0.10	0.18
Brothers and sisters speak to each other in: one language only (0) both English & French (1)	0.14	0.08	0.23
Mother's fluency in English: *speaking*	3.00	3.00	1.95
reading	3.00	2.98	1.86
understanding	3.00	3.00	2.27
Father's fluency in English: *speaking*	3.00	2.98	2.60
reading	3.00	2.98	2.60
understanding	3.00	3.00	2.73
Mother's fluency in French: *speaking*	1.00	1.23	3.00
reading	1.09	1.21	3.00
understanding	1.32	1.46	3.00
Father's fluency in French: *speaking*	1.41	1.44	3.00
reading	1.68	1.49	3.00
understanding	1.68	1.67	3.00

Table 4 (cont.)

Pilot Group Comparisons on Parent Questionnaire

	Experimental Class (N = 22)	English Controls (N = 38)	French Controls (N = 22)
Importance of learning the second language:			
For understanding the other group and their way of life	6.32	6.10	6.60
For getting a good job	6.05	6.08	6.10
To gain friends among the other group	6.05	6.10	5.77
For social recognition	2.91	2.92	4.57
To think and behave as the other group does	2.14	2.28	2.89
As a mark of education	1.68	2.69	2.65
To meet with varied people	7.00	6.70	6.18
For business or educational purposes	3.73	3.45	3.84
Contact with other culture:			
Try to speak other language	2.23	2.15	2.09
Read newspapers in other language	0.64	0.60	0.86
Read magazines in other language	0.59	0.45	1.18
Listen to radio broadcasts in other language	1.09	0.90	1.64
Other-group visitors to home	1.68	1.34	1.45
Attend plays and theater in other language	0.32	0.50	1.36

Reasons assigned less importance are, starting with the least: (1) as a mark of education; (2) to be able to think and behave like members of the other group; (3) for specific business or educational purposes; and (4) for social recognition or status. All these relatively unimportant reasons are instrumental in content except for (2). It is very instructive to realize that parents see the second-language learning situation mainly as an opportunity to develop skills that will enable one to meet new and varied people from another ethnolinguistic group, to understand their way of life, and to develop friendships with them, but *not* to so identify with them as to think and behave as they do. This restriction suggests that Canadian parents in Quebec today may be concerned about maintaining individual and cultural identity. At the same time, they appear very willing to develop intergroup social contact, friendship, and understanding. As we shall see later, this may constitute a basic conflict between parents' wishes and the self-views their children develop in the course of their schooling in French.

Finally, there are no differences between Experimental and English Control parents in the amount of contact they have with various French institutions and information media. Generally they have very little experience with French newspapers, magazines, radio, or theater. They do have somewhat more contact in the form of French-Canadian visitors in their homes, however (ratings in this case lie between "seldom" and "regularly"). In comparison, the French-Canadian parents have more contact with English-language institutions and media in that more of their ratings fall between the "seldom" and "regularly" level.

About a year later, after the children had finished grade I, the mothers were sent a questionnaire that focused more directly on their attitudes toward French and English Canadians. They gave their ratings of each ethnolinguistic group on a series of bipolar adjectives such as:

mean ____ : ____ : ____ : ____ : ____ : ____ : ____ kind

intelligent ____ : ____ : ____ : ____ : ____ : ____ : ____ stupid

Examples of how to use the seven-step scales were provided. For example, one can register an impression that English Canadians are, as a group, extremely kind, by checking the sixth or seventh positions on the scale, reserving the fourth position for an impression that English Canadians are neither kind nor mean. The adjectives used in the rating scales were solicited from second-grade children as descriptive terms *they* use to describe youngsters they like or dislike. For the parent questionnaires, the scales were rephrased to a more adult form in certain cases (e.g., "lazy ... industrious" instead of "lazy ... not lazy"; "stupid ... intelligent" instead of "dumb ... smart").

The data were first analyzed using an analysis of variance procedure. The parental group means for the Pilot Classes are presented in Table 5 along with indications of the statistically reliable differences between means, using simple t tests. In Table 5 scores have been converted so that in all cases a high mean score (i.e., one approaching the maximum of 7), indicates a more favorable overall rating. To illustrate, on the rating scale "short . . . tall," all three parental groups (Experimental, English Control, and French Control) have the impression that English Canadians are taller than French Canadians, but generally they see both English and French Canadians as relatively "short," since the average ratings fall mostly below the neutral point of 4. The line connecting 2.00 and 3.44 signifies a statistically reliable between-group difference. For present purposes, we are not interested in *within*-group differences, such as that between 4.30 and 2.00 for the English Control parents.

The following results are noteworthy. First, in no case is there a difference in the attitudes of the Experimental and the English Control parents toward English Canadians and French Canadians, even for personal attributes such as good . . . bad, intelligent . . . stupid, nice . . . not nice, mean . . . kind, etc. In other words, there is nothing to suggest that the parents of the Experimental Classes had a more charitable or friendly view of French Canadian people than the English Control parents.

Second, there is no evidence of denigration or hostility toward French Canadians on the part of either group of English-Canadian mothers. Small mean differences suggest that English-Canadian mothers view French Canadians as less good, less intelligent, or less kind than English Canadians in general. However, their tendency is also to see French Canadians as friendlier, happier, and prettier than English Canadians. The French Control mothers reveal an interesting stereotype: they see English Canadians as taller, thinner, less industrious, and somewhat less kind and less friendly than French Canadians, but not any less good or any more intelligent. Judging from the remarkably small amount of contact between English and French Canadians reported by these parents, one sees here no basic antagonisms or prejudices between the two ethnic groups that could not be ameliorated with more extensive social interaction. For example, the French Control mothers' belief that English Canadians are somewhat less kind and friendly would very likely change with more social contact. It seems then that the parental attitudes in the homes of the children involved in the experiment are based more on ignorance of the other group than prejudiced dislike or suspicion. The similarity of the outlooks of the Experimental and English Control parents gives us a firm starting point from which to judge the impact of the home-school language switch on the attitudes of the children.

Quality of teaching. In research of this type, it is extremely difficult to assure that the teachers of the various classes are comparable in ability, efficiency, and personality. No special attempt was made to do so in this investigation, but

Table 5

Attitude Profiles of Mothers of the Pilot Classes

Comparison of Mean Scores

People Rated: Mothers of:	English Canadians	French Canadians
(1) Short (1) – tall (7)		
Experimental Class	3.75	2.54
English Control Class	4.30	2.00
French Control Class	4.63	3.44
(2) Bad (1) – good (7)		
Experimental Class	3.75	3.38
English Control Class	3.35	3.33
French Control Class	4.50	4.63
(3) Stupid (1) – intelligent (7)		
Experimental Class	4.92	4.85
English Control Class	4.45	4.38
French Control Class	5.00	5.75
(4) Not nice (1) – nice (7)		
Experimental Class	4.33	3.85
English Control Class	3.70	3.71
French Control Class	4.50	5.00
(5) Weak (1) – strong (7)		
Experimental Class	4.83	4.69
English Control Class	4.50	4.43
French Control Class	4.88	5.63
(6) Not friendly (1) – friendly (7)		
Experimental Class	3.92	4.08
English Control Class	3.90	4.52
French Control Class	4.37	4.87
(7) Lazy (1) – industrious (7)		
Experimental Class	5.25	4.85
English Control Class	5.00	4.60
French Control Class	4.87	5.88

Table 5 (cont.)
Attitude Profiles of Mothers of the Pilot Classes

Comparison of Mean Scores

People Rated: Mothers of:	English Canadians	French Canadians
(8) Mean (1) – kind (7)		
Experimental Class	4.17	4.08
English Control Class	4.20	3.90
French Control Class	4.38	4.63
(9) Fat (1) – thin (7)		
Experimental Class	4.08	4.23
English Control Class	4.40	4.23
French Control Class	5.11	3.33
(10) Slow (1) – fast (7)		
Experimental Class	3.58	3.46
English Control Class	3.75	3.57
French Control Class	3.69	3.57
(11) Sad (1) – happy (7)		
Experimental Class	3.67	4.33
English Control Class	3.75	4.38
French Control Class	4.00	5.13
(12) Not pretty (1) – pretty (7)		
Experimental Class	3.67	3.92
English Control Class	3.60	3.62
French Control Class	4.13	4.25
(13) Not handsome (1) – handsome (7)		
Experimental Class	3.75	3.62
English Control Class	3.48	3.14
French Control Class	4.29	4.14

(The vertical lines indicate differences that are statistically reliable at beyond the .05 level of confidence.)

certain considerations give us confidence that the Experimental Classes were not specially favored with an unusually good set of teachers. In the first year, all four classes—the Experimental, two English- and one French-language Control—were situated in schools populated predominantly by children from middle-class families. The schools involved were all recognized as outstanding in the sense that they had active and progressive school boards and were pleasantly situated in residential areas offering generally attractive working conditions for teachers. Most of the teachers involved in the study had met the educational and experience requirements for permanent positions in their respective school commissions, and all had chosen to teach at the elementary level. There were several who did not meet these requirements, however, and as we shall see in each case the exceptions were in the Experimental Classes. More care than usual was taken to find teachers for the kindergarten and grade I Experimental Classes, since they had to be native speakers of French who would be willing to experiment in the sense that there were no guidelines available to them. The persons actually chosen had many more demands on their imagination and initiative than teachers following a conventional program. The young French-Canadian teacher who took over grade I had no experience with English-speaking children. For some reason, it took her much time to gain the affection of children and parents. In March she became ill and was replaced by an older and more experienced French-speaking teacher who was able to carry out the planned program with little apparent disruption. The replacement teacher was better able to keep the attention of the children and she soon enjoyed their affection and that of the parents. Fortunately for the purpose of the investigation, but unfortunately for the person in question, the grade I teacher of the English Control I Class also had to be replaced because of illness for a month and a half in February and March.

The grade II teacher available for the Experimental Class did not have the needed experience or training, so that throughout grade II the children were not at all privileged. In general, the teachers of the Experimental Classes at each grade level had the handicap, regardless of teaching experience, of adjusting to a very different type of student, with no frame of reference to help them and no relevant professional experience to draw on.

The academic program. The two-hour per day kindergarten program that all of the Experimental children attended was conducted exclusively in French from the first day on. The two teachers—one in charge of a morning class, the other, an afternoon class—were from France where they had taught at the "pre-maternelle" and "maternelle" levels, that is, with children four to six years of age. Their experience and talents and their ability to act as genuinely French monolinguals were extremely important features of the program. For instance, it meant that the children could be introduced to French in a natural way through plastic arts, music, and play so as to develop listening comprehension, vocabulary, and spontaneous verbal expression in the language. The goal of the kindergarten teachers was to prepare the children so that at grade I they could handle the content of the curriculum and function as though they were French-speaking youngsters, albeit somewhat slow and clumsy during the first several weeks. Thus the French-speaking atmosphere was established in the kindergarten. Still these classes were situated in an otherwise completely English-Canadian elementary school and once outside the classroom the children, at recess and when coming and going to school, were back in an English-speaking world. Selected French TV programs were a regular home assignment, though, extending in one sense the French atmosphere to the home.

The program of study that finally evolved for the Experimental Grade I Classes followed closely the curricula of the French-Canadian school systems of Montreal and that of lycées in France. Some of the books and materials were French-Canadian, some French (i.e., from France), and some had joint Canadian and French authorship. All of the materials used, however, were designed for children who spoke French as a native language, that is to say, it was in no sense a program of French taught as a second language. The programs of study of each grade level focused attention on the development of expected academic skills, with language purposely made incidental, except for French Language Arts which was taught in the same way that it would be taught to French-speaking children.

The principals of the elementary schools involved in the experiment were satisfied that the curricula for both kindergarten and grade I were comparable in level of difficulty and comprehensiveness to those of the English-Canadian schools in the Greater Montreal region.

An important question immediately arises: What does the teacher actually do in a classroom when she speaks a language that is totally strange to the children? Rather than describe in detail the texts, materials, lesson plans—which in most regards are standard—we felt it would be more instructive to describe classes in action as seen by an experienced teacher visiting the school for the first time. The teacher in question was Mme. Benoite Noble, who has taught some twenty years in France, England, and Canada with both French- and English-speaking elementary age pupils. She visited each class from kindergarten to grade V for two hours about a month after the beginning of the school year. Her insightful impressions are presented in Appendix B, and the reader may want to return to these descriptions as we follow the children through the various grades.

The testing procedure. Each spring, starting at the grade I level, the Experimental and Control Classes were given an extensive battery of individual and group tests devised to assess their intellectual and cognitive development, including: achievement tests in French and English Language Arts; listening comprehension in both languages; English and French speaking skills; foreign sound discrimination tests; tests of problem solving and computation skills in arithmetic given in French and English; measures of cognitive flexibility and creativity; verbal and nonverbal IQ tests; and attitudinal inventories designed to measure the children's attitudes toward their own and other ethnolinguistic groups.

In an attempt to reduce the "Hawthorne" effect of having only one group treated as an "experimental" class, care was taken in the selection of the control classes to make them somewhat special in their own right. The French Control Class, for example, took part in a well-publicized school-wide experiment in modern methods of teaching mathematics, and the school from which the English Control II Class was drawn was reputed for its methods of teaching English and French as school subjects.

Thus, we tried to assure that the classes were equated as closely as possible in terms of measured intelligence, socioeconomic background, parental attitudes toward the other language group, teachers' experience and skill, and program of study. Our apparent success in equating the Experimental and Control Classes was facilitated by restricting the selection to the middle band of the socioeconomic spectrum, and the results, of course, must be interpreted with this social-class restriction in mind. Currently we are replicating the study with children from lower socioeconomic backgrounds.

The Testing Procedures Used with the Pilot Classes

The testing was conducted by a small team of research assistants, some monolingual, some bilingual, who were experienced in administering group and individual tests. They visited the schools several times during the year, and spent from two to three weeks each spring conducting the end-of-year testing. This testing was distributed over a two- to three-week period, so that the children would not become fatigued or disinterested and so that the testing would not disrupt totally the regular school work. Care was taken to treat all groups alike with regard to the order of tests administered, the time of day involved, and the personnel conducting the tests or interviews. Teachers were not present during the testing sessions. For the Experimental groups from grade I on, instructions were given in French for French-content tests and in English for those with English content. Special rooms were provided in each school for individual or small group testing; unfortunately, in some schools these rooms were much quieter and more comfortable than in others.

A description of the measures employed. Measures 1-4, described below, were taken from the Metropolitan Achievement Tests (1959), Primary I Battery, designed to establish achievement levels as of the end of grade I in word knowledge, word discrimination, reading, and arithmetic concepts and skills. The raw scores were transformed into standard scores, the standardization being based on the results of testing large numbers of first-grade pupils in the United States. Children have a limited amount of time to complete each test.

1. *Word Knowledge in English.* This test measures the child's sight vocabulary, and requires a reading skill in English. The child is presented with a series of illustrations, with four words beside each. His task is to find the one word that best describes the illustration. For example, next to an illustration of a ball, he would search for the correct response among the four words: "pretty, here, ball, be." Total possible score was 35.

2. *Word Discrimination in English.* This measure, which also requires a basic ability to read English, assesses the child's skill in associating the spoken word with its printed form, a task requiring both auditory and visual discrimination. They were presented thirty-two sets of four words, with instructions to circle the word that was read aloud to them, first alone, then in a short sentence and then alone again. For example, they would hear "*and . . .* Bob *and* Frank . . . *and.*" and they were to circle the correct word among: "hand, am, and, summer." Total possible score was 35.

3. (a) *Reading Skills: Comprehension of English Sentences.* In this case, the child had to select the one sentence out of three that correctly described or defined an illustration. For example, next to a picture of a baby eating cereal, the choice was among these sentences: "Baby is eating his cereal. The baby has fun playing with his rattle. Someone wants the baby to stand up."

(b) *Reading Skills: Comprehension of Paragraph-length Material in English.* Here the child had to solve a riddle by finding the correct concept, or identify a concept by reading a short description. For example, the child would read these sentences: "I can fly. I can sing. I have a nest. Who am I?" and be expected to choose the correct answer from among: "a girl, a bird, a dog." Or, he would read: "Look, Tom. See the toy car. It is a big car." and answer the question: "The toy is: a car, a drum, a box." A total score, comprising both parts, was given each child. Total possible score was 46.

4. *Arithmetic Concepts and Skills in English.* This is a comprehensive measure of a child's mastery of basic numerical and quantitative concepts, his ability to solve verbal problems, and to add and subtract.

(a) *Numerical and Quantitative Concepts.* Separate items tested the following skills: (1) counting whole groups or parts of groups; (2) ordinals; (3) numbers of two or more digits; (4) money and time; (5) the concept of *one half*; (6) the concepts of *after, next to, biggest, before, least.* For example, the child would see an illustration of nine cars in a row and would be asked to put an X "on the sixth car," or to put an X "on half of them," or "on seven of them."

(b) *Verbal Problem Solving.* Here the child had to: (1) follow instructions; (2) add and subtract; (3) multiply and divide; and (4) enumerate. For example, the following questions centered around a large illustration: "See the pony ride picture. Find the row of numbers beginning with A. One of the numbers tells how many children are standing outside the pony ring. Put a cross in the box under that number in Row A." Note that this test calls for an ability to understand and follow often complicated directions presented orally.

(c) *Addition and Subtraction*. Children were asked to add or subtract dots

e.g., [•] and [::] are [ ]

or digits such as $9-4 = \underline{\hspace{1cm}}$.

A total score, based on all three parts, was determined for each child. Total possible score was 63.

5. *The Peabody Picture Vocabulary Test, in English*. This test, developed by Peabody (see Dunn, 1959), measures the child's auditory vocabulary. He is required to match a word, presented orally, to one of four illustrations. For example, the child would hear the word "kite" and search among four line drawings of a kite, a feather, an arrow, and some crayons for the appropriate picture. The test, of course, progresses to very complex concepts, such as "reaping," "deciding," or "imagining," with appropriate pictorial representations. Form B of the test was administered to the Experimental Class and the two English Control Classes. The first seventy items only were used at the grade I level.

6. *Word Association Analysis, English and French*. Each child heard a series of fifty-one words pronounced clearly one at a time by a reader whose voice was tape-recorded. The youngster was instructed and given practice in advance to say the very first word that came to mind when he heard each stimulus word. Several weeks prior to the actual testing, all children were given a ten-minute practice run with thirty "practice" stimulus words. The list of English words was given to the Experimental Class and to one of the English Control Classes; a list of French translated equivalents was given to the Experimental and the French Control Classes. There was a two-week delay period between the retesting of the Experimental Class in the "other" language; half of these pupils were tested first with the English list and half started with the French list.

The responses of the children were tape-recorded so that the time to respond could be measured, and so that each response could be recorded and classified according to the following scheme. Each response was categorized according to a system developed by Ervin (1961) and expanded by Entwisle (1966). *Syntagmatic* responses are those that commonly form an associational sequence with the stimulus word, that is, one where there is a syntactic link between the stimulus word and the response given. Typically the stimulus and response words are not in the same grammatical form class; for example: *bird* - flew; *red* - flower; *table* - spoon; *eat* - dinner are all syntagmatic type responses. We included certain responses in the syntagmatic category when a simple connecting word was omitted such as "the" or "to," so that *across* - street or *allow* - go were were included. However, we did not permit the omission of the connector "and," "with," or any conjunctions, the verb "is," or possessives. Thus *bird* - nest was not included (since *bird's* - nest or *bird* in the nest would be correct), nor was *table* - eat (although Ervin does include this as a syntagmatic response), because one would likely have to fill in with "eat *at the* table" or some other sequence of more than one word. We decided that *bird* - dog and *street* - car were not syntagmatic for six-year-olds who we presumed did not know about this special type of dog or those old-fashioned modes of transportation.

The contrast is made with *paradigmatic* responses, and these have two essential features: (1) they are of the same grammatical form class as the stimulus (even though they may, in other contexts, fall in some other grammatical class), and (2) they cannot be linked by a determiner to form a commonly occurring verbal sequence or run. Paradigmatic responses include superordinates (e.g., *rèd* - color, since the word "red" is both a noun and an adjective, and since "red color" does not form a common verbal run); subordinates (e.g., *color* - red); coordinates (e.g., *red* - blue); negatives (e.g., *clear* - not clear); and opposites (e.g., *fast* - slow).

Syntagmatic responses could be of two general types: a syntagmatic sequence or statistical *run*, such as *table* - spoon or *across* - street, or a syntagmatic *change*, which is not a common verbal sequence but is a change in grammatical form class, ruling out the paradigmatic classification. Although there were relatively few syntagmatic change responses, they were still analyzed as a separate type, as were *rhyming* responses (e.g., *say* - day), *transformations* (e.g., *kill* - killed), and *irrelevant* or *idiosyncratic* reactions (e.g., *street* - four).

In this analysis, then, attention is directed to the relative importance given to syntagmatic and paradigmatic forms of responses by the Experimental and Control Classes of children. The work of Ervin and Entwisle has demonstrated that "the paradigmatic shift" appears to be an important clue to linguistic and cognitive maturity. On the basis of their research, they argue that there is an orderly developmental sequence in children's associations. Very young children typically give *anomalous* responses (such as rhyming, transformation, and irrelevant reactions) where there is no apparent semantic or grammatical relation between the stimulus word and the response other than an acoustical one. As children mature, syntagmatic responses are the most typical until later, when paradigmatic responses predominate. Ervin (1961) presented strong evidence for this shift with her study of associational changes from kindergarten through grade VI. We are essentially interested here in seeing whether the Experimental group of children are as linguistically (and cognitively) far along in English as the English Control children are, and at the same developmental level in French as the French Control children. The mode of analysis permits one to see if the groups differ in their tendencies to give anomalous type responses, simple syntagmatic runs (such as *table* - cloth, *bird* - flew) or the presumably more mature paradigmatic reactions (such as *table* - chair, *bird* - animal).

The English responses were coded by two monolingual English-speaking judges and the French by two monolingual French-speaking judges; all responses were then reviewed and checked by two bilinguals. The instructions for the English version of the test were in English and those for the French version in French. The scores are percentages of the total number of responses given.

With similar ends in mind, we calculated each child's associational latency, that is, the average time taken to respond to the stimulus words. The rationale was that the Experimental and Control children might give similar type responses even though the Experimentals might still be more sluggish in responding, reflecting the play of more complicated mediation processes, such as translation from one language to the other. Since all responses were tape-recorded, it was simple to measure the time taken to respond, and to establish averages for each child. Scores for this measure are average latencies in seconds.

7. *Speaking Skill in English.* Each child was presented a filmstrip story of "The Lion and the Rat" accompanied by a dialogue in English, narrated by an adult. Immediately after, the child was asked to retell the story, and his production was tape-recorded. Several types of ratings were made by two linguistic judges, working independently:

(a) *Overall Expressive Ability* was measured on a 1-5 (poor to excellent) scale according to the child's ease of talking, word choice, and thought patterns, or errors in substance.

(b) *Grammatical Errors* were counted and are presented as percentages of errors out of the total number of words spoken.

(c) *Enunciation* was also scored on the same 1-5 scale and reflected the child's ability to pronounce words distinctly in contrast to running words together.

(d) *Rhythm and Intonation,* also rated on a 1-5 scale, reflects the general form of spoken English in terms of its rhythm and intonation.

(e) *Time of Production* and

(f) *Number of Words Produced* were actual counts made from the taped recordings, and are presented as separate scores.

8. *Speaking Skills in French.* This measure is essentially similar in form to the one just described (number 7). In this case, the film was entitled "Le Loup et l'Oiseau," narrated by an adult native speaker of French, with instructions given in French. The child's retelling of the story was tape-recorded and analyzed for: (a) *Overall Expressive Ability*; (b) *Grammatical Errors*; (c) *Errors of Liaison*; and (d) *Rhythm and Intonation.* Categories (a) and (d) were rated by a French language teacher on a five-point scale: (1) Nul ou mal; (2) Passable; (3) Moyen; (4) Assez bon; and (5) Bon, with native speakers of French as the point of reference. Categories (b) and (c) were scored as percentages of the total number of words spoken.

9. *Phoneme Production, in French.* This is a measure of the child's ability to

produce phonemic units in French. Each child was presented a series of nineteen French phrases spoken by a French-speaking adult, and, after each had been articulated twice, he was to reproduce the phrase. His responses were recorded on tape, analyzed, and scored by a specialist in French according to their approximations to nativelike control. The rating scale used ranged from 0 (nul), 1 (mal), 2 (moyen), to 3 (bon), with French-speaking children as a point of reference. Sample items are: "Avez-vous vu la lune?" (repeated twice) or "Onze saintes." In the first example, the child had to differentiate the "u" sound of "vous" from that of "vu" and "lune."

The nineteen phonemic units used were suggested by linguists as particularly difficult ones that must be mastered in learning to speak French perfectly. These French sounds, represented orthographically, are u, é, è, eille, eu, ô, ot, eur, â, alle, in, on, un, an, j, r, pn, pt (as in "p'tit"), and cl. The instructions were given in French. Since a rating of 3 is the best score, a perfect total score would be 57 (3x19).

10. *School Commission Mathematics Test, in French*. This test (entitled "Test de Rendement en Calcul") was designed by the Catholic School Commission of Montreal to measure two skills, *solving identities* (fifteen items) and *addition and subtraction* (fifteen items). Sample items, given in French, are:

Fill in the square so that the two boxes are equal.

3 + 5		□ +2

Put an X on the largest answer.

1 + 2	6 - 5	3 - 1	7 - 5	5 - 4

Instructions were given in French. The total possible score was 30.

11. *Reading Skills in French: Word Discrimination and Sentence Comprehension*. This is a test of French reading skills, "Test de Rendement en Français," constructed by the Catholic School Commission of Montreal. All instructions are given in French, and the highest possible score was 30.

The first ten items deal with *word discrimination*. The children were presented two groups of thirty printed words and were asked to find within each group the five words read aloud twice by the examiner. In a shortened form, an example might include a group of words such as: "cabane, boule, joue, école, café, zéro, roche, mine, lavabo" and the child would have to underline those he heard read to him, such as "école, café, joue."

The second group of ten items measure *sentence comprehension*. The children were asked to select from three printed sentences the one most closely associated with that read aloud to them. Thus, if they hear the sentence, "Papa a avalé," they would choose among three alternatives, such as: "Papa a bu. Papa a lu. Papa a joué."

The third group of ten items deal with *word order*—in this case the ability to reorder words that are unordered in a sentence. For example, given the array, "lave je lavabo le" they would indicate which word would most likely be last in a well-ordered sentence.

12. *Word Discrimination in French*. This is a French version of that described in 2 above, with thirty-two rather than thirty-five items. All instructions and examples were given in French. In this version, the children would hear an adult read "*et* . . . Jean *et* Paul . . . *et*," then they would choose among words such as "elle, et, vert, sans" for the correct response. Total score possible was 32.

13. *Phoneme Discrimination in Russian*. It has often been said that early bilingualism has a generally favorable effect on the learning of other languages and that the mastery of two contrasting phonemic systems carries with it a general sensitivity to language sounds. Arguments favoring this possibility were given by Peal and Lambert (1962) and supporting evidence was presented in a study by Yeni-Komshian (1965). More recently, Rabinovitch and Parver (1966) compared monolingual and bilingual college students on their capacity to discriminate Russian phoneme sequences, with Russian being a totally foreign language for both groups. They found the bilinguals to be very much superior to the monolinguals in making these discriminations. The procedures used by Rabinovitch and Parver were therefore adopted and pretested for this study. It was our belief that the bilingual experience of the children in the Experimental Class of first graders might favor the development of such a skill at an early age. On the other hand, the work of Kittell (1959, 1963) suggested that the cognitive advantages of bilingualism, rather than showing themselves in the first three grades, do not generally appear until grade V or so. Thus, if we failed to find a generalized ability to discriminate foreign sounds at this time, we might look for it during the next year or two, as the same children progressed in their development of bilingual skills.

The children were tested individually with directions given in the native language. They were first taught the meaning of the terms "same" and "different" (or "pareil" and "pas pareil") and were given practice runs. Each child heard fifty-three pairs of Russian syllables tape-recorded by a Russian-speaking linguist. The child, listening through earphones, had to decide if the two sound sequences heard in a pair were the same or different; actually both members of sixteen of the sound pairs were identical and thirty-seven were different. A perfect score would be 53.

14. *June Retesting of Intelligence*. The Progressive Matrices test (sets A, Ab, and B) developed by Raven (1956) was readministered to all children in June to determine whether any systematic or class-wide changes had taken place in intelligence for the children in the Experimental Class in comparison with those in the Control Classes. In this case, the covariance procedure controlled statistically for variations in both the initial Raven scores and the various aspects of home background.

These then were our research plans, our attempts at equating experimental and control classes, and the measures developed for evaluating the program's impact. Our expectations of how the children in the Experimental Class would likely stand relative to the comparison groups at the end of grade I are discussed in the next chapter, where we get the first signs of what goes on when children switch to a second language as the medium of instruction at school.

Chapter Three

The Standings of the Pilot Classes at the End of Grade I

What sort of impact does a home-school language switch have on first-grade children? To answer this question, we will examine first the children's English-language skills, comparing those in the Experimental Class who had no formal training in English during the year with those in the English Control Classes. The orienting question for this comparison is the following: Have the children trained in a second language suffered in their native language development relative to the controls? Or have they instead been able to develop generalizable skills in the course of their French training that are transferable to English, their native language? The reasoning here is that the Experimental children may use English privately (e.g., through translation) to give meaning to concepts introduced in the new language. That is, they may find it easier to cope with the demands placed upon them if they become skilled translators, at least at first. Because of their unique experience they might also become skilled at comparing and contrasting the two language systems. Since they had learned to read in French, they might also develop techniques on their own for transferring reading skills from French to English. The interesting question then is whether they would be able to transfer and relate notions developed through French into already known English concepts, to note and make use of contrasts and similarities in the structures of French and English, and to generalize the reading skills they have established in French to English. It is equally possible of course that the demands of this strange educational experience would retard the children's development in both languages, and obfuscate any new ideas presented to them through French.

The Comparative Standing of the Pilot Classes
in English at the End of Grade I

The test results are presented in Table 6. Note first that on tests requiring English word knowledge (Test 1), English word discrimination (Test 2), and reading skills (Test 3), the Experimental Class is clearly poorer than either of the English Control Classes. These tests are designed and standardized for English-speaking children who have followed a normal first-grade program in their native language, and all three require a reading ability in English. The statistical tests of significance indicate that the average performances of the Experimental and English Control Classes fall at quite different points, especially in the case of English reading skills. Nevertheless, the Experimental group still falls at the 50th percentile in terms of nationwide norms for English-speaking first graders on both Test 1 and Test 2 and at the 15th percentile on English reading skills, Test 3. Thus, the Experimental Class performs at the general average for their age level in English word knowledge and word discrimination, both calling for reading skill in English; it is on tests of sentence and paragraph comprehension that they fall below the average. These findings provide strong evidence for a transfer of skills from French to English, especially since the parents had been urged not to introduce or encourage English reading at home on an informal basis. Nearly all the youngsters and apparently most of the parents complied with this request.

During all three tests and particularly during the reading skills test, it was amusing and instructive to hear the spontaneous comments of the children in the Experimental Class when they were asked to follow each word in the written instructions accompanying the English texts, as these were read aloud by the examiner. Several complained that this was a "new" or "funny" writing system for them; but when encouraged to follow along so as "to get the knack of reading English," they seemed both puzzled and pleased that it was possible. In fact, we had the impression that only a small amount of practice would be needed to transfer reading skills acquired in a nonnative language to the native language. Research directed specifically to this notion would be of great value and interest to both educators and psychologists.

The Picture Vocabulary test (item 5 in Table 6) measures the child's competence with English-language terms and concepts. Note that the Experimental Class is in no way behind the two English Canadian Control classes in this skill. Many of the more difficult items in this test, we believe, were new concepts for the children, ones they would not have encountered except through French. Thus, certain concepts included in this measure were also likely transferred from French to English.

The children in the Experimental Class were indistinguishable from the English Controls in terms of their overall expressive ability, enunciation, and rhythm and intonation in spoken English (item 7 in Table 6). However, they did

Table 6

Test Results for the Pilot Classes at the End of Grade I, 1967

Test Number and Name	Experimental Class		English Control I		English Control II		French Control		Grand Mean	F Ratio	df
	Mean	Adjusted	Mean	Adjusted	Mean	Adjusted	Mean	Adjusted			
1. Word Knowledge, English	48.38	48.85	57.95	59.27	55.58	54.02	—	—	53.90	13.15**	2,62
2. Word Discrimination, English	48.21	48.50	59.95	60.99	57.23	56.08	—	—	55.06	15.31**	2,62
3. Reading Skills, English	35.20	36.46	57.27	58.64	54.67	52.09	—	—	48.62	40.54**	2,61
4. Arithmetic Concepts, English	54.36	55.23	54.64	54.95	58.67	57.47	—	—	55.90	.60	2,61
5. Picture Vocabulary, English	60.16	60.39	58.78	59.77	60.53	59.15	—	—	59.85	.22	2,50
6. Word Association Analysis *English*											
Associational Latency (secs.)	3.41	3.28	3.12	3.27	—	—	—	—	3.27	.00	1,36
Paradigmatic (%)	62.02	61.03	68.44	69.68	—	—	—	—	64.88	1.39	1,36
Syntagmatic Runs (%)	28.46	28.91	18.03	17.48	—	—	—	—	23.83	4.17*	1,36
Syntagmatic Changes (%)	4.70	4.74	4.08	4.02	—	—	—	—	4.42	.43	1,36
Irrelevants (%)	4.74	5.55	3.26	2.24	—	—	—	—	4.08	2.77	1,36
Rhymings	.32	.09	3.15	3.45	—	—	—	—	1.58	11.61**	1,36
Transformations (%)	.24	.28	3.05	3.00	—	—	—	—	1.49	3.73	1,36

Table 6 (cont.)
Test Results for the Pilot Classes at the End of Grade I, 1967

Test Number and Name	Experimental Class		English Control I		English Control II		French Control		Grand Mean	F Ratio	df
	Mean	Adjusted	Mean	Adjusted	Mean	Adjusted	Mean	Adjusted			
6. Word Association Analysis (cont.)											
French											
Associational Latency (secs.)	4.14	4.31	—	—	—	—	3.76	3.60	3.95	1.84	1,42
Paradigmatic (%)	49.56	50.66	—	—	—	—	50.76	49.66	50.16	.02	1,41
Syntagmatic Runs (%)	30.83	30.80	—	—	—	—	15.49	15.53	23.16	12.77**	1,41
Syntagmatic Changes (%)	5.47	5.69	—	—	—	—	2.70	2.48	4.08	5.31*	1,41
Irrelevants (%)	12.16	11.77	—	—	—	—	13.18	13.56	12.67	.25	1,41
Rhymings (%)	.24	.11	—	—	—	—	2.31	2.44	1.27	5.31*	1,41
Transformations (%)	1.62	.83	—	—	—	—	15.15	15.95	8.39	12.97**	1,41
7. Speaking Skills in English											
Overall Expressive Ability	4.71	4.75	4.95	4.93	5.77	5.75	—	—	5.13	1.28	2,57
Grammatical Errors (%)	2.81	2.78	1.07	.95	1.66	1.81	—	—	1.89	4.28*	2,57
Enunciation	5.83	5.83	6.33	6.42	5.86	5.78	—	—	6.00	1.22	2,57
Rhythm and Intonation	5.75	5.80	6.29	6.30	5.23	5.16	—	—	5.75	3.09	2,57
Time of Production (secs.)	49.17	49.12	35.52	33.67	35.82	37.64	—	—	40.38	3.55*	2,56
Number of Words Produced	44.08	45.86	47.48	46.08	56.36	55.76	—	—	49.18	1.91	2,57
8. Speaking Skills in French											
Overall Expressive Ability	1.92	1.78	—	—	—	—	4.25	4.41	3.04	69.22**	1,41

Test Number and Name	Experimental Class		English Control I		English Control II		French Control		Grand Mean	F Ratio	df
	Mean	Adjusted	Mean	Adjusted	Mean	Adjusted	Mean	Adjusted			
8. Speaking Skills in French (cont.)											
Grammatical Errors (%)	10.41	10.43	—	—	—	—	1.55	1.53	6.16	58.48**	1,41
Errors of Liaison (%)	2.58	2.73	—	—	—	—	.23	.07	1.45	13.71**	1,41
Rhythm and Intonation	1.85	1.69	—	—	—	—	4.38	4.53	3.06	81.21**	1,41
9. Phoneme Production in French	42.15	42.21	—	—	—	—	56.14	56.08	48.40	120.20**	1,38
10. School Commission Math, French	17.36	16.67	—	—	—	—	16.16	16.85	16.76	.01	1,41
11. Reading Skills in French	16.20	15.65	—	—	—	—	15.13	15.70	15.67	.00	1,40
12. Word Discrimination in French	28.33	28.38	—	—	—	—	23.72	23.68	25.98	5.03*	1,40
13. Phoneme Discrimination in Russian (Error Scores)	19.60	19.60	16.80	15.51	—	—	18.28	19.30	18.33	1.82	2,60
14. June Retest of Intelligence	23.17	23.66	27.45	28.03	25.92	24.94	—	—	25.46	6.20**	2,61

*The F ratios are marked as statistically significant at the .05 level of confidence with a single asterisk and at the .01 level with two asterisks. When only two groups are compared these can be read as t-test differences with the means indicating which group scored higher or lower. When three groups are compared, the Newman-Keuls method for making multiple group comparisons was used. Using this procedure, the following breakdowns were established:

Tests 1, 2 and 3, English Control I > English Control II > Experimental (i.e., each reliably different from the other).

Test 7 (error scores) Experimental > English Control I; English Control I = English Control II.

Test 7 (time scores) Experimental > English Control I; Experimental > English Control II; English Control I = English Control II.

Test 14 English Control I > Experimental; English Control I > English Control II; English Control II = Experimental.

distinguish themselves in two important respects: they made significantly more grammatical errors in their story-telling productions than the Controls, and they produced utterances at a slower rate than the Controls. This suggests that they were slower at selecting words and constructing sequences of ideas in English.

With regard to the children's word associations in English (item 6), note first that the Experimental Class associates as rapidly as the English Controls; that is, there is no difference between groups in associational latency, or in the number of irrelevant or idiosyncratic responses produced. The Experimental children, however, do give reliably more "syntagmatic runs" (common verbal sequences) in English, although this is not by itself a symptom of linguistic retardation since they are comparable to the Controls in the number of paradigmatic responses given. Overall, then, the Experimental Class is basically similar to the English Controls in giving English associations, although they do have more common associational chains of ideas.

Standing in French skills at grade I. How well do children progress linguistically in a second language when that language is used as the sole medium of instruction for the child's first year at school? Do they begin to acquire nativelike command of the language? Considering first French-speaking skills (measure 8), it is clear that the Experimental children are definitely poorer than the French-speaking first-grade Controls in their overall expressive ability, number of grammatical errors, errors of liaison, and rhythm and intonation. However, their mean score of 1.78 for overall expressive ability in French represents, in the eyes of the judge, a rating which falls just short of "passable" on a five-point scale extending from *nul* or *mal* to *bon*. This average rating reflects good progress, since the linguistic judge used native speakers as her point of reference. Thus, although the children of the Experimental Class are well below the French Control Class in all aspects of speaking skills, including errors of grammar and liaison, they apparently are beginning to progress toward nativelike command.

As a group, they are also clearly poorer than the Controls on French phoneme production (item 9). However, their mean score of 42.21 which translates to a rating of 2.22 on a scale running from 0 (*nul*), to 1 (*mal*), to 2 (*moyen*), to 3 (*bon*) makes them, as a group, better than average when native speakers are used as the point of reference. They have apparently progressed somewhat further in mastering the basic sound units of the language (e.g., phoneme distinctions) than in integrating those units into smooth and accurate speech patterns (e.g., liaison, rhythm and intonation, and overall expressive skill).

In contrast, the skills involved in understanding and responding flexibly to spoken French appear to have developed more readily than the productive skills. Thus on Test 11, which measures competence in French word discrimination, sentence comprehension, and word order, the Experimental children perform as well as the French Controls. It is especially instructive to see that the Experimental Class scored significantly *better* than the French Controls on Test 12, a measure of word discrimination in French. Here the children are required to associate the sound of a French word with its printed form, and it is difficult to explain why they surpass the Controls on this test. Possibly, in their attempts to cope with a new language, they may have developed a type of linguistic detective capacity to help search out and link up efficiently the written and oral forms of new words. Whatever the final explanation may turn out to be, it is important to realize that the Experimentals are either as good or better than the French comparison group in these relatively more passive French language skills.

In the French word association data (item 6), there are several noteworthy comparisons. First, the Experimental children respond as rapidly as the French Controls when giving associations in French, without giving more irrelevant or idiosyncratic associations.[1] However, they produce many fewer transformation and rhyming responses than the French Controls. This could mean either that they show limited flexibility and ingenuity in their French and English associations, or that they have moved farther away from childish play with the sounds of language. We have no way of settling this issue at the moment. It is certain, though, that the Experimental children give more syntagmatic responses (both runs and changes) than the French Controls do. Thus, they have a bilingual tendency to overemphasize syntagmatic responses, but again they do not give any fewer paradigmatic responses than the French Controls.

Standing in mathematics at grade I. What effect does a year's training conducted exclusively in French have on the Experimental children's mastery of a nonlanguage subject matter like mathematics? Here, the Experimental Class can be compared with both English and French Control Classes. The Experimental children do as well as both groups of English Controls on Test 4, a measure of comprehension of arithmetic concepts which was administered in English. This indicates that they have not suffered in any way, even on a test

---

[1] Although there is no reliable difference between groups in the number of irrelevant responses, nevertheless both the Experimental and French Control Classes give about 11 to 13 percent responses of that type. Note that the Experimental children give many more irrelevant responses in French (11%) than they do in English (5%), and that the French Controls in general give many more irrelevant responses than the English Controls. One cannot determine from these data whether there is some difference in the structural or semantic systems of the French and English languages that account for these differences or whether these samples of children are unrepresentative in some sense.

There is another interesting finding that is more incidental to our main study, i.e., the French Controls give a much larger proportion of transformation responses (15%) than do the English Controls (3%). Again, it would be valuable to determine whether there is some aspect of the French language that prompts so many more transformational responses from six-year-old children.

presented to them with English instructions and examples. Similarly, on Test 10, a standard French measure of mathematical concepts, the Experimental Class does as well as the French Controls. Thus, the Experimental group seems to experience no difficulty, relative to the Controls, when solving problems presented in either of their languages.

Standing in foreign language sound discrimination at grade I. Does bilingual experience of this sort contribute to a general sensitivity to foreign language sounds? In discriminating Russian phonemes (item 13), there are no reliable differences between the Experimental and either the French or the English Control groups, indicating that the Experimental children show no special skill in this regard.[2] It will be of interest nonetheless to see if a further year of experience in French does have the beneficial effect suggested by the work of Kittell (1959; 1963).

Standing in measured intelligence at grade I. Does a year's academic experience in a nonnative language affect the Experimental children's general intelligence? Research by Peal and Lambert (1962) suggested that we might expect some improvement in the Experimental children's general intelligence or "cognitive flexibility" because of their bilingual experience. On the other hand, one might expect to find that the language switch would cause some sort of mental confusion that would manifest itself in a regression or retardation of intellectual development. Of course, retesting IQ after only a nine-month period of schooling offers a very short time period for changes of any sort to take place. This comparison, then, will also be of more interest as we continue to examine the Experimental children at later stages of the program. In fact, the June retest with the Raven Progressive Matrices test (item 14) does show a reliable difference among groups: the Experimental children score lower than one of the English Control Classes, but no differently from the second English Control Class. Thus, there is *some* evidence for a relative lack of intellectual development in the Experimental Class, but not one that can be unambiguously attributed to differences in academic training.

Summary and Conclusions, Grade I Pilot Classes, 1967

After the kindergarten and grade I experience with the home-school language switch, we have the following answers to the major questions that guided our evaluation.

Do first-grade children trained through a second language suffer in the development of their native language, or do they develop general skills through

---

[2]We are grateful to Mrs. Renée Stevens for conducting this phase of the study, to Dr. J. G. Nicholson of McGill's Russian Department for making the master tapes, and to the authorities of the Lakeshore Regional School Board for permitting us to pretest the procedure.

the medium of the second language that can be transferred or related to similar processes in their native language? On tests of English word knowledge, word discrimination, and reading skill, the Experimental Class clearly falls below the English Controls. This was to be expected since they have had no training in English. However, the fact that their mean scores on two of these tests fall at the 50th percentile on American norms and that in English reading skills they reach the 15th percentile suggests that a good deal of transfer of skills from French to English has taken place. We presume then that their native language was in some way active as they followed the various subject matter presented through French.

They have no difficulty, relative to the Controls, in *comprehending spoken English*; and in *English-speaking skill*, they were as competent as the Controls in overall expression, enunciation, and rhythm and intonation. They did, however, make more grammatical errors, and had a slower rate of verbal output in reconstructing a story, suggesting a relative slowness in selecting words to construct sequences of ideas in English. However, their *word associations in English* came as rapidly as those of the Controls, and they gave no more irrelevant or idiosyncratic responses. Still, they showed a greater tendency to use common chains of ideas and to be somewhat less imaginative than the Controls in their English associations.

How well do children progress in their control of a second language when it is used as the sole medium of instruction for the first year of schooling? Do they approach nativelike command? With regard to *speaking skills in French*, the Experimental Class was definitely poorer than the French Controls in reconstructing a story, overall expression, errors of grammar, liaison, and rhythm and intonation. Nonetheless, the mean ratings of linguistic judges indicate that they are making good progress toward nativelike skill. Similarly, their ability to produce appropriate French phoneme distinctions was poorer than that of the native-speaker Controls and yet they were judged to be at the *moyen* level, with native speakers as the frame of reference. Thus, they have progressed further in the mastery of basic sound units in French than in the ability to integrate those units into smooth and accurate speech patterns.

At the same time, they are as efficient as the Controls on tests of French word discrimination, sentence comprehension, and word order. They also appear to be as flexible and creative in these more receptive aspects of French as the native-speaker Controls. The Experimental Class turns out to be even more clever than the Controls in associating the sound and printed form of French words. Our guess is that they have developed, as a consequence of the extra attention they must give in studying through the medium of a new language, a type of "linguistic detective" capacity—an enhanced sensitivity in searching out and linking up the written and oral forms of French words. Their *verbal associations* in French were given as rapidly as those of the Controls, and the content of their associations was no more irrelevant or idiosyncratic. They were nonetheless somewhat less flexible in the forms of associations given and more likely to produce common associative chains of ideas, even though they gave as many paradigmatic responses as the French Control children. It is of interest that in both languages the Experimental children show a disproportionate number of common associational chains. Their bilingual experience at this stage may have produced a general stereotyped mode of responding when spontaneous associations are called for.

What effect does a year's schooling conducted exclusively in a second language have on children's development in a nonlanguage subject matter such as mathematics? When compared to either English or French Control Classes, the Experimental children do just as well on arithmetic tests designed for pupils following a conventional first-grade program. Thus, they are able to follow directions and work out practice problems presented in either language, and their French training in mathematics is easily applied in an English-language context.

Does bilingual experience of this sort contribute to a general ability to differentiate language sounds, even those of a thoroughly strange language? Although previous research suggested that bilingual experience appears to foster a general sensitivity to the sound systems of foreign languages, we found no supporting evidence with our test of Russian phonemes: The Experimental Class was no better than the monolingual Controls on this measure. There are indications from other studies that the development of such a sensitivity may occur at a later age, and it will be valuable to look again for such an advantage as the experiment continues.

Finally, *does this type of bilingual experience affect the children's intelligence?* Previous research and theory suggested that bilingual experience can enhance cognitive or mental flexibility, but the results of the study to date offer no support for such an enhancement, nor for intellectual confusion or retardation of any sort. It will be particularly interesting to watch for changes of either sort in following years.

Although these findings are both instructive and encouraging, they must be interpreted with caution. The number of children involved has purposely been kept small. Even though every effort was made to equate the four classes on factors that could bias the comparisons, we must now determine whether the outcomes just discussed are reliable; that is we must determine if they will reappear with new groups of children following essentially the same program. This concern with replication is expressed in the following chapter where we examine carefully a new set of comparison classes to see if they show the same general pattern of outcomes. If this important matter is settled, we can then, with much more confidence, watch two separate Experimental Classes—the Pilot group we have just discussed and a Follow-up group to be introduced now—as they progress through grades II, III, and IV.

Chapter Four

The Follow-up Classes at the End of Grade I

Because the home-school language-switch program developed in response to a strong community-based desire to have children become fully bilingual, the year-by-year results of the experiment are viewed with much more than an academic interest by the parents, teachers, and school administrators involved in the program. The educational potential of the idea has also stimulated an interest among those responsible for bilingual education in various communities and settings around the world. Although the first-year results with the Pilot Classes were extremely encouraging, we nevertheless wanted to be more sure of the stability and generalizability of the results. To this end we compare here the end-of-year performances of a new set of first-grade pupils, comprising different Experimental, English, and French Control Classes. Our hope was to be able to replicate the first year results.

General Procedure

The overall plan remains the same: the purpose is to examine the effects of a year's schooling plus kindergarten, conducted exclusively in a second language, on the linguistic and mental development of first-grade children. Attention is given to the program's influence on their native and second-language skills, and their progress with the academic content of the first grade curriculum. The Follow-up Control Classes had the following characteristics: English Control I was a group of twenty-six first graders in the same school as the majority of the Experimental Class, but who were following a conventional English-language program; English Control II was a first-grade class of twenty-eight children from a school in Westmount, a middle-class district of Montreal; and the French Control Class comprised twenty-five first graders from a French-Canadian Catholic school in the St. Lambert district. The Follow-up Experimental Class actually comprised two separate classes, one of twenty-five children, the other of thirteen children, in separate English-language elementary schools. Each class with its own French-speaking teacher was full-sized, that is, each comprised about thirty students.

Because we wanted to make the results applicable to typical middle-class school systems in North America, we urged the administrators and teachers *not* to screen children out of the Experimental Classes who were thought to be slow learners or otherwise unlikely to cope with this special type of first-grade program. Even so, the parents of one or two children were dissuaded from participating by child psychiatrists, but at least two children with diagnosed "perceptual-motor problems" did remain in each of the Experimental Classes. As we shall see, these children subsequently adjusted well and became indistinguishable at the upper-grade levels from the other children in their overall performance. One gets an idea of the range of abilities from Table 7 which summarizes the intelligence scores for each class on the Progressive Matrices Test (Raven, 1956). Note that in all cases, the majority of scores range from the 50th to the 95th percentile, and that the Follow-up Experimental Class has one student below the 10th percentile. Thus, the program was not restricted to only the brightest students, and, as is evident from Table 8, there are no reliable differences in mean intelligence scores between the Experimental and the Control Classes.

The mothers of the children in the Follow-up Classes were interviewed in the same fashion as the parents of the Pilot Classes. Details were gathered about parental values, aspirations, and child training practices that have been found to influence academic intelligence and academic achievement (cf., Bloom, 1964; Davé, 1963; Wolf, 1963). A revised version of the interview schedule permitted us to survey all parents by telephone. However, fewer questions were asked this time, so that the Pilot and Follow-up groups' scores are not directly comparable. Class comparisons of these scores, presented in Table 8, show that there was a reliable difference among groups for one of the five major themes only, that of "home guidance and facilities for school learning." The English Control II Class rated reliably lower than all others in this regard.

In addition, the parents of all Experimental and Control children in the Follow-up Classes were surveyed to collect basic demographic and attitudinal information. Their responses, summarized in Tables 9 and 10, may be compared directly with the responses of the Pilot Class parents (see Tables 3 and 4 in Chapter II). In general, it is clear that the Experimental and Control parents are relatively alike in their background and attitudes. For the most part, they are life-long residents of Quebec, they have limited facility in "the other" language, they use their native language for family contacts, and they all attach importance to learning "the other" language.

Table 7

Follow-up Class Comparisons of Raven's Intelligence Scores at Start of Grade I, 1968

Percentiles	Scores of the Standardization Group*	*Percentage of Students Falling in Percentile Groups:*			
		Experimental Class	English Control I Class	English Control II Class	French Control Class
95	23 or over	25	48	33	29
90	21-22	11	5	11	19
75	17-20	36	33	26	43
50	14-16	25	9	22	5
25	11-13	0	5	7	5
10	10 or less	3	0	0	0
		N = 36	N = 21	N = 27	N = 21

*A sample of 300 Dumfries (Scotland) children, six years of age, at start of grade I.

Table 8

Follow-up Class Comparisons on Measures of Intelligence and Components of Socioeconomic Status at the Start of Grade I, September 1967

	Experimental N = 38	English Control I N = 26	English Control II N = 28	French Control N = 25	F-ratio
Intelligence, September Testing					
Raven Scores	19.74	21.35	20.39	20.40	n.s.
Home and Family Characteristics					
1. Emphasis on Education	3.79	3.50	3.59	3.70	n.s.
2. Quality of Linguistic Environment	3.56	3.58	3.69	3.38	n.s.
3. Home Guidance and Facilities for School Learning	3.83	3.62	3.18	3.80	6.40[a] df 3,105, p<.01
4. Enrichment of Home Environment	3.52	3.55	3.43	3.14	n.s.
5. Educational Facilities	4.25	4.14	4.07	4.13	n.s.
School Attendance					
Percentage of School Days Missed	4.14	6.85	5.74	1.47	10.46[b] df 3,118, p<.01

[a]The multiple-group comparison, tested with the Newman-Keuls technique (Winer, 1962), reveals that the English Control II group is significantly lower (at the .01 level) than all other groups.

[b]The Newman-Keuls test shows that the French Control class has significantly fewer absences than all other groups (.01 level) and that the English Control I class has significantly more absences than the Experimental class (.05 level).

As was the case with the Pilot Classes, the Experimental and English Control parents view French Canadians and English Canadians in a similar light on twelve of thirteen attitude scales which suggest to us that the sample of children included in the Follow-up Experimental Classes were not preselected to have unusually favorable attitudes toward French Canadians. This fact becomes important when we begin to discuss in Chapter 9 the long-range attitudinal consequences of the home-school language-switch program.

There was no evidence in terms of school attendance to suggest that the experimental program was more demanding or less interesting (see Table 8). The only reliable difference noted was that between the French Control Class, which had fewest absences, and the English Control I Class, which had most. Visits to the classes during the year revealed no apparent differences in discipline or attention problems.

We again made no attempt to equate the Follow-up Classes on the basis of quality, efficiency, or personalities of teachers. However, the school principals in this case too were confident each new first-grade teacher was fully trained and experienced and that each had selected elementary teaching as her specialty. The first-grade teachers for the Follow-up Experimental Classes were both from France and had teaching experience in France and in Canada. The curriculum used was essentially the same as that of the Pilot Classes, drawing on French materials used both in French Canada and France at the grade I level.

The same covariance procedure (Snedecor, 1956) used to analyze the Pilot Class data was employed again. This technique statistically adjusts each of the dependent variables for initial differences in IQ and home environment characteristics, and the adjusted mean scores are then tested by analysis of variance.

Measures Used with the Follow-up Grade I Children, 1968

Essentially the same battery of tests was used again with the Follow-up Classes; but certain modifications were introduced, and these are described below. The numbers refer to the listing of tests in Table 11.

5. *Picture vocabulary.* A French translation of Form A of the Peabody Picture Vocabulary Test was administered to the Experimental and French Control Classes. Half of the Experimental students received the English version (Form B) first and the French version (of Form A) one week later, with the order reversed for the remainder of the class. The first eighty-five plates of the test were used making the total possible score 85.

6. *Listening comprehension in English.* An entire class listened to two stories narrated in English, each one presented first in its entirety, then in two parts. After each part, the children were asked six true-false questions. For example, a section of one story ran as follows: "A little rabbit wanted to sleep. He stretched out in the green grass among white flowers. He opened his mouth very wide as

Table 9

Parent Questionnaire for the Follow-up Classes

	Experimental Class (N = 34)	English Controls (N = 52)	French Controls (N = 22)
Mother's residence in Quebec	3.47	3.48	3.95
Father's residence in Quebec	3.47	3.60	3.95
Mother speaks to children in: one language only (0) both English and French (1)	0.15	0.10	0.00
Father speaks to children in: one language only (0) both English and French (1)	0.30	0.20	0.09
Brothers and sisters speak to each other in: one language only (0) both English and French (1)	0.25	0.18	0.00
Mother's fluency in English: *speaking*	3.00	3.00	1.82
reading	3.00	3.00	1.91
understanding	3.00	3.00	2.05
Father's fluency in English: *speaking*	3.00	3.00	2.45
reading	3.00	3.00	2.45
understanding	3.00	3.00	2.45
Mother's fluency in French: *speaking reading*	1.03	1.25	2.82
reading	1.27	1.25	2.86
understanding	1.41	1.41	2.86
Father's fluency in French: *speaking*	1.71	1.81	3.00
reading	1.76	1.79	3.00
understanding	2.03	1.79	3.00

	Experimental Class	English Controls	French Controls
Importance of learning the second language:			
For understanding the other group and their way of life	6.38	5.88	6.18
For getting a good job	6.56	6.77	6.73
To gain friends among the other group	5.94	6.19	6.73
For social recognition	4.79	3.25	4.14
To think and behave as the other group does	3.38	2.85	2.23
As a mark of education	2.06	2.56	3.59
To meet with varied people	6.74	6.65	6.73
For business or educational purposes	4.71	4.94	1.55
Contact with other culture:			
Try to speak other language	1.82	2.02	1.82
Read newspapers in other language	0.59	0.77	1.59
Read magazines in other language	0.53	0.79	1.14
Listen to radio broadcasts in other language	0.91	0.96	1.45
Other-group visitors to home	1.56	1.52	1.23
Attend plays and theater in other language	0.29	0.37	1.14
Combined Subscores:			
Average residence in Quebec, mother and father	3.47	3.54	3.95
Average language usage of parents with children: (0 = one language, 1 = both languages)	0.22	0.15	0.05
Average language usage of all family members: (0 = one language, 1 = both languages)	0.26	0.16	0.03
Mother's overall fluency in English	3.00	3.00	1.92
Father's overall fluency in English	3.00	3.00	2.45
Mother's overall fluency in French	1.23	1.30	2.85
Father's overall fluency in French	1.83	1.79	3.00
Total of contact scores	1.00	1.07	1.39

Table 10

Attitude Profiles of Mothers of Follow-up Class Pupils

Characteristic	People Rated: Mothers of:	English Canadians	French Canadians
(1) Short – tall	Experimental Class	4.16	1.85
	English Control Class	4.00	2.50
	French Control Class	4.53	3.07
(2) Bad – good	Experimental Class	3.53	3.35
	English Control Class	3.59	3.28
	French Control Class	4.36	4.43
(3) Stupid – intelligent	Experimental Class	4.74	4.35
	English Control Class	5.06	4.50
	French Control Class	5.20	5.21
(4) Not nice – nice	Experimental Class	3.53	3.55
	English Control Class	3.94	3.56
	French Control Class	4.29	4.57
(5) Weak – strong	Experimental Class	4.74	4.40
	English Control Class	4.94	4.72
	French Control Class	4.86	4.86
(6) Not friendly – friendly	Experimental Class	3.00	3.65
	English Control Class	4.18	4.11
	French Control Class	4.07	4.79
(7) Lazy – industrious	Experimental Class	5.58	4.10
	English Control Class	5.29	4.44
	French Control Class	4.71	5.29

Comparison of Mean Scores

Comparison of Mean Scores

People Rated:

Mothers of:	English Canadians	French Canadians
(8) Mean – kind		
Experimental Class	3.79	3.70
English Control Class	4.18	3.89
French Control Class	3.93	4.29
(9) Fat – thin		
Experimental Class	4.11	4.30
English Control Class	4.24	4.00
French Control Class	4.71	3.29
(10) Slow – fast		
Experimental Class	3.68	3.15
English Control Class	3.53	3.11
French Control Class	3.62	3.92
(11) Sad – happy		
Experimental Class	3.32	3.90
English Control Class	3.59	4.11
French Control Class	3.57	4.64
(12) Not pretty – pretty		
Experimental Class	3.47	3.80
English Control Class	3.35	3.44
French Control Class	3.64	3.79
(13) Not handsome – handsome		
Experimental Class	3.58	3.10
English Control Class	3.24	3.11
French Control Class	3.64	3.71

Note: Entries connected by a solid line differ significantly (p <.01) he yawned." They were asked questions such as: "Did the rabbit want to sleep? Did he stretch out in his bed? Did he open his mouth to yawn?" With a total of twenty-four questions, the maximum possible score was 24.

7. *Word association analysis, English and French*. Modifications were made in the analyses of the children's word associations. When an associational response satisfied the criteria for more than one category, it was classified with the following priorities: category (a) (see below) was given priority over (b) through (f), category (b) was given priority over (c) through (f), and so forth.

(a) *Syntagmatic*: Stimulus and response words that occur in immediate sequence (forward or backward) or that are separated by a single determiner such as *a* or *the* in ordinary continuous speech were considered syntagmatic. The sequence had to be one likely to occur in children's speech; thus *DEAD—Drunk* is not considered a syntagmatic response for children of this age, although it would be for adults. The word "not" following a verb stimulus was classified as syntagmatic, e.g., *ALLOW—not*.

(b) *Paradigmatic* responses are those that occur in the same word class (e.g., noun, verb, adjective) as the stimulus word, even if each can also occur in other classes. The opposite or negation of a word was considered paradigmatic, e.g., *CLEAR—unclear*. *SOFTLY—hard* was called paradigmatic because it was presumed that the children were responding "hard" to the "soft" stem of "softly." Furthermore, "hard" is sometimes used as an adverb, as is "softly", e.g., "He hit the ball hard." Similarly, *COLOR—red* and *FIVE—six* were classified as paradigmatic.

(c) *Semantic clusters* are responses that are semantically related to the stimulus word, but do not fit categories (a) or (b), e.g., *EAT—plate*.

(d) *Rhyming responses*: e.g., *SAY—day*.

(e) *Transformations* (excluding negation) of stimulus words, e.g., *KILL—killing*.

(f) *Idiosyncratic* responses are those with no obvious relation between the stimulus and response, e.g., *RUN—spinach*.

The associations were classified by two judges working independently. The scores in Table 11 are percentages based on the total number of responses given.

Each child's associational latency (i.e., his average time to respond to stimulus words) was also calculated, on the assumption that the Experimental and Control Classes might give similar types of responses even though the Experimentals could be slower in responding if they used more complicated mediation processes, such as translation from one language to the other. Scores for this measure are average latencies, in seconds.

8. *Speaking skills: Story retelling*. Each child, tested individually, listened to a tape-recorded story consisting of six or seven sentences, and then retold the story in his own words. His output was tape-recorded. For the Experimental Class, half of the children received a French story on one day and several days

later an English story. The other half heard the English story first, then the French. Counts were made of the following features of each child's story, transcribed from tape to cards: the total number of words used in retelling the story; the number of adjectives; the number of different adjectives; the number of nouns; the number of different nouns; the number of verbs; the number of different verbs; the number of grammatical errors; and his overall comprehension of the theme and sequence of the story, rated on a five-point scale ranging from *poor* to *excellent*.

Ratings. The stories were then randomized on a master tape, and two perfectly bilingual judges independently rated the stories on five-point scales for the following linguistic features: *overall expression*, consisting of ease of talking, word choice, thought patterns, and errors of substance; *grammatical correctness; enunciation* (in French, enunciation and liaison); and *rhythm and intonation*. Each child's score is the average of the two judges' ratings.

9. *Speaking skills: Story creation.* Each child was presented sets of comic-strip type pictures and asked to make up a story suggested by the sequence of pictures in the set. Half of the Experimental children were tested in French first; the other half, in English first. The children's productions were *rated* and *counted* in the same manner as in 8 above.

12. *Listening comprehension in French.* A French version of test 6 described above. Total possible score is 24.

13. *Picture Vocabulary Test, in French.* A translated version of the standard Peabody Picture Vocabulary Test. Total possible score is 85.

16. *Speaking skills: Story retelling in French.* A French version of measure 8 described above.

17. *Speaking skills: Story creation, in French.* A French version of measure 9.

19. *Lorge-Thorndike intelligence.* This measure of intelligence uses pictorial materials and oral instructions. Level I of the test is standardized for first-grade pupils. It consists of three subtests. The first, containing twenty-five items, tests vocabulary by asking the child to circle one of five pictures which represents the word he hears read aloud. The second subtest (twenty-five items) requires the child to circle the picture (out of five alternatives) which does not belong (e.g., basketball; football; cat; baseball; tennis ball). The third subtest (twenty-five items) calls for an ability to determine which two pictures (out of five) go together. Subtest and total scores are given in Table 11; the highest possible total score is 75.

Results for the Grade I Follow-up Classes, 1968

As is generally the case in attempts at replicating, conditions are rarely the same from one time period to another. Even though the same program was followed for the Pilot and Follow-up Classes, different teachers, principals, and school buildings were involved; a different team of university students conducted the testing and interviewing; and changes were introduced in the mode of analysis and many of the testing procedures. These differences, of course, can be advantageous, for if we find the same pattern of results from year to year despite the variations introduced, we will be that much more convinced that the conclusions drawn are reliable and of general value. The results for this new set of grade I classes are presented in Table 11.

Reading ability and word knowledge in English. On the tests calling for an ability to read and make judgments about English words (items 1, 2, and 3 in Table 11), the Experimental children are significantly poorer than those in the two English Control Classes, as would be expected since the Experimental Class had no academic training in English. Still, when compared with the North American norms, the Experimental Class falls between the 20th and 40th percentiles on these tests. These results add further support to the idea that children trained to read in a nonnative language are very efficient at transferring the basic skills to the native language.

Vocabulary and listening comprehension in English. In terms of their passive command of English, measured by the Picture Vocabulary and the Listening Comprehension tests (items 5 and 6), the Experimental Class demonstrates the same capacity in English as that of either English Control group, even for concepts that they would likely only have encountered in school through French. In this respect, too, the results square nicely with those of the Pilot Classes.

Speaking skills in English. With regard to speaking skills in English (measures 8 and 9), the Experimental children were judged to be as competent as the English Controls in overall expression, grammar, enunciation, and rhythm and intonation, both when retelling a story (8) and when creating a story based on a series of comic-strip pictures (9). In fact, their grammar was rated significantly better in the story retelling task. In that case, they used more words than either English Control Class, they used the greatest number of adjectives, nouns, and verbs, and they displayed a more diversified repertoire of adjectives than at least one of the Control Classes. In addition, their story comprehension was judged reliably better than that of either Control Class. When asked to create a story without the aid of a verbal model, they were still similar to the Controls except that they used fewer adjectives and had a less diversified range of nouns than one Control Class. Yet their story comprehension was significantly better than either Control Class. There appear then to be no signs of their having trouble with English grammar, as was the case with the Pilot Class at grade I, and they showed more comprehension than the Controls and a richer descriptive repertoire of English terms when retelling a story.

Table 11

Test Results for the Follow-up Classes at the End of Grade I, 1968

Test Number and Name	Experimental Class		English Control I		English Control II		French Control		Grand Mean	F Ratio	df
	Mean	Adjusted	Mean	Adjusted	Mean	Adjusted	Mean	Adjusted			
English Competence											
1. Word Knowledge[a] (S.S.)	42.44	42.87	59.00	58.67	56.88	56.59	—	—	51.37	29.40**	2,72
2. Word Discrimination (S.S.)	45.94	46.59	58.90	58.35	58.00	57.58	—	—	53.09	20.20**	2,73
3. Reading Skills (S.S.)	39.17	39.89	58.48	57.50	56.78	56.57	—	—	49.65	40.48**	2,75
4. Arithmetic Concepts (S.S.)	55.86	55.88	54.05	53.65	54.96	55.25	—	—	55.12	0.91	2,75
5. Picture Vocabulary	64.00	64.26	62.85	62.37	65.11	65.13	—	—	64.09	0.92	2,73
6. Listening Comprehension	22.17	22.34	22.37	21.93	22.15	22.23	—	—	22.21	0.19	2,72
7. *Word Association Analysis*											
Associational Latency (secs.)	4.06	4.15	3.86	3.69	—	—	—	—	3.98	0.96	1,48
Paradigmatic (%)	60.94	60.80	62.93	63.18	—	—	—	—	61.67	0.15	1,49
Syntagmatic (%)	19.50	20.14	13.89	12.79	—	—	—	—	17.43	4.15*	1,49
Semantic Clusters (%)	7.35	8.07	4.96	3.73	—	—	—	—	6.47	7.79***	1,49
Idiosyncratic (%)	9.49	9.64	9.03	8.77	—	—	—	—	9.32	0.05	1,49
Rhymings (%)	0.35	0.16	2.48	3.35	—	—	—	—	1.13	5.61*	1,49
Transformations (%)	1.27	1.18	4.07	4.22	—	—	—	—	2.30	10.29**	1,49

Table 11 (cont.)

Test Results for the Follow-up Classes at the End of Grade I, 1968

Test Number and Name	Experimental Class Mean	Adjusted	English Control I Mean	Adjusted	English Control II Mean	Adjusted	French Control Mean	Adjusted	Grand Mean	F Ratio	df
8. Speaking Skills; Story Retelling Ratings											
Overall Expressive Ability	2.36	2.42	2.03	1.95	2.15	2.13	—	—	2.21	1.48	2,69
Grammar	3.00	3.04	2.74	2.68	2.80	2.79	—	—	2.81	3.29*	2,69
Enunciation	2.80	2.86	3.00	2.88	2.87	2.87	—	—	2.87	0.00	2,69
Rhythm and Intonation	2.39	2.35	2.13	2.11	2.46	2.52	—	—	2.35	1.73	2,69
Counts											
Number of Words	63.47	63.36	49.80	50.19	48.27	48.12	—	—	55.11	3.85*	2,71
Number of Adjectives	4.59	4.58	4.10	3.93	2.46	2.61	—	—	3.77	4.37*	2,71
Number Different Adjectives	3.26	3.27	3.40	3.33	1.92	1.97	—	—	2.86	4.47*	2,71
Number of Nouns	14.00	14.01	10.45	10.40	10.77	10.79	—	—	12.06	3.90*	2,71
Number of Different Nouns	9.44	9.49	8.05	8.14	8.12	7.97	—	—	8.66	2.24	2,71
Number of Verbs	11.21	11.10	8.20	8.23	8.58	8.70	—	—	9.60	3.58*	2,71
Number Different Verbs	8.32	8.23	7.30	7.40	7.00	7.04	—	—	7.64	0.92	2,71
Number of Grammatical Errors	0.12	0.05	0.05	0.10	0.31	0.36	—	—	0.16	2.46	2,71
Story Comprehension	2.18	2.23	1.45	1.36	2.19	2.19	—	—	2.00	11.24**	2,71
9. Speaking Skills; Story Creation Ratings											
Overall Expressive Ability	2.56	2.65	—	—	2.89	2.78	—	—	2.71	0.41	1,52
Grammar	2.64	2.62	—	—	2.93	2.94	—	—	2.77	3.96	1,52
Enunciation	2.56	2.55	—	—	2.61	2.62	—	—	2.58	0.13	1,52
Rhythm and Intonation	2.55	2.63	—	—	2.94	2.85	—	—	2.72	1.37	1,52

Test Number and Name	Experimental Class		English Control I		English Control II		French Control		Grand Mean	F Ratio	df
	Mean	Adjusted	Mean	Adjusted	Mean	Adjusted	Mean	Adjusted			
Word Counts											
Number of Words	44.29	46.48	49.45	49.94	54.85	51.64	—	—	49.02	0.43	2,73
Number of Adjectives	1.14	1.23	0.75	0.71	2.41	2.32	—	—	1.46	4.68*	2,73
Number Different Adjectives	0.89	1.03	0.75	0.73	1.33	1.17	—	—	1.00	0.63	2,73
Number of Nouns	6.97	7.43	8.95	8.99	10.52	9.89	—	—	8.62	2.29	2,73
Number Different Nouns	4.54	4.77	5.60	5.65	7.59	7.26	—	—	5.80	6.94**	2,73
Number Verbs	8.94	9.27	9.15	9.08	8.74	8.37	—	—	8.93	0.34	2,73
Number Different Verbs	6.97	7.34	7.10	6.99	6.74	6.34	—	—	6.93	0.84	2,73
Number Grammatical Errors	0.46	0.44	0.05	0.10	0.11	0.10	—	—	0.24	1.13	2,73
Story Comprehension	2.89	2.88	2.60	2.60	1.93	1.93	—	—	2.50	21.34**	2,73
French Competence											
10. Reading Skills	15.29	15.36	—	—	—	—	17.11	16.98	15.93	2.05	1,46
11. Word Discrimination	25.28	25.35	—	—	—	—	25.60	25.47	25.39	0.01	1,48
12. Listening Comprehension	15.15	15.15	—	—	—	—	19.45	19.45	16.74	19.79**	1,46
13. Picture Vocabulary	53.85	53.81	—	—	—	—	63.48	63.54	57.53	27.45**	1,47
14. Phoneme Production	38.35	38.35	—	—	1967–	1967–	56.14	56.08	—	—	—
15. *Word Association Analysis*											
Associational Latency (secs.)	5.78	5.76	—	—	—	—	3.76	3.79	4.90	12.58**	1,52

Table 11 (cont.)

Test Results for the Follow-up Classes at the End of Grade I, 1968

Test Number and Name	Experimental Class		English Control I		English Control II		French Control		Grand Mean	F Ratio	df
	Mean	Adjusted	Mean	Adjusted	Mean	Adjusted	Mean	Adjusted			
Paradigmatic (%)	42.55	42.50	—	—	—	—	49.43	49.49	45.39	2.36	1,55
Syntagmatic (%)	16.71	16.73	—	—	—	—	11.60	11.58	14.60	4.52*	1,55
Semantic Clusters (%)	10.67	10.60	—	—	—	—	6.86	6.95	9.09	2.72	1,55
Idiosyncratic (%)	12.11	12.17	—	—	—	—	10.54	10.45	11.46	0.36	1,55
Rhymings (%)	2.87	2.88	—	—	—	—	4.90	4.89	3.71	1.86	1,55
Transformations (%)	3.81	3.91	—	—	—	—	13.47	13.32	7.81	8.36**	1,55
16. *Speaking Skills: Story Retelling Counts*											
Number of Words	57.91	57.13	—	—	—	—	57.27	59.54	57.74	0.07	1,35
Number of Adjectives	2.78	2.68	—	—	—	—	2.18	2.49	2.63	0.05	1,35
Number Different Adjectives	0.94	0.93	—	—	—	—	0.73	0.75	0.88	0.18	1,35
Number of Nouns	11.69	11.55	—	—	—	—	9.82	10.21	11.21	0.62	1,35
Number Different Nouns	5.62	5.54	—	—	—	—	5.55	5.79	5.60	0.10	1,35
Number of Verbs	10.00	9.86	—	—	—	—	10.82	11.23	10.21	0.57	1,35
Number Different Verbs	6.31	6.18	—	—	—	—	7.82	8.19	6.70	4.94*	1,35
Number Grammatical Errors	3.78	3.76	—	—	—	—	1.00	1.06	3.07	13.76**	1,35
Story Comprehension	1.69	1.63	—	—	—	—	2.27	2.45	1.84	5.47*	1,35
Ratings: Bilingual Judges											
Overall Expressive Ability	1.48	1.44	—	—	—	—	2.00	2.13	1.62	10.85**	1,33
Grammar	1.53	1.49	—	—	—	—	2.18	2.29	1.71	26.48**	1,33
Enunciation and Liaison	1.97	1.94	—	—	—	—	2.45	2.54	2.10	5.42*	1,33
Rhythm and Intonation	1.65	1.58	—	—	—	—	2.27	2.45	1.82	10.83**	1,33
Ratings: French Teacher Judges											
Overall Expressive Ability	2.10	2.05	—	—	—	—	2.73	2.86	2.26	7.23*	1,34
Grammar	2.39	2.36	—	—	—	—	2.82	2.90	2.50	5.62*	1,34
Enunciation and Liaison	2.58	2.54	—	—	—	—	3.05	3.17	2.70	4.16*	1,34

Test Number and Name	Experimental Class Mean	Experimental Class Adjusted	English Control I Mean	English Control I Adjusted	English Control II Mean	English Control II Adjusted	French Control Mean	French Control Adjusted	Grand Mean	F Ratio	df
17. Speaking Skills: Story Creation Counts											
Number of Words	56.18	56.00	—	—	—	—	64.18	64.72	58.18	1.35	1,36
Number Adjectives	2.00	1.88	—	—	—	—	2.55	2.89	2.14	1.33	1,36
Number Different Adjectives	0.55	0.52	—	—	—	—	0.73	0.81	0.59	0.70	1,36
Number Nouns	12.42	12.36	—	—	—	—	12.18	12.36	12.36	0.00	1,36
Number Different Nouns	6.61	6.58	—	—	—	—	7.36	7.45	6.80	0.65	1,36
Number Verbs	9.03	8.96	—	—	—	—	11.00	11.21	9.52	3.46	1,36
Number Different Verbs	6.39	6.39	—	—	—	—	8.82	8.84	7.00	12.38**	1,36
Number Grammatical Errors	6.82	6.78	—	—	—	—	1.09	1.20	5.39	24.68**	1,36
Story Comprehension	2.45	2.49	—	—	—	—	3.00	2.88	2.59	2.14	1,36
Ratings: Bilingual Judges											
Overall Expression	1.71	1.70	—	—	—	—	3.14	3.16	2.08	39.87***	1,34
Grammar	1.34	1.33	—	—	—	—	3.00	3.02	1.77	83.19***	1,34
Enunciation and Liaison	2.21	2.24	—	—	—	—	3.00	2.92	2.42	9.35***	1,34
Rhythm and Intonation	1.98	1.98	—	—	—	—	3.32	3.32	2.33	28.39***	1,34
Ratings: French Teacher Judges											
Overall Expression	2.66	2.65	—	—	—	—	3.41	3.43	2.85	7.28*	1,36
Grammar	2.26	2.27	—	—	—	—	3.02	2.98	2.45	28.42**	1,36
Enunciation and Liaison	2.67	2.70	—	—	—	—	3.05	2.97	2.77	0.90	1,36
Rhythm and Intonation	2.42	2.40	—	—	—	—	3.48	3.54	2.69	12.96**	1,36
Intelligence Measures											
18. June Retest, Raven's	24.00	24.61	24.05	23.48	25.11	24.74	—	—	24.38	0.82	2,73

Table 11 (cont.)
Test Results for the Follow-up Classes at the End of Grade I, 1968

Test Number and Name	Experimental Class		English Control I		English Control II		French Control		Grand Mean	F Ratio	df
	Mean	Adjusted	Mean	Adjusted	Mean	Adjusted	Mean	Adjusted			
19. Lorge-Thorndike											
a. Vocabulary	17.86	17.99	17.89	17.96	18.12	17.89	--	--	17.95	0.01	2,72
b. Not-belonging	17.03	16.98	18.00	17.86	18.08	18.24	--	--	17.59	3.67*	2,72
c. Go-together	14.58	14.81	14.84	14.63	14.65	14.49	--	--	14.67	0.10	2,72
Totals:	49.19	50.07	48.26	47.42	50.85	50.26	--	--	49.51	1.55	2,72
Foreign Language Sensitivity											
20. Russian Phoneme Discrimination (Errors)	14.03	14.21	17.22[b]	16.98[b]	--	--	--	--	15.42	22.19	1,54

(a) Entries for the first four tests are mean Standard scores. They are based on different norms and are not comparable to the corresponding entries in Table 6 – 1967.

(b) Control students who had no second-language experience were selected from the English Control Group I and from the French Control. Their scores are combined to form these means.

* p < .05

** p < .01

English and French word associations. The results for the word association analysis are essentially the same as those for the Pilot Classes, even with the changes in methods of analysis. The Follow-up Experimental children are as rapid at associating in English as the Controls and they give no more idiosyncratic responses. Although they did produce reliably more syntagmatic responses in both English and French, the proportion of paradigmatic responses is equivalent to that of both English and French Control groups. Thus, as with the Pilot Experimental Class, there is evidence here also for a greater reliance on common verbal sequences in both languages, but not for an underuse of paradigmatic responses. There are then no symptoms of cognitive or linguistic retardation, as would be the case had we found a delay in making the paradigmatic shift. It is of special interest that this same pattern turned up with both Pilot and Follow-up groups, because it provides an instructive insight into a transition period in the development of bilingualism, a period where the Experimental children appear to rely on the sequential properties of both the native and target languages. Their significantly greater use of semantic clusters in English, but not in French (see measure 15), suggests that they also seem to rely on the semantic properties of the native language. Hence, the Experimental children may transfer the semantic structures of English into their use of French—a possibility that should be studied very carefully in follow-up research. Apparently, the attention focused on semantic clustering reduces the number of transformations given, a tendency noticed with the Pilot Classes. Thus, rather than producing transformational variants of the stimulus words to the same degree as the Controls, the Experimental children have a proclivity instead to give semantically related associations.

As was the case with the Pilot Experimental Class, the children in the Follow-up Experimental Class produce reliably fewer rhyming responses in English. This may be interpreted to be either a lack of playfulness with their native language, or, following Ervin (1961), as a sign of maturity since they are less tied to the sound properties of words. In any case, as we shall see, the tendencies to overstress syntagmatic and understress rhyming responses disappear by grade II, suggesting that the period of transition in which associational structures are affected by second-language schooling is short-lived.

Reading, word knowledge, vocabulary, and comprehension in French. With regard to their competence in French, the 1967 and 1968 patterns of results are very similar. In reading and word discrimination skills (measures 10 and 11), the Follow-up Experimental Class scores as well as the French Control, making them, after kindergarten and grade I, as competent in their receptive control of written French as native speakers. On the other hand, they are reliably poorer on our test of French listening comprehension (12), a measure of ability to understand, store in memory, and answer questions about the details of a story told to them in French. Judging from their scores on the French version of the

Picture Vocabulary Test (13), they also fall significantly short of nativelike command of French vocabulary. But actually, the groups differ by only ten points on this measure, meaning that the Experimental Class failed on ten concepts that the Controls passed. Many of these concepts may not have been introduced into the academic program, that is, concepts such as: *acrobatie* (stunt), *communication* (communication), *délice* (delight), *entonnoir* (funnel), *diriger* (to direct), *comptoir* (counter), *tache de rousseur* (freckle), *insigne* (badge), and *cueillette* (harvesting).

Speaking skills in French. Their skill in producing French sounds is also significantly below the level of native speakers, but again the question is, "How far below?" The Experimentals scored 38.35 out of a possible 57.00, while the French Control Class scored 56.08, and in terms of the linguist's ratings, their average score reduced to 2.01—a score of *moyen* with French native speakers as the point of reference. This is essentially the same figure that was found for the Pilot Class at grade I. The sounds that gave the children, as a group, particular difficulty are those listed first in the following series: *pn, pt, â, in, eille, ô, j, cl, eur, é, un, u, an, alle, ot, è, on, r, eu.* These are placed in rank from poor to good, with a sharp break occurring between the first two (*pn* and *pt*) producing the most difficulty and the last three (*eu, r, on*) which were clearly well controlled.

The ability of the Follow-up Experimental Class to retell or create stories in French is summarized by tests 16 and 17 in Table 11. In terms of statistical counts, the Experimental children make reliably more grammatical errors, especially errors of gender and agreement, and they have a more stereotyped stock of verbs than the French Controls, both when retelling and when creating stories in French. At the same time, they use as large a vocabulary and as varied a range of nouns and adjectives as the French Controls. Although they are reliably less able to comprehend a story told to them, they nevertheless score as well as the Controls on story comprehension when creating a story themselves. Overall, then, their production and comprehension in French is good when compared with that of the French Control Class.

Two teams of judges evaluated the tape-recorded productions of each child as he retold or created stories in French. One team comprised two perfectly bilingual French-Canadian university students who rated the outputs of all groups of children, thus assuring between-language comparability of judgments. In the training session prior to rating, they discussed their own criteria for evaluating the French samples and decided to be very demanding in the sense that they would use perfect bilinguals, such as themselves, as their frame of reference. On the five-point rating scale, they reserved position 5 for "superb" productions, 4 for those "very good or worthy of note," 3 for "passable or good," 2 for "below average, more mistakes than should be, but not poor," and 1 for "poor construction, redundant, needing prompting, etc." Incidentally, it was their opinion that the average French Canadian, adult or child, would likely fall between positions 2 and 3, whereas the continental French speakers would typically fall between positions 3 and 4! The second team consisted of two very experienced French-Canadian teachers who specialize in teaching French at the elementary school level. Their frame of reference was the typical French-Canadian child whom they had taught for fifteen years in one case and twenty-five years in the other. Their scale also ranged from poor (1) to excellent (5), but as can be seen in items 16 and 17 of Table 11, their ratings differed substantially from those of the bilingual judges. The bilingual judges rated the Experimental Class between positions 1.3 and 2.2, and the French Controls between 2.1 and 3.3, while the French teachers placed the Experimental Class between the 2.0 and 2.7 positions and the French Controls between 2.9 and 3.5. Both teams found that the groups differed most on rhythm and intonation and least on enunciation and liaison. Thus, the children's command of French is rated about one position lower on a 5-point scale than that of the Controls, somewhere between "poor" and "average" with native speakers as the point of reference. Their speech samples were considered relatively good in enunciation and liaison and relatively poor in rhythm and intonation and, when based on stories created without a model, in grammar as well. All four judges summarized their general opinions of the children by stating that those in the Experimental Class would likely be indistinguishable from natives if placed in a completely French environment for a month or two. They also volunteered the opinion that they had rarely encountered English-speaking high school or university students after many years of study with as good a command of French language sounds.

Word associations in French. The free associations in French of the Experimental Class are produced more slowly than is the case for the French Controls. There was no significant difference in latencies with the Pilot Classes. Similar to the Pilot Experimental Class, the Follow-up also gave significantly more syntagmatic responses and fewer transformation responses. It is interesting that both experimental classes favor common sequential runs in both languages. The fact that this trend appeared with two different samples of children speaks to its reliability and the likely value of special research on the matter.

Skill in arithmetic. When tested for ability to compute and solve arithmetic problems in English (4), the Experimental Class performs as well as the English Controls. All groups, in fact, fall between the 75th and 80th percentile on national norms. This result is impressive since all arithmetic concepts for the Experimentals were taught via French whereas this test was administered and presented in English. Apparently, the concepts they learned through French were well assimilated. It may well be that as they assimilate new mathematical notions through French, they simultaneously apply them to their everyday experiences in an English milieu.

Measures of intelligence. The end-of-year reassessments of intelligence are presented in rows 18 and 19 of Table 11. Contrary to the Pilot Class findings, the Follow-up Experimentals show no intellectual retardation on the Progressive Matrices test when compared with the two English Control groups. Likewise, there is no difference among groups on the total scores of the Lorge-Thorndike measure of intelligence. Hence, there is no sign of the children having developed an intellectual handicap or an intellectual advantage as of grade I. We shall see if any advantages or disadvantages become apparent as the children move up in grades.

Sensitivity to foreign-language sounds. Finally, when tested for sensitivity to the sounds of Russian, a totally foreign language for all children, the Experimental Class performs similarly to the Controls. Even though the overall averages are in the expected direction, there is no reliable evidence at grade I that the Experimental Class has developed a generalized sensitivity to foreign-language sounds.

Summary of Findings and Conclusions

In view of the substantial similarity of results obtained with two different sets of first-grade classes, one can make a more forceful set of conclusions than was the case with the Pilot Class data alone. What particularly impresses us is the fact that many changes were introduced from year to year: the methods of instruction, the teachers, the tests themselves, and the modes of analysis of test results.

If one asks whether kindergarten and first-grade schooling conducted entirely in a second language retards children's development in their native language, the answer is a qualified "No," at least for children with the range of intelligence and the home backgrounds of those studied here. In the first place, the Experimental children's breadth of vocabulary and listening comprehension in English were at the same level as those of the English Control Classes at the end of grade I. When reconstructing a story related to them, their expression, enunciation, rhythm, and intonation were also as good as that of the Controls and their grammar was better (a finding that contrasts with the Experimental Pilot Class whose grammar was poorer). Their stories were fuller, more descriptive and diversified, and they showed better comprehension of the story than was the case for the Controls. When creating a story on their own, their overall comprehension is still better, although in that case they show less descriptive diversity than one of the Control Classes. Thus, with regard to oral production and comprehension of English they are generally as competent as the Controls, and in certain respects more so.

Second, their associational responses indicate that they rely relatively heavily on common sequential patterns in English (syntagmatic responses), a tendency noted also when producing associations in French. However, there is no evidence of linguistic or cognitive retardation to the extent that these are reflected in the use of paradigmatic responses; neither the Pilot nor the Follow-up Experimental groups differ from the Controls in this regard. They do, however, distinguish themselves from the Controls by overemphasizing semantic relationships and underemphasizing transformation and rhyming responses in their associations. These differences form the basis of the qualifications attached to the "No" given above. As we shall see, at the end of grade II, this qualification is lifted completely, but it is nevertheless valuable to have a reliable index of the type of cognitive effects this mode of developing bilingualism tends to engender, even though they turn out to be ephemeral.

In the third place, we have twice found that the English reading skills, word knowledge, and word discrimination of the Experimental children are statistically poorer than those of the Controls, as would be expected since they have purposely had no academic or home training in reading English. What is noteworthy is that they nonetheless score between the 20th and 40th percentiles on North American norms for these three skills. We interpret this rather amazing skill with the written forms of English as a fascinating instance of transfer of essential skills from French to English, suggesting to us that the learning of French for these children may in part take place through English. This of course is only a hypothesis, but one well worth investigating separately. Our reasoning runs like this: The children very likely start the program with a good deal of translating from French to English. They may soon become very efficient at both translating and comparing, in their own way, the two languages. Translating and contrasting of this sort would provide a basis for the transfer of concepts, notions, and skills from French to English. In other words, the task of breaking the foreign code may give the Experimental children insights into their own native code through comparison and translation. The claim that one really gets to know his own language through the study of a second one is often made by teachers of classical languages. Perhaps we will come to attach greater significance to this possibility as more research is centered on children following home-school language-switch programs.

How well do children progress linguistically in a second language when it is used as the medium of instruction for kindergarten and the first year of schooling? The answer is, "Remarkably well." Drawing on the results from the Pilot and Follow-up Experimental Classes, we see that their reading and word discrimination skills in French are at the same level as those of the French Control group. Although they are significantly poorer than the Controls in listening comprehension and in receptive command of vocabulary, they nevertheless appear to have a substantial understanding of abstract and complex French concepts. Their mastery of French phonemes was also clearly not at the level of native speakers, and yet linguistic judges rated their phoneme production as "average" using native speaking children as a reference frame. When retelling or creating stories in French, they compare surprisingly well with the French Controls on overall comprehension and on vocabulary depth and diversity. When their taped productions in French are analyzed, they are definitely not mistaken for native speakers of French, mainly because of their relatively poor command of rhythm and intonation. Still, in terms of enunciation and liaison they perform surprisingly well.

How do children trained in this fashion compare on tests of achievement in a subject like mathematics taught exclusively through the second language? The fact that they scored as well as the two English Control groups, falling at the 80th percentile on national norms, with the testing conducted in English, strengthens the notion that the information and training they received via French is transferred efficiently into English. It may well be that the information they receive in French is thought through or reprocessed with English language equivalents, or that the information is processed simultaneously in the two languages from the start.

Does this type of bilingual experience affect the sensitivity of these children to the sounds of a completely novel third language? With two separate testings, there is no reliable evidence after the kindergarten and grade I years for a generalized sensitivity with phonemes attributable to the bilingual experience.

Finally, does the bilingual experience affect the measured intelligence of the Experimental children? We noted that the Pilot Experimental Class was significantly lower on their June retest of intelligence than one Control group, but not different from the second Control Class. For the Follow-up Classes there was no difference among groups on either of two comprehensive measures of intelligence. There is then no evidence of intellectual confusion or retardation attributable to the training received. Neither is there any evidence at the end of grade I for an intellectual advantage attributable to their bilingual experience.

Our purpose here was essentially to check on ourselves by repeating our original evaluation of the impact of schooling in a second language with a second set of first-grade classes. The two sets of results are similar enough to generate confidence in the outcomes, and now we can turn to year-by-year assessments for both Pilot and Follow-up groups. In the next chapter, we see how they are doing at the end of grade II.

Chapter Five

The Pilot and Follow-up Classes at Grade II

The school setting for the Pilot Experimental Class did not change for grade II. It was again situated in a small, neighborhood elementary school where English was the language of all academic matters except for the few experimental classes. Even for them, those in the experiment, however, English was the natural language of social interaction outside of class. Still, the principal and all of the teachers were sympathetic to the experiment, making the atmosphere for those in the experimental program a friendly and considerate one.[1] Judging from discussions with teachers and visits to the classes, there were no signs in grade II that the experimental program was oppressive or unpleasant in any way. Nor did the Experimental Classes have more absences from school. For example, the mean number of absences in the year, corrected for total number of school days, showed that the Pilot Experimental Class missed fewer days than the English Control.

The English and French Control Classes continued schooling in their respective native languages, whereas the Experimental children followed a French-language curriculum except for two thirty-five minute periods of English Language Arts taught each day by a specialist in that subject matter. Her aim was to cover the core of the standard second-year program in English as concisely as possible. In other words, the Experimental Classes were taught English not as students of a second language but as ordinary second-grade English-speaking pupils. Otherwise, they followed an all-French program with content appropriate for their grade level in terms of the standards set by the regional school board. All textbooks, workbooks, and readers were written in French, published in Canada, and prepared for native speakers of French, except for those used in the English Language Arts program.

---

[1] We have not examined the attitudes of other children in the school toward the experimental program or the pupils enrolled. The reactions of these other children may have created a quite different climate of feeling that we are unaware of.

While there was only seventy minutes of formal English instruction daily, English was nonetheless the language of instruction for music, art, physical education, and the library period. Thus English was used for 40 percent of the complete grade II curriculum. From our point of view, this amount of English seemed high. It was particularly unfortunate that the "fun" subjects—art, music and physical education—were given exclusively in English, since these subjects provide excellent opportunities for the children to express themselves spontaneously in French. Since there were few other outlets in the curriculum for spontaneous expression and discussion, the actual percentage of French to which the Experimental children were exposed was small considering that their linguistic environment outside of the classroom was essentially English.

As the classes moved up to grade II, they had new teachers who, with one exception, were fully qualified and experienced at the second-grade level. The exception was the teacher of the Pilot Experimental Class who had not completed her own secondary schooling and had no previous teaching experience. Being in charge of the Pilot Class also meant that she necessarily had no experience with the home-school language-switch plan. We do not mean to imply that this teacher was ineffective, but merely to indicate that from a research point of view there was certainly no bias of teacher qualifications and experience favoring the Experimental Class in this case. The teacher in question was French-Canadian, meaning that the Pilot Experimental Class had French-Canadian teachers in both grades I and II (except for a European French replacement teacher who took over for the last two months of grade I).

The number of students in each class at the grade II level was as follows: the grade II Pilot Experimental Class, twenty-two; English Control I, sixteen; English Control II, twenty-three; and French Control, twenty. For the grade II Follow-up Experimental Class, thirty-three (from two classes); English Control I, twenty; English Control II, twenty-two; and French Control, nineteen. In each Experimental Class, a few additional children were allowed to join the program after the kindergarten year. They are not included in our statistical analyses, however. Thus, the Experimental Classes were actually comparable in size to others in the school. The Control children were, of course, located in different classrooms or in different schools; they too were in full-sized classes with other children not involved in the experiment.

At the grade II level, problems of dwindling numbers in the original Control Classes began to arise. Some families had moved out of the region, and in the case of the French Controls, several of the original class were placed in special schools. The two original Pilot English Control Classes were combined and treated as one group for statistical purposes, but the French Control group became very small. For this reason, we shifted our attention to tests in French and in English for which city-wide or national norms were available. Starting with grade II, for example, the Commission des Ecoles Catholiques de Montréal

(CECM) kindly allowed us to use their own tests to measure the Experimental pupils' achievement in French and mathematics. This permitted us to assess their progress in terms of city-wide norms for French-speaking children at the grade II level.

In contrast to the dwindling numbers of Control pupils, the Pilot and Follow-up Experimental Classes remained almost intact, suggesting that the parents may have been reluctant to move to other neighborhoods where their children would not be able to benefit from a similar program. The testing was carried out during the month of May. The principal of the French Control school requested that the testing in her school be concentrated into three days. This was done without disrupting the overall testing schedule by increasing the size of our team of assistants so that on alternative days, parallel testing could be conducted in the Experimental and English Control Classes. To facilitate the testing we took certain shortcuts. For example, we did not collect new grade II data on the French phoneme production test, since we knew from the grade I results that French-speaking children achieved nearly perfect scores, as would be expected. Similarly, we collected word associations from only half the French Control Class, since the gathering of free associations is an individualized and time-consuming procedure.

Normally there was less than a one-week interval between the administration of a given test to the Experimental and to the Control groups. In cases where the Experimental children received both French and English versions of the same test, one half of the class received the English version first; the other half, the French. After a two-week delay, the second version of the test was administered, insuring a minimum of carry-over from one version to the other.

The majority of the research assistants were fully bilingual, and their ability to administer both French and English tests helped to make the testing conditions comparable from one class to another.

In the analysis of results, the same covariance procedure was used again, statistically adjusting each of the dependent variables for initial (i.e., start of grade I) differences in nonverbal IQ (Raven, 1956) and in home environment characteristics (Bloom, 1964; Davé, 1963; Wolf, 1963). The adjusted mean scores were then tested by analysis of variance.

Measures Used with the Pilot and Follow-up Classes at Grade II

In most cases, the tests and measures administered to the grade II children were standard extensions of those used with the first graders. This is clearly so for standardized tests such as the Metropolitan Achievement (Primary II Battery) and the Peabody Picture Vocabulary. Others, like the word association and speaking skills measures, were identical in format for both grade levels with scoring provisions to accommodate age differences, where necessary. A few, such as the Lorge-Thorndike Intelligence Test and certain subtests of the

Metropolitan series, however, were changed in format to be appropriate for the grade II level (e.g., the test of problem arithmetic required the older children to read problems themselves rather than answer questions read aloud to them). The tests actually administered are described briefly below. The numbering corresponds to the entries in Table 12, where the statistical results are summarized.

1. *English word knowledge*. Similar to the corresponding test given in grade I, but standardized for second graders. For the last twenty items, written descriptions rather than illustrations were used as stimuli, and these had to be matched with printed words. Standard scores are used for tests 1-6 in Table 12.

2. *English word discrimination*, and 3. *English reading skills*. These are comparable to the grade I tests except for more difficult vocabulary.

4. *English spelling skills*. Consists of thirty dictated words, each presented in a context to make its meaning unmistakable.

5. *English listening comprehension*. Comparable to that used for grade I level with more complex and involved stories. Total score possible was 24.

6. *Peabody Picture Vocabulary Test, English and French*. One hundred items were presented in English and in French. Total score possible was 100 for each version. The same crossover procedure employed with the first graders was used again (i.e., half of the Experimental Class started with the English version; half, with the French).

7. *Speaking skills in English: Story retelling*, 8. *Speaking skills in English: Story creation*, and 9. *Word association analysis in English*. These were the same tests as given at the grade I level. For the Pilot Classes two sets of judges made the ratings, as in the grade I analysis. For the Follow-up Classes, however, two trained linguists did the rating.

10. *French reading skills*. A more advanced test than that used with first graders, and also a relatively difficult one, even for the French Control children. In the first section, dealing with *word recognition and spelling ability*, children read a story in unison with certain words deleted, and were asked to fill in the missing words which they heard read aloud one time only. Spelling had to be perfect. There were eighteen items. The second section tests *sentence comprehension* and here the children read a story, silently, twice and were asked twelve rather difficult questions, requiring an understanding of the meanings of words. They gave spontaneous one-word answers. Section three was similar to the *word order* subtests given in grade I but with longer sentences and higher level vocabulary. Total score possible was 40. (This test was not used with Follow-up Classes.)

11. *French listening comprehension*. Comparable to that used at grade I with more complex stories. Total possible score was 24. For the Follow-up Classes a new and somewhat more difficult version was constructed; it had twenty items.

12. *Peabody Picture Vocabulary Test, in French.* See item 7 above.

13. *French phoneme production;* 14. *Speaking skills in French: Story retelling;* 15. *Speaking skills in French: Story creation;* and 16. *Word association analysis, in French.* These are the same tests used at grade I.

17. *Arithmetic concepts (English).* Forty-two items that provide a comprehensive measure of the child's ability to use basic numerical and quantitative concepts.

18. *Arithmetic computation (English format).* Consists of thirty exercises in addition and subtraction.

19. *June retest of intelligence: Raven's.* Same as that given at grade I. Note that for all classes involved, this was the third time they had taken the Progressive Matrices Test (i.e., for the Pilot Classes, September 1966, June 1967, and June 1968; for the Follow-up Classes, September 1967, June 1968, and June 1969).

20. *Lorge-Thorndike intelligence (1959).* The Level 2 form was used at this grade level; the format is the same as the Level 1 test, but the items are more demanding.

21. *Russian phoneme discrimination.* Same procedure as used with grade I.

The Follow-up Classes

The following new measures were used with the Follow-up but not the Pilot Classes at the grade II level. The numbering refers to entries in Table 13.

9. and 18. *Decoding skills: English and French versions.* This was a group test developed by Samuels, Reynolds, and Lambert (1969) as an index of pupils' ability to understand (decode) English and French descriptive messages spoken by either children their own age or adults. Each child was given two twelve-page booklets; one containing sets of six abstract designs; the other, six photographs of a woman's face. The designs of each set were very similar except for subtle variations in lighting or details. The children listened to a series of twenty-four tape-recorded descriptions, and selected from their booklets the one design or photograph being described. Two tapes were used, one with child speakers and one with adult speakers. The total possible score was 12 for decoding of children's descriptions and 12 for adult's descriptions. Separate English and French versions were developed. The procedure is described more fully in Samuels, Reynolds, and Lambert (1969).

12. *Rendement en français.* New versions of this test are prepared yearly by the CECM for use with French-speaking children at all grade levels. At the grade II level there were five subsections:

(a) *Sentence completion.* The child is asked to find the missing word, among a series of words provided, in order to complete a sentence. There were eight incomplete sentences given, making a total possible score of 8.

(b) *Parts of speech.* The child is asked to decide which words in a list are verbs or adjectives. Total score possible was 8.

(c) *Gender*. From four lists of words, the child is asked to select feminine and masculine nouns. Total possible score was 4.

(d) *Word completion*. The child must discover which word in a set of five incomplete words can be correctly completed with a given letter. Total possible score was 5.

(e) *Verb tense*. The child selects from a series of short sentences the one whose verb is in the present, past, or future tense. Total possible score was 5.

13. *French word discrimination*. This measure was developed to assess the same skills required in the English Word Discrimination Test of the Metropolitan battery. In the French version, the children hear an adult read aloud sequences like "*et . . .* Jean *et* Paul *. . . et*," and they are asked to choose the word they heard from among a list such as *elle, et, vert, sans*. Total possible score was 32.

24-27. *Creativity measures*. The creativity tests are of two types, both purporting to measure flexibility of thinking or spontaneous inventiveness. In the first part the child is asked to name as many *unusual uses* as he can for three common objects: (a) a brick, (b) a skipping rope, and (c) a safety pin. In the second part, he describes what the *consequences* would be if, for example, (d) *animals could talk*; if there were (e) *no clocks or watches in the world*; and (f) *if everyone could do as he liked*. The Control Classes were given all six items whereas the Experimental Classes were presented three items in one language and three in the other, at different sittings. Half the Experimental Class received items (a), (c), (e), for example, in English and (b), (d), (f) in French, while the other half took the same six subtests with languages reversed.

Responses were scored as follows: (1) reponses similar as to general idea were grouped together, so that a child who said a brick can be used to build a house, a bookcase, a garage, etc., would receive one point only; (2) responses that were nonsensical were not counted, nor were completely nonutilitarian or irrelevant responses (actually very few responses of this type occurred); (3) any responses given by less than one-tenth of the total number of children were awarded 2 points; all other (more common) responses were awarded one point only. Total scores were averaged over the number of items answered.

The creativity measures were introduced because earlier research had suggested that they assess an ability to switch sets and to use one's imagination constructively, an ability Peal and Lambert (1962, 1964) found to be more characteristic of bilingual than monolingual ten-year-olds. More recently, Torrance, Wu, Gowan and Aliotti (1970) also found a superiority of bilinguals over monolinguals on originality and elaboration in tests of creativity. Creativity nonetheless is a complex ability, and although certain specialists place great faith in the measures adopted here (e.g., Guilford, 1950; Getzels, 1962; Torrance et al., 1970), others such as Cronbach (1970) suggest that caution be used in the interpretation of creativity scores, because more research on their possible meanings is clearly needed.

Results for the Pilot Classes
at the End of Grade II

The results to be discussed are summarized in Table 12, where the average performance scores of the various classes and the statistical tests of significance are presented. The following results were obtained with the Pilot Classes at the end of grade II.

English Language Competence

Reading skills, spelling, and vocabulary in English. There is an extremely impressive array of evidence here showing that the Pilot Experimental Class at the end of grade II, with a very minimum of training in English, is in no way inferior to the English Control Classes in the development of native-language skills. On tests of word knowledge and word discrimination (items 1 and 2 in Table 12) which require a facility in matching printed words with their meanings in one case and with their sounds in the other, the Experimental Class scores as well as either English Control group. Moreover all three groups fall between the 85th and 90th percentiles on nationwide norms. In reading skills (item 3), measured by tests of comprehension of English sentences and paragraphs, the Experimental pupils' score is equivalent to Control II but reliably lower than that of Control I. In this instance, then, their relative standing is intermediate, but the Class as a whole nevertheless falls at about the 80th percentile. Even on the Metropolitan Spelling Test (item 4), the Experimental Class is equivalent to both Control groups, the average score falling at the 87th percentile. One would not necessarily expect the Experimental children to have developed an equivalent degree of skill in spelling, since they had so little training in English and since the spelling systems of French and English often differ in subtle ways. Their performance on the Peabody Picture Vocabulary Test (item 7) which demands a knowledge of complex concepts in English is also equivalent to that of both Controls, as is their facility at storing and recalling the details of a story read to them (item 8).

The performance of the Pilot Experimental Class at the end of grade II becomes especially interesting if one keeps in mind that all of the skills called for in these tests are normally *taught* and laboriously *drilled* in school. One way to interpret their unexpected performance is to argue that the conventional pace of elementary education in North America is so slow, even in the best schools, that children who have had a year or more "vacation" can catch up rather easily. Even if this were the case, it is still noteworthy that this group of students could "catch up" with such apparent ease. One might also interpret the performance of the Experimental Class in terms of maturation. The argument could run as follows. Delaying the formal teaching of reading skills and conceptual

Table 12

Test Results for the Pilot Classes at the End of Grade II, 1968

Test Number and Name	Experimental Class Mean	Adjusted	English Control I Mean	Adjusted	English Control II Mean	Adjusted	French Control Mean	Adjusted	Grand Mean	F Ratio	df
English Competence											
1. Word Knowledge[a] (S.S.)	56.33	56.40	55.35	57.69	57.48	55.69	—	—	56.49	0.20	2,51
2. Word Discrimination (S.S.)	55.00	55.06	55.35	56.54	55.39	54.46	—	—	55.25	0.24	2,51
3. Reading Ability (S.S.)	53.59	54.52	55.71	59.63	55.61	51.82	—	—	54.92	3.58**	2,52
4. Spelling (S.S.)	57.41	57.65	58.18	61.75	58.22	55.35	—	—	57.92	2.48	2,52
5. English Listening Comprehension	22.68	22.66	22.81	22.53	23.09	23.32	—	—	22.87	0.65	2,50
6. English Picture Vocab.	75.24	74.69	75.00	76.41	75.21	74.87	—	—	75.17	0.39	2,49
7. *Speaking Skills in English:*											
Story Retelling											
Linguistic Ratings											
Overall Expression	2.98	3.05	2.32	2.50	3.07	2.91	—	—	2.88	0.96	2,45
Grammar	2.84	2.85	2.64	2.68	3.00	2.97	—	—	2.86	0.56	2,45
Enunciation	3.20	3.17	2.73	2.75	3.55	3.57	—	—	3.25	3.42*	2,45
Rhythm and Intonation	3.11	3.11	2.09	1.94	3.09	3.17	—	—	2.90	7.88**	2,45
Word Counts											
Number of Words	80.27	78.27	51.73	50.93	69.14	70.69	—	—	66.25	5.19*	2,38
Number of Adjectives	6.09	6.01	3.00	2.91	4.27	4.37	—	—	4.29	6.21**	2,38
Number Different Adjectives	4.91	4.90	2.07	2.09	3.36	3.35	—	—	3.31	8.41**	2,38
Number of Nouns	17.18	16.87	11.53	11.12	14.68	15.12	—	—	14.27	4.89*	2,38
Number Different Nouns	11.73	11.48	7.87	7.79	10.68	10.86	—	—	10.04	4.71*	2,38

Test Number and Name	Experimental Class		English Control I		English Control II		French Control		Grand Mean	F Ratio	df
	Mean	Adjusted	Mean	Adjusted	Mean	Adjusted	Mean	Adjusted			
7. *Speaking Skills in English:*											
Word Counts (cont.)											
Number Verbs	14.36	14.03	8.00	8.28	11.82	11.79	—	—	11.21	6.31**	2,38
Number Different Verbs	10.73	10.51	6.53	6.61	9.32	9.37	—	—	8.77	5.00*	2,38
Number Grammatical Errors	0.18	0.19	0.13	0.10	0.14	0.16	—	—	0.15	0.18	2,38
Story Comprehension	2.27	2.18	2.00	2.01	2.45	2.50	—	—	2.27	1.51	2,38
8. *Speaking Skills in English:*											
Story Invention											
Linguistic Ratings											
Overall Expression	3.35	3.26	2.70	2.68	3.47	3.58	—	—	3.22	3.85*	2,45
Grammar	3.05	2.99	2.60	2.59	3.22	3.29	—	—	2.99	5.75***	2,45
Enunciation	2.97	2.91	2.60	2.63	3.20	3.24	—	—	2.95	3.33*	2,45
Rhythm and Intonation	3.30	3.17	2.63	2.56	3.57	3.76	—	—	3.22	6.96***	2,45
Word Counts											
Number of Words	67.67	68.55	42.06	38.59	66.23	67.91	—	—	60.19	6.74***	2,49
Number of Adjectives	1.52	1.48	0.56	0.37	1.77	1.95	—	—	1.36	2.98	2,49
Number Different Adjectives	1.52	1.50	0.56	0.49	1.36	1.43	—	—	1.20	1.83	2,49
Number of Nouns	12.86	13.07	6.12	5.33	11.55	11.92	—	—	10.54	13.77***	2,49
Number Different Nouns	7.10	7.20	4.37	3.86	7.36	7.64	—	—	6.46	10.79***	2,49
Number of Verbs	12.90	13.28	6.56	6.64	11.59	11.18	—	—	10.69	7.20***	2,49
Number Different Verbs	9.00	9.09	5.62	5.56	9.55	9.51	—	—	8.29	5.12*	2,49
Number Grammatical Errors	0.33	0.32	0.06	0.12	0.18	0.15	—	—	0.20	0.90	2,49
Story Comprehension	3.00	2.99	2.25	2.21	2.23	2.26	—	—	2.51	12.70**	2,49
9. *Word Association Analysis,*											
English											
Associational Latency (secs.)	2.70	2.81	3.54	3.46	—	—	—	—	3.19	1.00	1,20
Paradigmatic (%)	61.41	59.73	70.10	72.18	—	—	—	—	65.30	3.70	1,29

Table 12 (cont.)

Test Results for the Pilot Classes at the End of Grade II, 1968

Test Number and Name	Experimental Class		English Control I		English Control II		French Control		Grand Mean	F Ratio	df
	Mean	Adjusted	Mean	Adjusted	Mean	Adjusted	Mean	Adjusted			
9. *Word Association Analysis, English (cont.)*											
Syntagmatic (%)	16.17	16.28	11.76	11.63	—	—	—	—	14.20	1.33	1,29
Semantic Clusters (%)	6.94	6.94	5.51	5.52	—	—	—	—	6.30	0.73	1,29
Idiosyncratic (%)	12.99	14.90	4.06	1.70	—	—	—	—	9.00	9.98**	1,29
Rhymings (%)	0.30	0.33	1.22	1.19	—	—	—	—	0.71	1.06	1,29
Transformations (%)	1.88	1.90	4.41	4.39	—	—	—	—	3.02	7.66**	1,29
French Competence											
10. French Reading Skills	17.86	18.73	—	—	—	—	18.33	16.80	18.03	0.64	1,24
11. French Listening Comprehension	18.95	19.15	—	—	—	—	21.38	21.09	19.94	2.33	1,23
12. French Picture Vocabulary	71.23	71.66	—	—	—	—	76.92	76.13	73.24	6.08*	1,25
13. French Phoneme Production	42.23	42.23	—	—	—	—	—	—	—	—	—
14. *French Speaking Skills:*											
Story Retelling											
Linguistic Ratings:											
Bilingual Judges											
Overall Expression	1.93	1.94	—	—	—	—	2.73	2.72	2.42	7.82**	1,27
Grammar	1.61	1.61	—	—	—	—	2.70	2.70	2.28	20.22**	1,27
Enunciation and Liaison	2.21	2.28	—	—	—	—	2.93	2.89	2.65	5.39*	1,27
Rhythm and Intonation	2.21	2.19	—	—	—	—	2.80	2.81	2.57	3.53	1,27
Linguistic Ratings: French Teacher Judges											
Overall Expression	2.86	2.91	—	—	—	—	3.45	3.42	3.22	3.41	1,27
Grammar	2.82	2.93	—	—	—	—	3.16	3.09	3.03	0.44	1,27
Enunciation and Liaison	3.04	3.13	—	—	—	—	3.18	3.12	3.12	0.00	1,27
Rhythm and Intonation	2.68	2.59	—	—	—	—	3.41	3.46	3.12	9.76**	1,27

Test Number and Name	Experimental Class		English Control I		English Control II		French Control		Grand Mean	F Ratio	df
	Mean	Adjusted	Mean	Adjusted	Mean	Adjusted	Mean	Adjusted			
Word Counts											
Number of Words	75.50	74.58	—	—	—	—	72.09	72.65	73.38	0.02	1,28
Number of Adjectives	2.14	2.21	—	—	—	—	2.04	2.00	2.08	0.05	1,28
Number Different Adjectives	1.14	1.32	—	—	—	—	0.96	0.85	1.03	0.77	1,28
Number of Nouns	16.36	15.50	—	—	—	—	12.39	12.92	13.89	1.62	1,28
Number Different Nouns	7.14	6.73	—	—	—	—	7.22	7.47	7.19	0.75	1,28
Number of Verbs	13.36	13.10	—	—	—	—	12.22	12.38	12.65	0.12	1,28
Number Different Verbs	9.07	8.39	—	—	—	—	9.13	9.55	9.11	0.66	1,28
Number Grammatical Errors	4.86	4.91	—	—	—	—	0.83	0.79	2.35	46.57**	1,28
Story Comprehension	2.79	2.71	—	—	—	—	2.96	3.00	2.89	0.43	1,28
15. *French Speaking Skills:*											
Story Creation											
Linguistic Ratings:											
Bilingual Judges											
Overall Expression	2.00	2.04	—	—	—	—	3.03	2.98	2.46	19.80**	1,29
Grammar	1.40	1.40	—	—	—	—	2.85	2.86	2.05	62.62***	1,29
Enunciation and Liaison	2.29	2.30	—	—	—	—	3.18	3.16	2.68	16.57***	1,29
Rhythm and Intonation	2.24	2.26	—	—	—	—	3.26	3.24	2.70	29.75***	1,29
Linguistic Ratings: French											
Teacher Judges											
Overall Expression	3.24	3.31	—	—	—	—	3.79	3.70	3.49	2.58	1,30
Grammar	2.57	2.57	—	—	—	—	3.28	3.28	2.90	12.97**	1,30
Enunciation and Liaison	3.02	3.06	—	—	—	—	3.32	3.28	3.16	2.20	1,30
Rhythm and Intonation	3.14	3.16	—	—	—	—	3.71	3.69	3.40	4.20*	1,30

Table 12 (cont.)
Test Results for the Pilot Classes at the End of Grade II, 1968

Test Number and Name	Experimental Class		English Control I		English Control II		French Control		Grand Mean	F Ratio	df
	Mean	Adjusted	Mean	Adjusted	Mean	Adjusted	Mean	Adjusted			
Word Counts											
Number of Words	76.05	76.91	—	—	—	—	68.44	67.43	72.54	0.61	1,30
Number of Adjectives	1.24	1.25	—	—	—	—	3.33	3.32	2.21	10.67**	1,30
Number Different Adjectives	0.57	0.49	—	—	—	—	1.28	1.37	0.90	2.66	1,30
Number of Nouns	16.00	16.25	—	—	—	—	12.33	12.04	14.31	2.69	1,30
Number Different Nouns	8.24	8.48	—	—	—	—	7.61	7.33	7.95	1.15	1,30
Number of Verbs	13.00	12.89	—	—	—	—	11.33	11.46	12.23	0.59	1,30
Number Different Verbs	9.33	9.27	—	—	—	—	7.67	7.74	8.56	1.78	1,30
Number Grammatical Errors	7.57	7.76	—	—	—	—	1.06	0.84	4.56	45.12**	1,30
Story Comprehension	3.52	3.49	—	—	—	—	3.33	3.37	3.44	0.15	1,30
16. *French Word Association Analysis*											
Associational Latency (secs.)	4.97	5.85	—	—	—	—	7.34	6.37	6.10	0.05	1,31
Paradigmatic (%)	54.06	55.64	—	—	—	—	58.92	57.33	56.49	0.09	1,33
Syntagmatic (%)	19.89	17.79	—	—	—	—	13.91	16.01	16.90	0.20	1,33
Semantic Clusters (%)	7.09	6.40	—	—	—	—	8.87	9.57	7.98	3.78	1,33
Idiosyncratic (%)	12.79	14.34	—	—	—	—	9.90	8.35	11.34	1.45	1,33
Rhymings (%)	1.21	0.76	—	—	—	—	1.96	2.41	1.59	2.70	1,33
Transformations (%)	3.36	3.64	—	—	—	—	5.13	4.85	4.25	0.30	1,33

Test Number and Name	Experimental Class		English Control I		English Control II		French Control		Grand Mean	F Ratio	df
	Mean	Adjusted	Mean	Adjusted	Mean	Adjusted	Mean	Adjusted			
Arithmetic Competence											
17. Problem Solving (S.S.)	54.60	55.54	51.06	52.73	57.48	55.42	—	—	54.70	0.47	2,50
18. Computations (S.S.)	62.30	63.27	48.71	49.36	57.30	55.98	—	—	56.53	9.05**	2,50
Intelligence Measures											
19. June Retest, Raven's	28.27	28.27	28.94	30.23	27.65	26.76	—	—	28.21	2.03	2,51
20. *Lorge-Thorndike*											
Total	49.86	50.14	50.29	50.73	49.83	49.24	—	—	49.97	0.20	2,52
Vocabulary	15.68	15.52	14.59	14.71	17.09	17.15	—	—	15.90	4.35*	2,52
Not-belonging	17.23	17.44	18.65	18.85	17.22	16.86	—	—	17.61	2.42	2,52
Go-together	17.41	17.58	17.06	16.98	17.35	17.24	—	—	17.29	0.58	2,52
Foreign Language Sensitivity											
21. Russian Phoneme Discrimination (Errors)	13.27	13.01	15.21[b]	15.63[b]	—	—	—	—	14.03	1.08	1,27

(a)   Entries for tests 1-6 are mean Standard scores.

(b)   Control Subjects who had no second-language experience were selected from both English and French control classes. Their scores are combined to form these means.

* $p < .05$
** $p < .01$

development in the native language for a year may provide a shortcut in the time needed for learning. From the data available at this point in the program, we cannot build a convincing counterargument to the maturation possibility, although we can emphasize that we noted a similar catching-up process in operation even at the first-grade level.

In our attempts to understand the children's performance, we have come to favor the hypothesis that the Experimental children may never have been on "vacation" in English at all. Instead, they may have transferred basic skills of reading, concept development, word manipulation, and verbal creativity *through* French to English by reprocessing in English all the information they received through French, or by simultaneously processing in French *and* English. The possibility we see in these results (which is only an idea to be tested with further experimentation) is that children of normal intelligence, trained through a second language, process new information encountered in class both in the second language—thereby developing skill with that language—as well as in the native language. The idea is that they do this naturally in order to draw on and relate the notions presented in the second language to their reservoir of English conceptual knowledge, built up through infancy and childhood. As a consequence they help themselves comprehend and understand both the content of the new material and the nature of the new code through which that content is presented. In other words, it is our hunch that these children consider the new language as a code to be broken, and, through contrasts made with their native language, they become with time increasingly more clever at relating and translating academic content between French and English, and at relating and contrasting linguistic codes. It has often been argued by specialists of the classical languages that training in Latin or Greek develops a deeper awareness and understanding of one's native language (at least for speakers of languages linguistically related to Latin or Greek). Similarly we propose that learning through a second, linguistically related language may have a favorable influence on children's performance in their *native* language. The possibility will also be discussed below that this contrastive linguistic experience may favorably affect the mastery of academic *content* as well.

An example of this interplay can be drawn from results on the Peabody Picture Vocabulary Test. Consider some French concepts that the third- and fourth-grade child is expected to understand, according to the age norms accompanying the Peabody test: *meringue, excaver, arctique, cérémonie, assaillir, chimiste, escarpement, lamentation, sentinelle, submerger, canine, évaluation, confiné, précipitation*, and *amphibie*. As the child develops the meanings of these new words in French, he will certainly draw on past experiences and basic notions already symbolized and given substance with English names. Osgood's theory of meaning and his research on the development of "assigns" clearly supports such a line of speculation (see Osgood, 1952). For example, the context in which the concept *canine* is introduced and the amplifications provided by the French teacher will prompt the Experimental children to draw on their past experiences with dogs and dog-related events. Then as the notion is developed in French and the use of this new word is stabilized in the child's memory, he will quite incidentally have developed an equivalent and presumably new concept in English, i.e., canine. Note the correspondence between the English and French terms in the sample of items taken directly from the French version of the Peabody test: *canine, excavate, arctic, ceremony, assail, chemist, escarpment, lament,* and so forth. Thus, when given the English version of the Peabody test, the child has a great number of items already at his disposition. In addition to concepts that are cognates in English and French, the children must also come to understand such words as *pignon* (gable), *sondage* (probing), *hisser* (hoist), *déchirement* (bereavement), and *planer* (hover). As the meanings of these words are developed, a sharp *contrast* between languages is incidentally offered, and the child may be prompted, because of the lack of likely correspondence, to seek out on his own the English translation equivalents of such new notions which have been given substance with French symbols.

Speaking skills in English. Further supportive evidence for this general view is found when the children's abilities to retell or create stories in English are compared (items 7 and 8 in Table 12). When retelling a story, the Pilot Experimental Class is rated equivalent to both English Control groups on overall expression and grammar, and as equivalent to one Control and better than the other on enunciation, rhythm and intonation in English. When creating stories in English, they are rated as equivalent to one Control and better than the other on both expression and grammar; the same as both English Controls on enunciation; but poorer than one Control and better than the other on rhythm and intonation. Except for this last instance, they are, in general, either as efficient as or better than one Control Class or the other at retelling or making up stories in English.

When each child's stories are transcribed and analyzed in detail, we find that the Experimental Class has a vocabulary in English as rich and varied as that of the Controls, if not more so. In retelling stories, they generally show a richer and more varied vocabulary than English Control I, and they are similar to English Control II in depth and range of vocabulary. They also have a reliably *more* varied stock of adjectives than either Control Class. Moreover, they have as good command of English grammar as either Control and are as able to comprehend the material presented them. The same general picture emerges when the story inventions of each group are compared: The Experimental children use as many words and as many different words as one Control Class and are statistically better in these regards than the other. However, the Experimentals comprehend the stories they invent significantly better than do *either* of the Controls. Thus, the Experimental children's capacity to use English spontaneously is definitely as well developed as either Control Class at the grade II level.

Encoding and decoding skills in English. There is one other indication of how well the Experimental children handle English. A separate experiment was conducted during the 1967-68 school year with the grade II Experimental and English Control I children to assess their skill in communicating spontaneously and creatively in English (see Samuels, Reynolds, and Lambert, 1969). In that study, attention was directed to both the decoding and encoding abilities of the children, that is, their skill in *understanding* the descriptive messages of children their own age, and in *sending* messages to others. The decoding task is portrayed in Figure 1: a child hears a tape-recorded version of another child describing which block out of the six should be put next in order on the peg. For example, he might hear, "Next it's the one that looks like a girl with hair and hands and no feet and no tummy," as a description for the block at the top of the peg. His task was to decode this information correctly. For the encoding test, the same child had to describe in his own words which blocks he was putting on the peg at any time. This task calls for knowledge of children's everyday language, and the finding of special interest at this point is that the Experimental Class was as efficient as the English Controls in both decoding and encoding in English.

Word associations in English. As one examines the children's English word associations (item 9), the same pattern of comparability between classes becomes evident. The relative overuse of syntagmatic responses that characterized both Experimental Classes in the first year is no longer evident. Here the Experimental children are as rapid in giving their associations as the Controls. They give proportionately no more paradigmatic, syntagmatic, semantic clusters or rhyming responses than the Controls. However, they do give reliably more idiosyncratic and reliably fewer transformation responses than the Controls. It is difficult to interpret the meaning of their overuse of idiosyncratic responses. It could signify a relative lack of inhibition or a carelessness when thinking in English, especially when set to respond quickly, or it could mean that, as their facility with French progresses, there are more between-language routes along which associations can pass. Since there was no such tendency at the end of grade I, it will be of interest to see if this tendency shows up again with the grade II Follow-up Classes.

The major outcome of this analysis, nonetheless, is the similarity among classes in the forms of English word associations. The tendency for the grade I Experimental Classes to give disproportionately more syntagmatic responses than the English Controls is not apparent at the grade II level. If this outcome is replicated with the Follow-up Classes, we will be able to argue with greater assurance that the peculiar associational pattern noted after one year's academic experiences in a second language passes away in a relatively short time. Of course, other peculiarities could show up at other points in time as the children

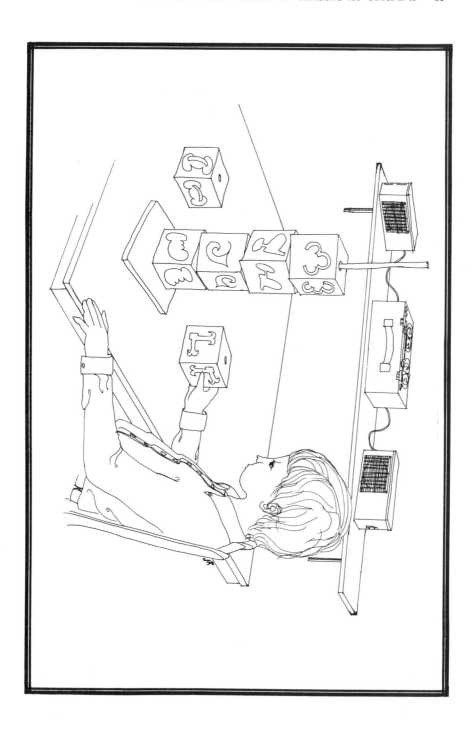

develop deeper degrees of bilingual skill, and we will watch carefully for such eventualities in the following grades.

Arithmetic competence. A third line of evidence suggesting beneficial transfer effects from French to English is to be found in the performance of the Experimental Class on tests of arithmetic skill (items 17 and 18 in Table 12). Keep in mind that mathematics was taught to the Experimental children exclusively through French. Their knowledge of mathematical concepts when tested through English is especially interesting. On test 17 (arithmetic concepts and problem-solving ability), they score as well as either group of English Controls, and, as a class, rank above the 90th percentile on national norms. On test 18, (measuring speed and efficiency in mathematical computations), they are significantly better than either Control Class. These results indicate very clearly that the French training they received in math had "gotten through" to them. There are two likely explanations: either they are amazingly clever in transferring the fruits of this training, and/or they are obliged by their training in French to relate new notions and concepts to their English reserve of basic meanings at the same time as they develop new complex ideas in French. The fact that they are even more skilled in the application of these ideas than the Controls (at this grade level) suggests that the processes of transferring and relating may make the newly developing concepts particularly vivid and meaningful, thereby speeding up the learning process itself. Although the results obtained support such an hypothesis, much more research of a detailed, experimental nature is, of course, called for to verify it.

French Competence

Reading skills and listening comprehension in French. On the test of French Reading Skills (item 10), the Pilot Experimental Class scores as well as the French Controls.[2] Likewise on the French Listening Comprehension Test (item 11) there is no difference between groups. Thus, in terms of these two more passive aspects of French competence, the Experimental Class is as good as native-speaker Controls.[3]

---

[2] On one subtest—that concerned with word order—the Experimental Class is significantly better than the French Controls ($F = 6.63, df = 1, 24, p < .02$.

[3] Certain of these comparisons involve only part of the French Control Class. For example, item 12 on Table 10 has only twenty-four degrees of freedom; this means that there are thirty-three children in the comparison, since nine degrees of freedom are lost because of the statistical covariance adjustments made, one df is lost for each variable adjusted and for each group compared. The French Control children have been placed in various second-grade classes in their school, and we were able to take the time of only a part of the total for certain tests. In these cases, there was no selection of the better or poorer children, so that the smaller numbers are likely representative of the total. Because small samples are involved, the need to replicate this study with another set of second-grade classes is obvious.

Vocabulary in French. On the French version of the Peabody Picture Vocabulary Test (item 12), the Experimental children fall behind the Controls, but even though this is a statistically reliable difference, it is of practical importance to realize that the two group means differ only by five units (71.66 versus 76.13), meaning that the Experimental Class, on the average, did not know five concepts that the Control Class did know. The concepts that gave them most difficulty were *attirail* (meaning junk; superfluous baggage; or funny attire), *cérémonie* (ceremony), *entonnoir* (funnel), *assaillir* (to assault), and *hisser* (to hoist). It is likely that these concepts had not been encountered in their reading or school work. At the same time more of the Experimental children knew certain concepts than did the French Controls, e.g., *non dressé* (bronco), *meringue* (as on a lemon pie), and *excaver* (excavate). Both classes, of course, had equal difficulty with the final 25 of the 100 items included in the test (i.e., numbers 76 to 100). From our perspective, then, the Experimental children have actually developed an extensive vocabulary of complex concepts in French, even when compared with native-speaker controls.

French phoneme production. The Experimental Class's control of the essential sounds of French is reflected in their score on the French Phoneme Production measure (item 12). There is evidence here for progress over their first-grade performance (42.23 for grade II versus 38.00 for grade I), when rated by the same judges, on the same scales. Their average score works out to a mean rating of 2.22 (42.23/19 on a three-point scale) signifying a judgment of their performance as lying between *moyen* and *bon*, with native speakers of French as a point of reference.

The sounds that presented the greatest difficulty to the children in the Experimental Class are presented at the start of the following list: *pt, in, pn, â, alle, eur, é, ô, eille, j, on, an, un, cl, u, r, ot, è, eu*. The order progresses from poorest performance to best, but there is a distinct break after *pt*, the sound that is clearly least well controlled, and another break before *è* and *eu*, the two sounds best under control.[4]

Impressive as their performance here is, one could interpret these results in a different light. Perhaps the Experimental children have leveled off in their progress with French sounds by the end of grade II, and with each year will have progressively fewer chances of reaching perfect, nativelike command of the French sound system. This possibility should be considered seriously, because it may signify that starting French at kindergarten age and sustaining it in a classroom environment only is both too late and not enough, from one point of

---

[4]It would be of interest and value to study why certain sounds show improvement from year to year, while others apparently do not, e.g., why is it that certain sounds such as *alle* and *eille*, and *an* and *on* shift in relative positions from one year to another?

view. However, many parents and educators do not feel that developing *perfect* control of pronunciation in a second or foreign language is the most important aspect of bilingual skill to strive for.

In any case, the four linguistic judges, when asked about this feature of the children's pronunciation, felt that the children *would* be indistinguishable from native speakers *if* placed in a completely French environment for a "month or so." At the same time, the judges felt that the children's command of the sounds was extremely good and that, as a group, they did not have a "typical" English accent in their use of French.

Speaking skills in French. The analyses of the children's oral productions when retelling or creating stories in French (items 14 and 15 in Table 12) also reveal an extremely high level of skill on the part of the Pilot Experimental Class. The statistical counts of the stories they told indicate that they have as good comprehension as the Controls of the themes in the stories and as rich and varied a vocabulary in French. Still they make significantly more grammatical errors than the Controls.

The same two sets of judges who helped us with the grade I analysis (described in Chapter 4) rated the children's productions as of the end of grade II. The same discrepancies between the ratings of the bilingual and the French teacher judges are apparent here as with the first graders. The more demanding bilingual judges find the Experimental children reliably poorer on overall expression, grammar, enunciation, and liaison; but no different from the Controls in their rhythm and intonation. The French teacher judges, in contrast, find the Experimental Class comparable to the Controls on all aspects except rhythm and intonation. The mean ratings assigned by the bilingual judges range between 1.61 and 2.28 for the Pilot Experimental Class and between 2.70 and 2.89 for the French Control Class, translating to an overall "low average" rating for the Experimental Class compared to a "passable" rating for the French Controls. The ratings of the relatively more lenient French teachers ranged from 2.59 to 3.13 for the Experimental Class and from 3.09 to 3.46 for the French Control Class, making the groups even closer in their judgments.

The picture is only slightly different when the judgments deal with the children's spontaneous creations (item 15). In this case, the Experimental children make relatively more grammatical errors than they do when simply retelling a story, and in both instances, they make significantly more errors of grammar than do the Controls. They also have a less diversified stock of adjectives than the Controls, which was not the case for story retelling. Otherwise, the overall size of their vocabulary, the diversity of nouns and verbs used, and their degree of story comprehension are the same as those of the Controls. The ratings of the bilingual judges in this case show a larger difference between groups, and in no aspect is the Experimental Class rated as high as the Controls. The French teacher judges also make a greater differentiation of the two classes in this case, especially with regard to grammatical correctness: the Experimental Class is significantly poorer than the Controls in their command of grammar and in their rhythm and intonation. In terms of overall verbal expression, enunciation, and liaison, however, the French teachers find no difference between the Classes when story creation is involved. In summary, then, the Experimental Class, when evaluated by two teams of judges, each with its own criteria, is relatively well judged in comparison with native speakers of French. As a group, they are placed about one step lower on a five-point scale than the Controls, between positions 2 and 3 on the scale. They are particularly poor in their control of French grammar, especially when creating stories on their own, but are relatively good in terms of enunciation, liaison, and overall expression.

Decoding and encoding skills in French. The same measures of decoding and encoding skills as described above were used a second time to assess the Experimental children's ability to communicate with children their own age in French. Remember that their normal experience in French is restricted mainly to the classroom and to interaction with an adult, the teacher. That is, they have relatively few opportunities for informal interaction in French with children their own age, except for their school-related contacts with one another in the classroom. Consequently, we anticipated that they might well be less efficient at French decoding and encoding than French-speaking children.

To test their abilities, the same procedure described for the English version was used in French. Their task was to follow descriptive instructions given to them by children who were native speakers of French. For example, with Figure 1 as a model, they might hear a description such as "ça ressemble à deux 3 colés ensemble" for the top block. For encoding, they had to give their own descriptive directions which French children could understand. Because the French Control Class was not available for retesting, we used a new control group of French children who were equated with the Experimental children for intelligence and social-class background.

It was surprising and reassuring to find that the Experimental Class performed as efficiently as the native-speaker controls on *both* the decoding and encoding tasks. Thus, even on this nonacademic measure of communication skill, the Experimental Class functioned at the same level as the French Controls at the end of grade II.

Word associations in French. In their word associations (item 16), the Experimental Class does not differ in any respect from the French Control Class. This means that their associations in French come as rapidly as those of the Controls;[5] they give no more idiosyncratic responses; and, perhaps most

---

[5] Note, however, that the Experimental Class is much slower when associating in French (5.85 sec.) than they are in English (2.81 sec.). This may mean that there is no difference in reaction time simply because the French Control Class was unusually slow.

important of all, they do not give proportionately more or fewer syntagmatic responses or semantic clusters than the Controls. Thus, by the end of grade II the Experimental children have become indistinguishable from the native-speaker Control Class in the structure of their French associations and (apparently) in their speed of associating. This important reversal from the grade I level will become more valuable if it is found to be reliable with the Follow-up Classes at grade II.

Intelligence Measures

Two different measures were taken of the children's intelligence at the end of their second year in the experiment, a retest using the Progressive Matrices Test (item 19), and the Lorge-Thorndike battery (item 20). On the Progressive Matrices test (19) there is no difference among group means, indicating that the slight depression in IQ, noted with the Pilot Experimental Class at the end of grade I, is no longer apparent. On the Lorge-Thorndike scales (20), the Experimental Class is equivalent to English Control I on the vocabulary subtest, but both are significantly poorer than the English Control II Class. On the other two subtests and on the total scale, however, the Experimental Class scores at the same level as either control. Thus, we have no symptoms at the end of grade II for any intellectual deficit associated with participation in the experimental program. At the same time, we also have no evidence at this stage for any intellectual advantage that can be ascribed to the experimental program.

Foreign Language Sensitivity

A comparison was made of ability to differentiate Russian phonemes between the Experimental Class and the children in the English and French Control Classes who had no second-language home experience. Although the Experimental Class, as predicted, was somewhat better than the Controls, the difference was not statistically significant.

Results for the Follow-up Classes
at the End of Grade II

As already mentioned, the reliability of the results of the overall experiment is given a difficult test when a second, follow-up set of classes is examined. Changes in teachers, philosophies of teaching, and methods of evaluating the comparative standing of the classes have all taken place from one year to the next. More important, perhaps, the Follow-up Experimental Class is out of the spotlight that was focused so directly on the Pilot Experimental Class. In other words, the atmosphere for this new class of second graders was less experimental and more relaxed than that of the Pilot Class. Most important, the teachers could see that other children had already succeeded in grade II, so that they could now profit from and experiment with the teaching procedures of the preceding year.

Comparisons among the Follow-up Classes at the end of grade II are presented in Table 13. Note that the two Follow-up English Control Classes, kept separate for the grade I analysis, have been combined to form one large English Control group.

English Language Competence

Reading, word knowledge, listening comprehension, and vocabulary. The results presented in items 1, 2, 3, 5, and 6 of Table 13 show that the Follow-up Experimental Class, like the Pilot Class at grade II, is similar to the English Controls in the development of English-language competence. Only on the spelling subtest (item 4) do they fall reliably below the Controls. Still in terms of nationwide norms, their mean score on that subtest reaches the 70th percentile. For reading, they are at the 75th percentile, for word discrimination at the 80th percentile, and for word knowledge at the 85th percentile.

Keeping in mind that the Experimental Class had only two daily thirty-five-minute periods of formal training in English Language Arts, these results are particularly noteworthy. Not only did the Follow-up Class do as well as the Controls on subtests of word knowledge, word discrimination, and reading, all of which call for reading skill in English, but they also performed as well as the Controls on the English listening comprehension test (item 5).

Of special interest is their performance on the Peabody Picture Vocabulary Test (item 6), where they score reliably better than the Controls. This outcome adds credibility to the hypothesis advanced earlier that positive transfer to English may take place through the training in French the children have received. Since many of the concepts included in the English test apparently would only have been encountered in French, some form of transfer across languages seems inevitable. When a count is made of those concepts in the English version of the Peabody test that were proportionately better understood by the Follow-up Experimental Class, we find the following: *assistance, observatory, erecting, horror, hive, locomotive, lubricating, soldering, dissatisfaction, casserole, oasis,* and *laden.* Note that all but *hive* and *laden* have cognates in French, suggesting that the favorable transfer may easily have taken place from French to English. This analysis indicates the potential value of a separate study of this type of transfer. For present purposes, however, the evidence is clear that after grade II, the Experimental children are not handicapped in any way in their development of English concepts and vocabulary.

Table 13

Test Results for the Follow-up Classes at the End of Grade II, 1969

Test Number and Name	Experimental Class		English Controls		French Controls		F Ratio	df
	Mean	Adjusted	Mean	Adjusted	Mean	Adjusted		
English Competence								
1. Word Knowledge (S.S.)	55.46	56.19	56.77	56.25	—	—	0.00	1,59
2. Word Discrimination (S.S.)	53.79	54.54	58.16	57.60	—	—	3.02	1,58
3. Reading (S.S.)	50.88	52.30	54.41	53.41	—	—	0.40	1,55
4. Spelling (S.S.)	50.33	51.86	58.55	57.47	—	—	6.58*	1,57
5. Listening Comprehension	12.54	12.64	12.69	12.62	—	—	0.00	1,57
6. English Picture Vocabulary	76.25	77.33	72.97	72.29	—	—	6.53*	1,54
7. *Speaking Skills in English: Story Retelling*								
Linguistic Ratings								
Overall Expression	6.94	7.04	6.74	6.64	—	—	1.38	1,58
Grammar	7.47	7.67	7.88	7.70	—	—	0.01	1,58
Enunciation	7.19	7.38	7.03	6.84	—	—	2.81	1,58
Rhythm and Intonation	9.08	9.04	8.97	9.01	—	—	0.01	1,58
Word Counts								
Number of Words	55.97	55.55	47.21	47.60	—	—	3.11	1,58
Nouns (% of total)	0.18	0.18	0.17	0.16	—	—	1.32	1,58
Different Nouns (%)	0.66	0.65	0.71	0.72	—	—	1.55	1,58
Adjectives (%)	0.09	0.10	0.09	0.08	—	—	1.75	1,58
Different Adjectives (%)	0.87	0.56	0.92	0.93	—	—	2.47	1,52
Verbs (% of total)	0.14	0.14	0.16	0.16	—	—	2.38	1,58
Different Verbs (%)	0.75	0.75	0.84	0.84	—	—	2.38	1,58
Story Comprehension Rating	2.41	2.35	2.15	2.20	—	—	0.16	1,58

Test Number and Name	Experimental Class		English Controls		French Controls		F Ratio	df
	Mean	Adjusted	Mean	Adjusted	Mean	Adjusted		
8. Speaking Skills in English: Story Invention								
Linguistic Ratings								
Overall Expression	7.00	6.94	7.32	7.38	—	—	1.89	1,58
Grammar	7.47	7.53	7.65	7.59	—	—	0.03	1,58
Enunciation	7.38	7.70	7.03	6.72	—	—	7.64**	1,58
Rhythm and Intonation	9.20	9.02	9.03	9.20	—	—	0.43	1,58
Word Counts								
Number of Words	47.34	44.99	57.59	59.81	—	—	5.62*	1,58
Nouns (% of total)	0.17	0.17	0.19	0.19	—	—	3.60	1,58
Different Nouns (%)	0.72	0.73	0.63	0.62	—	—	5.67*	1,58
Adjectives (% of totals)	0.01	0.01	0.01	0.01	—	—	0.51	1,58
Different Adjectives (%)	0.90	0.99	0.55	0.34	—	—	4.94*	1,58
Verbs (% of total)	0.18	0.18	0.17	0.17	—	—	1.56	1,58
Different Verbs (%)	0.78	0.78	0.77	0.77	—	—	0.08	1,58
Number Grammatical Errors	1.19	1.16	1.09	1.11	—	—	0.02	1,58
Story Comprehension Rating	3.78	3.81	3.47	3.44	—	—	2.51	1,58
9. Decoding Skill in English								
Children's Descriptions	7.19	7.12	7.28	7.34	—	—	0.16	1,62
Adults' Descriptions	7.97	8.25	7.62	7.39	—	—	2.45	1,62
10. Word Association Analysis: English								
Latency (secs.)	2.63	3.00	3.60	2.93	—	—	0.04	1,42
Paradigmatic (%)	79.97	75.55	69.62	73.24	—	—	0.20	1,63
Syntagmatic (%)	8.00	12.46	13.56	9.90	—	—	0.66	1,63
Semantic Clusters (%)	5.69	5.64	6.31	6.34	—	—	0.27	1,63
Idiosyncratic (%)	3.13	2.69	7.56	7.92	—	—	2.01	1,63
Rhymings (%)	0.75	0.90	0.67	0.55	—	—	0.45	1,63
Transformations (%)	2.50	2.60	2.15	2.08	—	—	0.32	1,63

Table 13 (cont.)

Tests Results for the Follow-up Classes at the End of Grade II, 1969

Test Number and Name	Experimental Class		English Controls		French Controls		F Ratio	df
	Mean	Adjusted	Mean	Adjusted	Mean	Adjusted		
French Competence								
11. Listening Comprehension	10.15	10.13	—	—	12.72	12.76	9.33**	1,43
12. Rendement en Francais	12.70	12.90	—	—	15.73	15.41	1.72	1,30
13. French Word Discrimination	31.86	31.98	—	—	30.33	30.14	9.69**	1,38
14. French Picture Vocabulary	69.45	69.59	—	—	76.65	76.40	18.11**	1,38
15. French Phoneme Production, 2.56 (with maximum possible of 3.00).								
16. *French Speaking Skills: Story Retelling*								
Linguistic Ratings								
Overall Expression	4.64	4.71	—	—	6.38	6.26	6.48*	1,36
Grammar	4.14	4.23	—	—	6.69	6.54	36.60**	1,36
Enunciation	5.32	5.37	—	—	6.06	5.98	1.63	1,36
Liaison	6.93	6.98	—	—	7.63	7.53	1.12	1,36
Rhythm and Intonation	5.50	5.57	—	—	7.56	7.44	14.44**	1,36
Word Counts								
No. of Words, total	35.27	35.03	—	—	64.44	64.82	25.21**	1,34
Nouns (% of total)	0.21	0.21	—	—	0.15	0.15	8.06**	1,34
Different Nouns (%)	0.76	0.76	—	—	0.63	0.61	6.24*	1,33
Adjectives (%)	0.06	0.06	—	—	0.03	0.03	5.85*	1,34
Different Adjectives (%)	0.88	0.88	—	—	0.84	0.84	0.28	1,17
Verbs (% of total)	0.15	0.15	—	—	0.14	0.14	0.33	1,34
Different Verbs (%)	0.80	0.82	—	—	0.72	0.70	2.93	1,33
Story Comprehension Rating	2.23	2.24	—	—	2.75	2.73	2.07	1,34
17. *French Speaking Skills: Story Invention*								
Linguistic Ratings								
Overall Expression	7.00	7.04	—	—	7.29	7.22	0.17	1,38
Grammar	4.90	4.98	—	—	6.29	6.16	8.84**	1,38

Test Number and Name	Experimental Class		English Controls		French Controls		F Ratio	df
	Mean	Adjusted	Mean	Adjusted	Mean	Adjusted		
17. *French Speaking Skills: Linguistic Ratings (cont.)*								
Enunciation	6.14	6.19	—	—	6.18	6.08	0.13	1,38
Liaison	7.69	7.71	—	—	7.76	7.73	0.01	1,38
Rhythm and Intonation	6.93	6.97	—	—	7.71	7.64	3.61	1,38
Word Counts								
No. of Words, Total	50.11	50.37	—	—	66.63	66.16	6.82*	1,36
Nouns (% of total)	0.23	0.23	—	—	0.19	0.19	7.81**	1,36
Different Nouns (%)	0.56	0.56	—	—	0.58	0.58	0.29	1,36
Adjectives (% of total)	0.01	0.01	—	—	0.03	0.03	7.20**	1,36
Different Adjectives (%)	0.65	0.66	—	—	0.37	0.36	5.14*	1,38
Verbs (% of total)	0.14	0.14	—	—	0.15	0.15	0.25	1,36
Different Verbs (%)	0.65	0.65	—	—	0.72	0.72	2.61	1,36
Number Grammatical Errors	4.15	4.13	—	—	2.94	2.99	2.68	1,42
Story Comprehension Rating	2.90	2.92	—	—	3.29	3.25	0.62	1,38
18. *Decoding Skills in French*								
Children's Descriptions	5.79	5.79	—	—	6.65	6.63	2.85	1,37
Adult's Descriptions	6.43	6.39	—	—	6.94	7.00	2.36	1,37
19. *Word Association Analysis: French*								
Associational Latency	3.55	3.52	—	—	—	—	—	—
Paradigmatic (%)	71.47	71.80	—	—	60.56	60.00	4.82*	1,40
Syntagmatic (%)	7.47	7.64	—	—	5.89	5.61	1.14	1,40
Semantic Clusters (%)	7.33	7.45	—	—	9.00	8.81	0.63	1,40
Idiosyncratic (%)	8.37	8.27	—	—	6.56	6.72	0.19	1,40
Rhymings	1.13	-1.14	—	—	5.44	5.44	18.79**	1,40
Transformations	2.80	2.09	—	—	12.89	14.07	23.47**	1,40
Arithmetic Competence								
20. Problem Solving (S.S.)	54.57	55.03	52.00	51.67	—	—	2.31	1,58
21. Computations (S.S.)	57.68	59.35	53.37	52.14	—	—	6.88*	1,58

Table 13 (cont.)
Test Results for the Follow-up Classes at the End of Grade II, 1969

Test Number and Name	Experimental Class		English Controls		French Controls		F Ratio	df
	Mean	Adjusted	Mean	Adjusted	Mean	Adjusted		
22. June Retesting Raven's	26.73	27.58	24.97	24.45	27.00	26.60	4.59*	2,72
23. *Lorge-Thorndike*								
Total	50.68	51.45	49.65	49.07	—	—	2.38	1,57
Vocabulary	16.54	16.75	17.24	17.08	—	—	0.15	1,57
Not-Belonging	18.14	18.31	16.76	16.63	—	—	4.10*	1,57
Go-Together	16.00	16.38	15.65	15.36	—	—	1.99	1,57
Creativity Measures								
24. Unusual Uses, French	4.73	4.85	—	—	4.56	4.21	0.28	1,32
25. Consequences, French	4.47	4.65	—	—	7.15	6.60	3.10	1,31
26. Unusual Uses, English	7.13	6.90	6.58	6.79	—	—	0.02	1,57
27. Consequences, English	6.66	6.26	5.44	5.81	—	—	0.23	1,56
Foreign Language Sensitivity								
28. Russian Phoneme Discrimination (errors)	12.50	11.60	13.33	14.83	—	—	1.52	1,40

*p > .05
**p > .01

English speaking skills. When the Follow-up Class is compared with the English Controls in ability to retell and invent stories in English (items 7 and 8), they again show no deficiencies. In fact, they appear to be ahead of the English Controls in certain respects. When retelling a story in English, the Follow-up children were rated by linguists as equivalent to the English Controls in overall expression, grammar, enunciation, and rhythm and intonation. Their vocabulary choice is as rich and varied as that of the Controls; they make no more grammatical errors; and their comprehension of the story is as good. When creating a story of their own, their enunciation is reliably better than that of the English Controls, with all other linguistic features equivalent. It is interesting to note that they use reliably fewer words in their invented stories which nonetheless show as much coherence as those of the Controls, and as much diveristy in the use of nouns and adjectives. The fact that the Experimental children distinguish themselves in their enunciation and vocabulary diversity in Egnlish on a test that provides no verbal structure is of special interest. It suggests that the French training may favorably influence these features of English usage. Theoretical speculations aside, the Follow-up Experimental Class's speaking skill in English, like that of the Pilot Class, is certainly as advanced as that of the English Control children at the end of grade II. Rather than showing signs of negative transfer from French, we interpret the findings as indicating that the training in French may have a beneficial effect, through vocabulary development and enunciation, on their expressive ability in English.

English decoding skills. The decoding measure provides a different index of the Follow-up Class's competence in English. Our interest here was in each pupil's ability to comprehend and use verbal descriptions in the solution of discrimination problems. The descriptions were collected from other children their own age and from adults. In order to decode successfully another child's descriptions, the listener must select the crucial features in a certain visual display that differentiates it from others very similar to it in a set. The children's descriptions, of course, come in the form of spontaneous and youthful imagery, while the adult descriptions demand an understanding of a different style of imagery and expression. The results (item 9) show that the Follow-up Class is as efficient as the English Controls in decoding either children's or adults' descriptions.

English word associations. It will be noted in item 10 of Table 13 that there are no reliable differences between the Experimental and Control Classes in their modes of associating in English. This finding is important since we now have evidence that neither the Pilot nor the Follow-up Experimental Classes at the end of grade II show signs of overusing syntagmatic and underusing paradigmatic forms of associational responses as they did at the end of grade I. Thus, the less mature associational pattern noted with the Experimental first graders is no longer evident by the end of the second year. The home-school language-switch program, then, may affect adversely the form of associations children give in both languages during kindergarten and grade I—that period when marked progress is made in learning the new language and relating ideas from one language to the other—but by the end of the following school year, it seems, no symptoms of this type of retardation remain. Furthermore, the overuse of idiosyncratic responses and the underuse of transformations noted in the English associations of the Pilot Experimental Class at grade II should be seen as unreliable outcomes, since no such trends are found with the grade II Follow-up Experimentals.

French Language Competence

Reading, word knowledge, listening comprehension, and vocabulary. The Follow-up Experimental Class scored significantly poorer on the French listening comprehension measure than the French Control Class (item 11). This means that, as a group, they were less able to hold in memory and retrieve the details of a story presented in French. This was not the case, it will be recalled, for the Pilot Class at grade II, who did not differ from the Controls on a slightly different form of this measure. However, on the 1969 version of the Test de Rendement en Français (item 12) which requires skill in rapid reading and verbal analysis, the Follow-up Class did not differ from the Controls, and on the word discrimination task (item 13) they scored reliably higher than the controls.[6]

Vocabulary in French. The Follow-up Class, as was the case with the Pilot Class, fell reliably below the French Controls on the French version of the Peabody Picture Vocabulary Test (item 14). In this instance there is an average difference of about seven score points separating the groups, meaning that the Experimentals missed seven concepts passed by the French Controls. They had difficulty, for instance, with such concepts as *insigne, fouet, tâche de rousseur, torsion, astiquer, ronger,* and *comptoir.* With certain concepts, though, the Experimental Class did better than the French Controls (e.g., *groupe, chef, aigle*), and both groups had trouble with concepts such as *sentinelle, poutre, planner, deuil,* and *pignon.* Neither group had difficulty with concepts such as *délice, descendre, pouf, porteur,* and *archer.* In general, the French Controls showed that they know about 76 of the 100 concepts comprising this measure compared to the Experimentals' 70, suggesting that school experiences with French, can, by the end of grade II, greatly narrow the gap between the Experimental and French Control Classes.

French phoneme production. The Follow-up Class progressed from the grade I level in their active control of the essential sounds of French (measure 15). At the end of grade II, their average score was 2.56, on a three-step scale ranging

---

[6]Note that both groups are close to the ceiling (32) on this test; but, even so, the distribution of scores clearly favors the Experimental Class.

from *poor* (1), to *average* (2), to *good* (3). This represents an above average performance in terms of the ratings. The sounds they produced especially well were: *onze, note, était, deux,* and *peur;* while they had more difficulty with *lune, soleil, chacun, pain,* and especially *pneu.* In general, then, the Experimental children have developed near nativelike skill with many of the basic sound units of the French language by grade II.

French speaking skills. Their speaking ability in French, assessed with the story retelling and story invention procedures (items 16 and 17), reveal a high level of attainment, especially on story invention.

Two linguists judged the tape recordings of their speech, using five-step scales that ranged from poor (1) to excellent (5). The ratings of both linguists are combined in the scores entered in Table 13, making a range from 2 to 10 with 6 as the average score. Native speakers of "standard" French served as the judges' reference model. Note that the judges did not, in general, use the "excellent" category even for the French Controls; thus the actual scores range between 4 and 8.

When *retelling* a story in French, the Follow-up Experimental Class, as a group, is rated approximately at 5 for overall expression, enunciation, and rhythm and intonation; about 4 on grammatical correctness; and about 7 on liaison. In comparison with the French Controls, whose ratings are distributed between 6 and 7.50, the Experimentals are significantly poorer in overall expression, grammatical correctness, and rhythm and intonation; but essentially the same as the Controls in terms of enunciation and liaison. When *inventing* stories in French (without a model to follow) the Experimental children are rated more favorably than when retelling someone else's story. That is, they are rated between 6 and 7.7 on all features except grammar, which falls to 5. In fact, except for grammar—they are not significantly different from the French Controls—an amazing level of attainment for English-speaking children. The tendency to perform better when inventing their own stories than simply retelling a story was also noted with the Pilot Experimental Class at grade II. This contrast suggests that young children learning a second language in this fashion may have developed a need and an ability to express their own ideas in their own ways, a possibility that warrants further study.

Statistical word counts were made of the types and varieties of words children used in their productions, and ratings were made of the degree of coherence or comprehension of their stories. When retelling a story, the Experimental children use significantly fewer words (thirty-five versus sixty-five words), but more nouns, adjectives, and more different nouns than the French Controls. There are no differences in the number or variety of verbs. Although the stories of the Experimental children are generally shorter, their comprehension scores are not reliably different from the Controls, suggesting that in this sense, they are efficient in their communication.

When inventing stories, their productions are also reliably shorter than those of the French Controls, but the difference is less pronounced (fifty versus sixty-six words on the average). They also use relatively more nouns and fewer adjectives.[7] There are no differences in the number or variety of verbs employed. As for grammatical errors, the Experimental children make reliably more errors than the Controls, especially errors of gender. They also make many errors of *syntax* or faulty construction (e.g., *je veux toi venir* rather than *j e veux que tu viennes*); and somewhat fewer errors of *contraction* (*à les* rather than *aux*), of tense (*demain je lisais*), and of *number* (*vous aime* for *vous aimez*). The French Controls make proportionately more errors of omission (*il est pas content* for *il n'est pas content*) than do the Experimentals. This analysis highlights those aspects of the language that pose difficulties at the grade II level and it will serve as an interesting reference point as we watch their progress with French in subsequent years.

In this analysis, we again found no reliable difference in the comprehension ratings given the Experimental and French Control groups. Even though the Experimental children have a relatively restricted vocabulary, marked by a proportionately larger number of nouns, they nevertheless display as much comprehension of the overall themes of the stories they retell or invent in French as do the French Controls.

French decoding skills. To assess the Experimental children's understanding of spontaneous, nonacademic language used by French-speaking children and adults, we used a French version of the language decoding procedure described earlier (item 18). The analysis showed that the Follow-up Class, like the Pilot, was as successful as the French Controls in decoding the descriptive comments of both French-Canadian children and adults. This second instance of the Experimental children's ability to follow nonschool forms of French suggests that they have capitalized on the opportunities available to them in bilingual Montreal to pick up informal uses of French. It would be valuable, of course, to study this possibility in detail with sociolinguistic surveys of the children in diverse social situations. In Chapter 9, we describe the results of one such study.

French word associations. One can interpret children's modes of free association as indicants of their thought processes. From this perspective, it seems that the French associations of the Follow-up Experimental Class (item 19 in Table 13) are as mature and sophisticated as those of the French Controls. In fact the Follow-up Experimental children gave significantly more paradigmatic associational responses in French than the Controls, and were essentially like the Controls in the proportions of syntagmatic responses, semantic clusters, and idiosyncratic responses which they produced. However, they did give signifi-

---

[7]No importance is attributed to the fact that the Experimental Class has a greater variety of adjectives; too few cases are actually involved, since the Experimentals generally use few adjectives.

cantly fewer rhyming and transformation responses, which was not the case for the Pilot Experimental Class at grade II, although it was for both Experimental Classes at the grade I level. It is difficult to interpret these group differences in rhymings and transformations. As mentioned earlier, they could indicate a lack of play with the language or, on the other hand, a tendency away from infantile clang-type associations. Thus, no special attention will be given this tendency, except to call it to the attention of those interested in free associations as a research topic. Overall, the Follow-up Class shows no signs of cognitive difficulty when functioning in French; in fact they seem to have made the paradigmatic shift somewhat earlier than the French Control Class.[8]

Arithmetic Competence

Problem solving and computations. Progress in arithmetic was assessed with subtests of the Metropolitan Achievement tests (items 20 and 21), even though the Experimental children had received their mathematics training exclusively in French. This change in the languages of training and testing should not presumably affect performance in computations, but one would imagine it might hamper problem solving. Actually, the Experimental Class scores higher than the English Control Class on *both* subtests, falling at the 85th and 90th percentile in contrast to the Controls, who score at the 75th percentile in both cases. The difference for the computational subtest is statistically significant, making a clear replication since the Pilot Experimental group also scored reliably better than the Controls at grade II. Of course, this better performance in arithmetic could mean that the Experimental Classes enjoy more talented teachers or more effective methods of teaching arithmetic. We could only rule out such an interpretation if we had much more comprehensive methods of equating the competence of teachers and the methods of instruction they use. As far as we could determine, however, the teachers of the Experimental Classes were not specially experienced in arithmetic, and the texts used in the Experimental Class are French versions of those used by the English Controls, both influenced by the "new" math, and both published in North America.

It is striking that the Experimental children by the end of grade II have been able to assimilate mathematical notions and procedures through French with no apparent difficulty. In the case of problem solving, they seem to be able to utilize with apparently equal ease the skills acquired through French when tested through the medium of English. This phenomenon merits special study.

Intelligence Measures

Three different measures of intelligence were used to assess the relative

---

[8]Certain tapes were destroyed during the analysis and, although we had transcribed the responses in advance, we could not compute the latencies for the French Control Class.

effects of the language-switch program on the intellectual development of the Experimental children: a spring retest of the Progressive Matrices test, a retest of the Lorge-Thorndike battery, and two forms of tests designed to measure "productive thinking" or "creativity." This much attention was given to possible changes in cognitive development because we felt it to be foremost among the concerns educators and parents have about the program.

Again, covariance corrections were made for each child's intelligence score and his home background environment. A few bilingual children in the Control Classes were excluded from these comparisons (items 22-27 in Table 13). With regard to the children's spring performance on the Progressive Matrices test (item 22), the Follow-up Experimental and the French Control Classes are about alike in mean scores (27.58 and 26.60), while the English Control Class is lower (24.45). Thus the significant difference noted for the overall comparison is due to the relatively low mean score of the English Controls, meaning that the Experimental children perform as well as one Control group and somewhat better than the other. There is, then, no evidence from either the Pilot or Follow-up Classes of intellectual retardation at the end of grade II; nor are there any such signs with the total score or any of the subtests of the Lorge-Thorndike measure. In fact, the Follow-up Experimental Class scores reliably better than the English Control Class on the "not-belonging" subtest. Instead of a deficit then, we have some evidence here for a possible intellectual advantage favoring the bilingual children; but this has only emerged with the Follow-up Class, and not the Pilot. Hence, it cannot be given undue emphasis.

The results on the creativity measures are interesting. When performing through French, the Follow-up Experimental children are as productive and imaginative as the French Controls. This point is stressed because one might expect the Experimental children to be handicapped in expressing the flow of their imaginative thoughts in French, but they appear to have no difficulty in this regard, relative to the French Controls. Likewise, they are as skilled as the English Controls when performing through English.

Foreign Language Sensitivity

As was the case with the Pilot Class, the Follow-up Experimentals also have fewer errors than the Controls on the Russian Phoneme Discrimination test, (11.60 vs 14.83), but the difference is not statistically significant. We have repeatedly found, from grade I on, small differences favoring the Experimental children, but in no case has a difference been large enough to meet significance levels. This means that up to the end of grade II, the Experimental children show no special sensitivity to foreign-language sounds. One might argue that the test has not been fair because it is difficult in bilingual Montreal to find purely "monolingual" controls, i.e., youngsters who have had *no* experience with the other language. Even so, we would expect, in light of the work of Rabinovitch and Parver (1966), a strong difference to appear at some age level, but as yet we have not seen one.

Summary of Findings and Conclusions
for the Grade II Classes

The general similarity and consistency of the grade II results for both Pilot and Follow-up Experimental Classes permit one to draw various conclusions that have important educational and psychological implications. The statements to be made are, of course, limited to children from middle-class families, in a Montreal socio-cultural setting. Whether they will hold for other social class groups or other social class groups or other settings can only be determined by separate long-range investigation.

(1) *What effect does such an educational experience, where kindergarten and the first two years of schooling are conducted mainly in a second language, have on the development of children's native-language skills?* On the measures used, there are no signs of retardation, except for some trouble with spelling in English. To the contrary, there are certain indications of a beneficial enrichment of native-language development flowing from the bilingual experience. The Experimental children's word knowledge, word discrimination, reading, and listening comprehension scores are at the same level as those of the English Controls; although significantly poorer in English spelling, they still score at the 70th percentile on national norms for spelling ability. In one instance—that of the Follow-up Class—vocabulary development in English is significantly better than that of the Controls. When retelling or inventing stories in English, their comprehension scores are as good as those of the Controls; their vocabulary is as rich and varied, or more so, especially for nouns and adjectives; their overall expression, grammatical correctness, and rhythm and intonation are at the same level as those of the Controls, and their enunciation in English is as good or better. Their ability to encode and decode English messages of a nonacademic nature is also as advanced as that of the English Controls, whether the messages are spoken by children their own age or adults. Their word associations in English at the end of grade II are similar in all regards to those of the Controls, including associational speed, and numbers of idiosyncratic responses. In contrast to the grade I findings, their associational responses are as "mature" in terms of the ratio of paradigmatic to syntagmatic responses. These extremely favorable outcomes indicate that the mainly French training received by the Experimental Classes has left no symptoms of confusion or retardation in the native language. In certain respects the training via French seems to have had a salutary effect on English competence.

(2) *How well do children progress in second-language competence when that language is used as the sole medium of instruction for kindergarten and the first year of schooling and as the major medium for the second year?* Compared to

their relative standing at grade I, there is, as expected, substantial progress in both the passive and active features of competence in French. This means that the Experimental children are, for example, at the same level as the French Controls in French word knowledge, word discrimination, and reading. However, they score significantly lower than the Controls in the French version of the picture vocabulary test, and, in the case of the Follow-up Class, in French listening comprehension.

Their abilities in spoken French are in many respects remarkable, although it is clear that at this stage they are not nativelike in their command of oral French. Their ability to produce the fundamental phonemes of French is rated above average. When retelling stories or creating new ones of their own, the Follow-up Class uses reliably fewer words than the French Controls, but their ratings for story comprehension (or coherence) are at the same level as that of the Controls. Thus, in one sense they are relatively efficient and selective in their use of French, since in both cases (story retelling and story invention) they have a reliably more diversified choice of vocabulary than do the Controls.

The linguists' ratings of the children's spoken French when retelling a story place both Pilot and Follow-up Experimental groups reliably below the French Controls, that is, somewhat below the "average" point on the scales for overall expression, grammar, and rhythm and intonation. However, they are essentially similar to the Controls in enunciation and liason. The composite picture, then, for both Experimental Classes at the end of grade II is that they have made great progress in pronunciation and control of the basic sound units of French at the same time as they lack competence relative to the French Controls, in the grammatical rules and in the smooth, rhythmic use of the language. There is, nevertheless, an interesting change in performance when they are asked to create their own stories. In that case their overall expression and rhythm and intonation are much better than when retelling a story. In fact the Follow-up group is above the average point and *at the same level* as the French Controls on overall expression, enunciation, liaison, and rhythm and intonation in the story creation task, falling below the Controls only on ratings of grammar and on actual counts of grammatical errors. Their most frequent errors comprise gender and syntax. This capacity in spontaneous story invention in contrast to story retelling suggests that the children following the experimental program may have emphasized the development of skills that enable them to express their *own* feelings and ideas in this new language in contrast to relaying other people's ideas and descriptions. This possibility deserves special examination in future research.

(3) *Linguistic development aside, how well do English-speaking children, trained as these youngsters were, function in a nonlanguage subject such as arithmetic taught exclusively through French?* The only nonlanguage subject we have been able to assess so far is arithmetic, including both its computational

and problem-solving aspects. The children were given standardized English language tests of arithmetic and were compared with the English Control Classes. What was particularly interesting about the comparison was that the Pilot and Follow-up Experimental Classes scored as well as the English Controls on problem arithmetic and significantly better on computational arithmetic. Whereas the Controls placed around the 80th percentile, the Experimentals scored at about the 85th. One wonders whether the mode of teaching or the texts favored the Experimental children in some way. From the information available to us, we know that the teachers involved in the Experimental program have no special training in mathematics, and the texts are French versions of those used by the Controls (i.e., standard, up-to-date approaches to arithmetic).

The major finding here is that these children have been as able as the Controls to process and assimilate mathematical notions and techniques through French. The development of their mathematical thinking is as evident in the supposedly silent language (English) as in the language of instruction. The fact that both Experimental Classes at the grade II level perform *better than* the English Controls in computational arithmetic deserves special consideration in future research. This might signify that they have acquired the techniques and ideas more efficiently and more thoroughly because of the second-language instruction.

(4) *Does a bilingual educational experience of this sort extended through grade II affect the Experimental children's sensitivity to language sounds in general?* To provide an answer to this question, the children were retested for their ability to differentiate Russian phonemes, a language totally foreign to all children included in the analysis. Both the Pilot and Follow-up Classes had fewer errors than the Controls, but neither was significantly better than the corresponding Control Class. There is then no generalized sensitivity to foreign language sounds in evidence at the first or second grade levels. This general trend of nonsignificant differences is of interest, because of the overwhelming differences in sensitivity favoring bilingual adults over monolingual adults reported by Rabinovitch and Parver (1966). The question now is: At what age does that sensitivity start to show itself with consistency?

(5) *Finally, does the home-school language switch extended through grade II affect favorably or unfavorably the measured intelligence of children?* The data for both Pilot and Follow-up Classes indicate that there is no form of intellectual retardation attributable to the bilingual experience, regardless of the measures of intelligence (Matrices, Lorge-Thorndike, or Creativity) used. On the other hand, there is no reliable evidence at the grade II level of intellectual enhancement, although certain favorable symptoms emerge with the Follow-up Class (but *not* with the Pilot) in the sense that they score significantly higher than the English Controls on the June retest of the Progressive Matrices and significantly higher on the "not-belonging" subsection of the Lorge-Thorndike test. Until these

trends become more general, however, we shall consider them as chance outcomes only. The fact that the Follow-up Class scored as well as both French and English Controls on the tests of creativity is promising since one might imagine that their stage of development in French would have hampered them in this form of assessment.

Chapter Six

The Pilot and Follow-up Classes at Grade III

At the start of the 1968-69 school year, the children in the Experimental Classes, previously located in smaller neighborhood schools, were moved into the St. Lambert Elementary School, a larger centrally located school in the same community. In all respects it, too, was a typical English-language Protestant school except for a few classes of French-speaking Protestant children who, with their own group of teachers, formed a separate academic stream within the school. Even though there was very little contact between the French and English sections, the bilingual nature of the school did have the effect of reducing somewhat the "experimental" aspect of the program.

By this time too a friendly spirit of cooperation had developed among the various people involved in the experiment—the parents, the school board members, the principal and teachers, and the research team. Through several discussion sessions, all had contributed suggestions and ideas for the curriculum to be followed in the Experimental Classes. For example, the content was to be as comparable as possible to that offered the regular English classes under the school board's jurisdiction without sacrificing the quality of the French language materials to be used. As in the earlier years, most of the texts and work books selected were ones widely used for native speakers of the language in Quebec schools. Thus, no French as a Second Language materials were considered. The actual content of the curriculum was reexamined at regular intervals and new developments in the field of French language education were exchanged and discussed.

The typical daily program was essentially the same for Pilot and Follow-up Experimental Classes: the day was divided into thirty-five-minute periods, the first one set aside for class routine and opening exercises, given in French; then there were two periods of English Language Arts, two of French Language Arts, one of mathematics, and additional once-a-week periods of natural science, physical education, music, art, and library. Although there were only seventy minutes of formal training in English per day, the "fun" subjects (physical education, music, and art) were still either conducted by English-speaking teachers or otherwise neglected unless the regular class teacher felt she could handle them herself.

The grade III Pilot Experimental Class was taught by a French-Canadian woman with experience only as a teacher of French-Canadian students at the high school level. One of the Follow-up Classes was taught by a French-Canadian teacher; the other, by a teacher originally from Belgium.

Measures Used with the Grade III Classes, 1969 and 1970

In general a similar but more advanced battery of tests was used in the spring of 1969 and again in 1970. The new tests of substantial modifications are described briefly below. The numbering refers to entries in Table 14 where the results for the grade III Pilot Classes are presented and Table 18 which summarizes the results for the grade III Follow-up Classes.

Measures of English Competence

The Metropolitan Achievement Test again served as the basic standardized measure for gauging the more receptive English skills of the children in the Experimental and English Control Classes. Form A of the Elementary Battery, appropriate for third-grade pupils, is divided into various sections with only a limited time allowed for each. Raw scores were transformed into standard scores (SS), making comparisons possible with the performance of large samples of North American pupils. Two new subtests were introduced at the grade III level.

Language usage in English (Table 14, item 5). Pupils are presented a series of twenty-four sentences, each containing one underlined word, with instructions to decide whether that word was used correctly (e.g., Tom *knowed* the right way to Jim's house). If incorrect, the correct form was to be written in a space provided. Most of the items involved agreement of case or number. The total possible score of 24 corresponds to a SS of 80.

Punctuation and capitalization in English (Table 14, item 6). In this case, each sentence had one or more circles above one part or another and the child was asked to indicate whether any change of punctuation or capitalization was needed (e.g., My father has an office in the tower building). The total possible score of 36 corresponded to a SS of 77.

Table 14

Test Results for the Pilot Classes at the End of Grade III, 1969

Test Number and Name	Experimental Class		English Controls		French Controls		F Ratio	df
	Mean	Adjusted	Mean	Adjusted	Mean	Adjusted		
English Competence								
1. Word Knowledge (S.S.)	56.11	56.41	56.76	56.59	—	—	0.01	1,44
2. Word Discrimination (S.S.)	56.11	56.84	55.09	54.68	—	—	0.69	1,44
3. Reading (S.S.)	49.32	49.84	52.75	52.44	—	—	0.83	1,42
4. Spelling (S.S.)	52.74	52.63	56.61	56.66	—	—	3.33	1,43
5. Language: Usage (S.S.)	56.89	57.13	60.91	60.77	—	—	2.20	1,42
6. Language: Punctuation (S.S.)	45.37	45.20	52.16	52.26	—	—	6.22*	1,42
7. Listening Comprehension	13.35	13.50	14.91	14.83	—	—	3.06	1,45
8. Picture Vocabulary	84.33	84.01	85.91	86.09	—	—	1.17	1,42
9. *Speaking Skills in English:*								
Story Retelling								
Linguistic Ratings								
Overall Expression	7.00	7.14	7.03	6.95	—	—	0.33	1,42
Grammar	9.11	9.03	8.83	8.88	—	—	0.33	1,42
Enunciation	7.00	7.13	7.35	7.28	—	—	0.19	1,42
Rhythm and Intonation	8.31	8.46	8.45	8.37	—	—	0.07	1,42
Word Counts								
Number of Words	56.53	57.58	59.48	58.94	—	—	0.08	1,41
Nouns (% of Total)	0.19	0.19	0.17	0.17	—	—	1.93	1,41
Different Nouns (%)	0.61	0.61	0.65	0.65	—	—	0.75	1,41
Adjectives (% of Total)	0.11	0.11	0.10	0.10	—	—	1.16	1,41
Different Adjectives (%)	0.89	0.91	0.86	0.85	—	—	1.28	1,39
Verbs (% of Total)	0.13	0.12	0.13	0.14	—	—	1.55	1,41
Different Verbs (%)	0.84	0.84	0.78	0.78	—	—	0.93	1,41
Story Comprehension Rating	2.94	3.03	3.09	3.05	—	—	0.01	1,41

Table 14 (cont.)
Test Results for the Pilot Classes at the End of Grade III, 1969

Test Number and Name	Experimental Class		English Controls		French Controls		F Ratio	df
	Mean	Adjusted	Mean	Adjusted	Mean	Adjusted		
10. *Speaking Skills in English:*								
Story Invention								
Linguistic Ratings								
Overall Expression	7.28	7.37	7.12	7.07	—	—	0.84	1,42
Grammar	8.56	8.59	8.85	8.83	—	—	0.43	1,42
Enunciation	7.39	7.49	7.58	7.52	—	—	0.01	1,42
Rhythm and Intonation	8.83	8.97	8.44	8.36	—	—	2.80	1,42
Word Counts								
Number of Words	56.61	54.06	67.79	69.18	—	—	0.45	1,42
Nouns (% of Total)	0.15	0.15	0.17	0.17	—	—	4.53*	1,42
Different Nouns (%)	0.71	0.70	0.67	0.67	—	—	0.27	1,42
Adjectives (% of Total)	0.01	0.02	0.01	0.01	—	—	1.47	1,42
Different Adjectives (%)	0.81	0.72	0.93	0.99	—	—	2.32	1,42
Verbs (% of Total)	0.17	0.17	0.17	0.17	—	—	0.01	1,42
Different Verbs (%)	0.78	0.78	0.77	0.77	—	—	0.10	1,42
Number Grammatical Errors	0.94	0.89	0.67	0.70	—	—	0.43	1,42
Story Comprehension Rating	3.94	4.00	3.73	3.70	—	—	2.37	1,42
11. *Decoding Skill in English*								
Children's Descriptions	7.86	8.05	7.21	7.09	—	—	3.22	1,46
Adults' Descriptions	7.24	7.33	8.00	7.94	—	—	1.05	1,46
12. *Word Association Analysis: English*								
Latency (secs.)	2.07	1.89	2.71	2.90	—	—	12.43**	1,33
Paradigmatic (%)	78.52	79.26	74.06	73.61	—	—	1.46	1,46
Syntagmatic (%)	12.10	11.47	11.32	11.71	—	—	0.01	1,46
Semantic Clusters (%)	4.67	5.06	7.26	7.02	—	—	2.41	1,46
Idiosyncratic (%)	2.81	2.42	3.15	3.39	—	—	0.26	1,46
Rhymings (%)	0.00	0.00	0.47	0.47	—	—	4.91*	1,46
Transformations (%)	3.33	3.47	2.06	1.98	—	—	0.68	1,46

Test Number and Name	Experimental Class Mean	Adjusted	English Controls Mean	Adjusted	French Controls Mean	Adjusted	F Ratio	df
French Competence								
13. Listening Comprehension	13.17	12.55	—	—	13.78	14.39	1.81	1,27
14. Rendement en Francais	12.47	12.01	—	—	18.50	18.99	21.42**	1,28
15. Picture Vocabulary	83.56	83.66	—	—	89.33	89.22	6.48*	1,27
16. French Phoneme Production	2.70 (with maximum possible of 3.00)							
17. *French Speaking Skills: Story Retelling*								
Linguistic Ratings								
Overall Expression	6.80	6.67	—	—	7.94	8.08	6.59*	1,29
Grammar (Ratings)	5.30	5.41	—	—	7.83	7.71	37.38**	1,29
Enunciation	6.90	6.75	—	—	7.11	7.28	2.07	1,29
Liaison	8.00	8.00	—	—	8.22	8.22	0.90	1,29
Rhythm and Intonation	6.90	6.88	—	—	8.56	8.58	23.29**	1,29
Word Counts								
Number of Words, Total	53.90	51.78	—	—	52.29	54.92	0.25	1,29
Nouns (% of Total)	0.18	0.18	—	—	0.15	0.15	4.27*	1,29
Different Nouns (%)	0.75	0.77	—	—	0.81	0.79	0.11	1,28
Adjectives (% of Total)	0.05	0.06	—	—	0.05	0.04	1.61	1,29
Different Adjectives (%)	0.90	0.89	—	—	0.97	0.99	1.75	1,29
Verbs (% of Total)	0.16	0.16	—	—	0.16	0.16	0.00	1,29
Different Verbs (%)	0.78	0.79	—	—	0.82	0.80	0.07	1,29
Story Comprehension Rating	3.57	3.40	—	—	3.00	3.21	0.22	1,29
18. *French Speaking Skills: Story Invention*								
Linguistic Ratings								
Overall Expression	7.65	7.51	—	—	8.11	8.26	2.40	1,29
Grammar (Ratings)	5.45	5.33	—	—	7.61	7.74	37.33**	1,29

Table 14 (cont.)
Test Results for the Pilot Classes at the End of Grade III, 1969

Test Number and Name	Experimental Class		English Controls		French Controls		F Ratio	df
	Mean	Adjusted	Mean	Adjusted	Mean	Adjusted		
Enunciation	7.20	7.14	—	—	7.22	7.29	0.14	1,29
Liaison	8.05	8.03	—	—	8.06	8.09	0.03	1,29
Rhythm and Intonation	7.25	7.14	—	—	8.67	8.78	25.64**	1,29
Word Counts								
Number of Words, Total	56.30	58.72	—	—	64.33	61.11	0.07	1,26
Nouns (% of Total)	0.24	0.24	—	—	0.17	0.17	18.33**	1,26
Different Nouns (%)	0.55	0.53	—	—	0.59	0.62	1.52	1,26
Adjectives (% of Total)	0.01	0.01	—	—	0.03	0.03	4.44*	1,26
Different Adjectives (%)	0.85	0.80	—	—	0.61	0.64	0.20	1,26
Verbs (% of Total)	0.15	0.15	—	—	0.14	0.14	0.23	1,26
Different Verbs (%)	0.79	0.81	—	—	0.67	0.64	10.70**	1,26
Number Grammatical Errors	4.15	3.92	—	—	1.13	1.41	4.88*	1,27
Story Comprehension Rating	4.05	3.99	—	—	4.06	4.13	0.08	1,28
19. *Decoding Skill in French*								
Children's Descriptions	8.00	8.11	—	—	7.94	7.83	0.17	1,27
Adults' Descriptions	7.28	7.28	—	—	7.39	7.38	0.02	1,27
20. *Word Association Analysis: French*								
Associational Latency	2.88	2.99	—	—	2.89	2.79	0.53	1,26
Paradigmatic (%)	72.58	74.92	—	—	63.50	66.03	2.64	1,28
Syntagmatic (%)	11.95	10.50	—	—	8.11	9.64	0.07	1,28
Semantic Clusters (%)	8.00	7.33	—	—	10.00	10.71	1.36	1,28
Idiosyncratic (%)	5.37	4.79	—	—	4.28	4.89	0.00	1,28
Rhymings (%)	0.21	0.18	—	—	0.89	0.92	3.37	1,28
Transformations (%)	2.32	2.49	—	—	8.39	8.20	4.81*	1,28
Arithmetic Competence								
21. Arithmetic Computations (S.S.)	51.63	52.29	55.63	55.27	—	—	1.07	1,45

Test Number and Name	Experimental Class		English Controls		French Controls		F Ratio	df
	Mean	Adjusted	Mean	Adjusted	Mean	Adjusted		
22. Arithmetic Problems (S.S.)	54.21	55.11	56.39	55.91	—	—	0.08	1,46
Intelligence Indices								
23. June Retest, Raven's	29.43	29.43	29.53	29.53	—	—	0.01	1,46
24. *Lorge-Thorndike*								
Total	53.50	53.60	52.89	52.83	—	—	0.10	1,46
Vocabulary	18.55	18.71	20.34	20.25	—	—	4.77*	1,46
Not-belong	18.50	18.59	17.29	17.23	—	—	3.50	1,46
Go-together	16.45	16.61	16.69	16.59	—	—	0.00	1,46
Creativity Measures								
25. Unusual Uses, French	7.05	6.84	—	—	4.74	5.05	2.96	1,26
26. Consequences, French	7.86	7.73	—	—	7.54	7.73	0.00	1,26
27. Unusual Uses, English	7.81	7.82	6.09	6.08	—	—	5.54*	1,40
28. Consequences, English	7.72	8.20	7.65	7.37	—	—	0.74	1,40
Foreign Language Sensitivity								
29. Russian Phoneme Discrimination (Errors)	12.16	11.46	11.77	12.78	—	—	0.32	1,23

* p <.05
** p <.01

Important modifications were made in the following measure: *English Picture Vocabulary*. The Peabody Picture Vocabulary Test (Dunn, 1959) was administered again to all children, this time with items 40 to 116. For the Pilot Classes, we scored from 1 to 116, making a total score of 116 possible (see Table 14), whereas for the Follow-up Classes we scored from 40 to 116, making the total possible score 76 (Table 18). The test progressed from relatively simple items such as captain, cobweb, and hydrant to more complex ones like incandescent, sconce, and hoary. *Speaking skills in English: Story retelling.* This test was given to the grade III Pilot Classes only. Each child individually listened to a tape-recorded story which he was asked to retell in his own words. His output was tape-recorded, and then transcribed from tape to cards. Two types of analysis were performed—linguistic ratings and word counts. Counts were made for the total number of different nouns, the number of adjectives, the number of different adjectives, the number of verbs, the number of different verbs, and the number of grammatical errors. The child's overall comprehension of the story was inferred from his retelling, and rated on a five-point scale, ranging from *poor* to *excellent*.

The linguistic ratings were made by two linguists who listened to a random arrangement of children's output thereby mixing Experimental and Control Classes. Their task was to rate the children on the following linguistic skills: *overall expression*, consisting of ease of talking, word choice, thought patterns, and errors of substance; *grammatical correctness, enunciation,* and *rhythm* and *intonation*. Each pupil's score was the total of the two judges' ratings, given on five-point scales. The following criteria were used to evaluate the children's English. For *overall expression*, a rating of 5 was given only if there were no errors of substance, little or no hesitation, wide vocabulary choice, and sophisticated syntax (such as the use of subordinators, e.g., *although*). The rating 4 indicated that some hesitation was noted; the vocabulary was appropriate, but more limited; and the syntax less elaborate (emphasis on coordination and casual expressions such as *then, so*). A rating of 3 was assigned when there appeared to be some confusion about substance, with some hesitation; sentences lacked connecting words or used *and* almost exclusively; and prompting was sometimes necessary. A rating of 2 indicated that the story was garbled, the vocabulary quite limited, and there was much hesitation, with the interviewer having to provide much encouragement. Syntax was often characterized by incorrect arrangements. A rating of 1 was assigned when the story was practically incomprehensible, with very limited vocabulary, much hesitation and much prompting.

For *grammatical correctness* a rating of 5 was given only if no errors (including antecedent problems, lack of parallelism) occurred. The rating of 4 was similar to 5, except that stylistic deviation did occur. A rating of 3 indicated that the story was generally correct with one or two errors (e.g., *-ed* added to a strong verb in past tense; pronoun switching). A rating of 2 was used for lack of concord and a generally unstructured story, while 1 meant that there was virtually no structure.

For *enunciation*, the rating of 5 indicated relatively great muscular tension with proper voicing and devoicing. The norm was the kind of English used by child actors. A rating of 4 was assigned when there was less muscular tension and some allophonic variation. The rating 3 was used for understandable mispronunciations; 2 similar to 3 but less understandable, and 1 for intensified and almost incomprehensible utterances.

For *rhythm and intonation* the rating of 5 was given only if the child had appropriate final contours, wide pitch range, and beats reasonably evenly spaced; 4 was similar to 5 but with less pitch variation; 3 indicated occasional inappropriate rising final contours; 2 meant that rising contours were the rule with uneven and uncertain pitch variation; and 1 meant that there was no final contour.

Measures of French Competence

Various measures were used to assess French competence, most of them similar in intent to those used to test competence in English. In each case, when both a French and English version of a particular test was used, one half of the Experimental Class received the French form first, followed two weeks later by the English form (with equivalent but different items). The remainder of the Class had the reverse order. The *French Listening Comprehension* test, designed by us, was similar to the English measure described above. The children listened to a story (about elephants) and then answered twenty "Yes–No" questions about its content. The *Test de Rendement en Français* (Table 14, item 14) was designed for French-speaking grade III children and consisted of five sections: (a) *Parts of speech* which directed the child to choose the noun, the verb, or the adjective out of a series of five words, following written instructions. The total possible score was 8. (b) *Odd item* which asked the child to choose the one word out of five which did not belong (e.g., *peuplier, bouleau, chêne, érable, étable*). Total possible score was 4. (c) *Sentence completion* instructed the child to select the one word most appropriate for an accompanying sentence (e.g., *J'ai prêté___briques à mon petit frère*) from a list such as *ces, ses, mais, mes, c'est*. There were five such items making the total possible score 5. (d) *Adjective type* where the child was to study a series of sentences each containing an underlined adjective (e.g., Claire porte un chapeau de paille *vert*). The task was to indicate whether the adjective: dit une qualité, dit à qui appartient, sert à montrer, sert à compter, ou dit le rang. The total possible score was 8. (e) In the case of *sentence substitution* the child had to replace an underlined word (e.g., *Faire* un calcul difficile) with the most appropriate alternative among five possible substitutions (*résulter, épeler, effectuer, inscrire, aplanir*). The total possible score was 10. For all sections combined, the overall total score possible was 35.

Speaking skills in French: Story retelling. This test was used for the Pilot but not the Follow-up Classes. The method of presentation and analysis was similar to that described for the English story retelling test. In addition to rating overall expression, grammatical correctness, enunciation, rhythm, and intonation, two linguists also evaluated the use of liaison, using five-point scales (ranging from *poor* to *excellent*). Again, the ratings by the two judges were combined, making 10 the maximum score obtainable. The word counts were similar to those of the corresponding English measures. The results for the Pilot class are given in Table 14, item 17.

In evaluating the French stories the following criteria were used by the linguists making the ratings. For *overall expression*, a value of 5 indicated absence of silence within a sentence, very good fluency and spontaneity, coherent and appropriate vocabulary; 4: some short silences, some unimportant words left out; 3: some words used in the wrong position, some words missing, intervention of the interviewer occasionally needed; 2: many construction errors, many words missing; and 1: a total break in sentence construction, no interpretation possible.

For *grammar*, a rating of 5 indicated no grammatical mistakes; 4: a few less evident mistakes (e.g., wrong auxiliary, wrong article); 3: some evident mistakes of gender, number, tense, etc.; 2: many errors, and 1: a total mishandling of French grammar.

For *liaison*, the rating 5 meant that all obligatory liaisons were present and no forbidden ones; 4: a few errors only; 3: four or five errors; 2: five or six errors; and 1: generally very poor use of liaison.

A rating of 5 for *rhythm and intonation* meant that proper intonation was used for all declarative, interrogative, and exclamatory statements; 4: a slight deviation from 5 with rising or lowering intonation at the wrong time and a displacement of stress; 3: slight deviations similar to 4 which could be attributed to English interference; 2: many errors similar to 3; and 1: a total break in the intonation contour, with random use of stress.

A rating of 5 for *enunciation* indicated mastery of thirty-six necessary phonemes, without English interference and without exaggerated French-Canadian allophones. The model adopted by the linguists, one of whom was a French Canadian, was "standard metropolitan" French. The rating 4 meant that the phonemes were mastered, but a little distortion was allowed; 3: one or two sounds were not mastered; 2: three to five sounds were not mastered; and 1 indicated that most French sounds were not mastered.

Results for the Pilot Classes
at the End of Grade III (1969)

English Language Competence

Reading, word knowledge, listening comprehension, and vocabulary. On the subtests of the Metropolitan Achievement Test (items 1 through 5 in Table 14), the Pilot Class performs at the same level as the English Controls. Only on the Punctuation subtest (item 6) do they score reliably below the English Controls. Their scores on the English word knowledge, word discrimination, and language usage tests fall at or above the 80th percentile on national norms, whereas the scores for reading and spelling in English lie at the 55th and 65th percentiles respectively. Interestingly enough, on these two measures, the Controls also score relatively low, suggesting that the programs of English Language Arts in Montreal elementary schools may underemphasize reading and spelling. In any case, at the end of grade III the pupils in the Pilot Class, with only two thirty-five-minute periods a day of formal training in English as a subject, are equivalent to the English Controls in all aspects of English language competence except punctuation.

The Pilot Class is also equivalent to the English Controls in listening comprehension (item 7), meaning that they are as able to comprehend and remember the details of an English passage, presented orally. Similarly, their performance on the Peabody Picture Vocabulary Test (item 8) is equivalent to that of the English Controls, indicating that they very likely profit a good deal, through transfer, from vocabulary training and other features of their academic experiences conducted in French.

Thus, except for their command of English punctuation rules (which were not given special attention in their English Language Arts program), the Pilot Class shows no retardation relative to the Control children in these more passive or receptive features of English language competence. The fact that the Experimental Class can maintain as high a level of achievement and competence in English as the Controls with such an abbreviated program of training should be of special interest to educators, particularly since they have made substantial progress in French at the same time.

Speaking skills in English. The relative performance of the Pilot Class on tests of expression in English is equally reassuring. When retelling a story (item 9), the linguistic ratings of their overall expression, grammar, enunciation, and rhythm and intonation signify that they are at the same achievement level as the English Control children. The statistical counts of their productions also confirm the equivalence of the Pilot and Control Classes.

The same holds for their ability to invent stories in English, without the aid of a model. In terms of word counts, the stories they make up are somewhat shorter and have reliably fewer nouns. Yet in all other respects, including the story comprehension rating and the number of grammatical errors, they are similar to the Controls. Since their stories are shorter but apparently just as complete and well-formed, one could argue that they are in one sense more efficient in English verbal expression, a trend already noted at the grade II level.

Decoding skills in English. The decoding abilities of the various grade III groups are summarized in item 11. Here we also see that the Pilot Class is as efficient as the Controls in comprehending and making use of the descriptive speech of English-speaking children and adults. Apparently the extensive experience in French and the limited formal training in English has not hampered the children of the Pilot Class in developing appropriate age-level skills in the informal uses of English.

Word associations in English. Several features of the free associations of the Pilot Class deserve special comment (item 12). First, there are no further signs at the grade III level of an overuse of syntagmatic responses as was the case for both Pilot and Follow-up Classes at the end of grade I. It is very evident that by the end of grade II they had surmounted the early difficulty they had had in making the "paradigmatic shift," and no recurrence is seen at grade III. Second, the Pilot Class is reliably faster than the English Controls at the grade III level in producing associations in English. Although more rapid, they are not more reckless in the sense that they do not give disproportionate numbers of idiosyncratic or semantic cluster responses. Thus, the children's mode of thinking in English as reflected by their verbal associations is similar to that of the English Controls in terms of paradigmatic and syntagmatic type responses at the same time that it is more rapid than that of the Controls.

French Language Competence

Listening comprehension, and Rendement en Français. The grade III Pilot Class performed at the same level as the French Controls on the test of French listening comprehension (item 13), meaning that the two groups are apparently comparable in ability to understand and remember complex information presented orally in French. In contrast, the Pilot Class scored significantly below the Controls (Exp $\overline{X}$ = 12.01, FC $\overline{X}$ = 18.99) on the 1969 version of the *Test de Rendement en Français* (item 14). Since there were no differences on this test between the French Controls and either the Pilot or the Follow-up Classes at the grade II level, we presume that some features of the 1969 version of the test were either inappropriate or particularly difficult for the Pilot Class children. The items that gave them particular difficulty were in subparts 1 and 4, presented in Table 15. In these subtests the children are asked to find "nouns," "verbs," and "adjectives," without a verbal context to guide them (part 1), and to identify the *type* of adjectives used in sentences. These traditional grammatical categories are given much less attention by teachers of the Experimental Classes, who place relatively more emphasis on verbal context as a means of developing vocabulary and abstract concepts. The format of the questions also posed a special problem; for example, in part 1, they were asked to search across rows for the correct answer, but because the vertical blocks were numbered (see Table 15) the children often confused columns for rows.

Table 15

Sample Items from the 1969 *Test de Rendement en Français*

Part 1. Dans chaque série de mots ci-dessous, trouve un *nom* :

	1	2	3	4	5
1.	succulent	sagement	compliment	excellent	défend
2.	soumis	hormis	concis	démis	avis
3.	préfère	mystère	austère	accélère	éphémère

Dans chaque série de mots ci-dessous, trouve un *verbe* (mot d'action):

	1	2	3	4	5
4.	encore	fort	éclore	mort	aurore
5.	butinent	pertinent	innocent	châtiment	comment

Dans chaque série de mots ci-dessous, trouve un *adjectif* (mot de qualité):

	1	2	3	4	5
6.	croit	émoi	adroit	soit	envoi
7.	fragile	argile	empile	domicile	assimile
8.	mèche	lèche	pèche	calèche	sèche

Part 4. Dans les phrases ci-dessous, les adjectifs sont soulignés.

    Indique la *sorte* pour chacun d'eux.

	1	2	3	4	5
	dit une *qualité:*	dit à qui *appartient:*	sert à *montrer:*	sert à *compter:*	dit le *rang:*

18. Claire porte un chapeau de paille *vert*.
19. Nous avons visité l'Expo *douze* fois.
20. Gilles dessine avec *sa* règle.

On the French Picture Vocabulary Test (Table 14, item 15) the Pilot Class, as a group, has improved substantially from the grade II to III levels (grade II $\overline{X}$ = 71.66, grade III $\overline{X}$ = 83.66), reflecting a gain comparable to that made by the French Controls. The Pilot Class was nonetheless still reliably below the French Control Class and again by some 5 to 6 points out of the 116 possible. The items that posed particular difficulty for the Pilot Class were terms like *astiquer, ronger, appareil, lamentation, poutre,* and *sonder.* Still in certain cases they had less trouble than the French Controls with such items as *gousse, incarcérer, machette,* and *meringue.* Both groups of course had difficulty with items at the upper end of the scale such as *inciter, embossé, généologiste,* and *concentrique.* On balance then, the Pilot Class showed substantial progress from their grade II performance level.

French phoneme production. As indicated in item 16, the Pilot Class has nearly mastered the basic sounds of French by the end of grade III. Their average score of 2.70 out of a possible 3.00 means that the linguists judging their competence place them, as a group, between *average* (2) and *good* (3), with native speakers of French as a frame of reference. The sounds mastered particularly well were: n*o*te, p*eu*r, d*eu*x, était, while those presenting more difficulty were: l*u*ne, chac*u*n, sol*ei*l, and p*ai*n. This pattern of relatively hard and easy sounds is very similar to that for the Follow-up Class at grade II although the average score, as expected, is higher at grade III. Thus, by the end of grade III the Experimental children have developed extremely good spontaneous control of the basic sound units of French. However, as we shall see, this does not necessarily mean that they have developed a comparable ability to integrate these basic sound elements into fluent oral productions.

French speaking skills. The Pilot Class's average scores for French story retelling and story invention are presented in items 17 and 18 of Table 14, where the ratings of two linguists have been combined to produce a scale ranging from 2 (poor) to 10 (excellent), with 6 as the "average" point. Note that the judges rarely used the "excellent" category, even for the French Controls, so that the assigned scores really range only from 5 to slightly over 8.

Several interesting comparisons are apparent here. First, the Pilot Experimental Class is rated above average and equivalent to the French Controls on liaison and enunciation, both when retelling and inventing stories in French. These two measures reflect a mastery of basic French sound units and an ability to fuse sounds appropriately at word boundaries. In sharp contrast, the Experimental children are clearly nonnative in their control of French rhythm and intonation and in their overall expression. In order to understand the meaning of this contrast, it may be valuable to examine certain details of the linguistic analyses. For *rhythm and intonation*, the linguists attended to basic French intonation contours and the recurrence of accent and stress, the children's use of intonation in declarative, interrogative, and exclamatory statements, and the succession of tonic accents. For *overall expression*, attention was given to fluency and spontaneity of productions and to the meaningful and appropriate use of vocabulary. Even by grade III, the home-school switch program has apparently not provided sufficient opportunities to the children to develop nativelike spontaneous expression in French. We will return to this matter later.

The second point of interest in items 17 and 18 is that Experimental children at grade III (similar to the Follow-up Class at grade II) scored farther above the average point and closer to the French Controls when inventing French stories than when retelling them. In fact, when creating stories on their own, their scores move up noticeably on the measure of overall expression (becoming equivalent to those of the French Controls), enunciation, and rhythm and intonation. The recurrence of this pattern strengthens the argument advanced earlier that the Experimental children seem to be particularly motivated and able to express *their own ideas* in French.

Third, it is also clear that the Pilot Class makes more errors than the Controls in French. Not only do the linguists rate them below the average point in this regard, but the actual counts also show that they make significantly more errors (see item 18). It is important then to ascertain what types of errors are habitually made, because routines to eliminate errors could easily be introduced into the grade II and III programs. With this purpose in mind, a detailed analysis was made of the errors the children made when inventing stories. It is interesting to learn that *gender* is the major type of error, occurring more frequently than all other types at both grade levels. Gender, of course, presents hardly any difficulty for native speakers of French, a phenomenon that attracted our attention in earlier research (Tucker, Lambert, Rigault, and Segalowitz, 1968). Because of that research, we believe one could easily tutor the Experimental children to become aware of the subtle cues embedded in French nouns that distinguish gender (cf. Tucker, Lambert, and Rigault, 1969).

The next most frequent types of errors noted at both age levels are those of *contraction* (e.g., *à les* instead of *aux*), *tense* (e.g., *demain je lisais . . .*), and *number* (e.g., *vous aime* instead of *vous aimez*). The grade II Experimental children also choose more faulty construction (e.g., *je veux toi venir* rather than *je veux que tu viennes*) than do the French Controls, but it is instructive to see that at the grade III level, the proportions of these types of errors are essentially the same for Experimentals and Controls.

It is also interesting and surprising to learn that the Pilot Experimental and French Control Classes make proportionately equal numbers of the following type errors: *wrong auxiliary* (e.g., *il a venu* rather than *il est venu*); *wrong pronouns* (e.g., *il le fait peur* for *il lui fait peur*); *faulty word order* (e.g., *il a un blanc chien* for *il a un chien blanc*); errors of *morphophonology* (*vieux homme* instead of *vieil homme*); *wrong article* (*les* rather than *des*); and *wrong preposition* (*dans l'hiver* rather than *en hiver*).

Thus, in general there are four major types of errors made by the Experimental children at the grade II level (gender, construction, contractions, and tense), while at grade III there are only two predominant types, gender and contractions. Errors of construction and word order apparently drop away with the additional year's experience in the language.

The *word counts* reveal that the total number of words produced by both groups is approximately the same as is the diversity of vocabulary. In fact, when inventing stories, the Experimental children have a significantly more varied choice of verbs, and use a greater number of nouns than do the French Controls. Both groups show essentially the same ability to comprehend and relate the general theme or meaning of the stories, according to the ratings assigned for story comprehension.

Thus, by the end of grade III the pupils in the Pilot Class approach very closely the normal French child of the same age and education in certain features of oral expression in French, especially enunciation and liaison which involve the basic sound units of the language. They do not, however, attain nativelike competence in terms of spontaneity and fluency in their French expression. Nevertheless, as a group, they are better at spontaneous expression of their own ideas in French than in relaying other people's ideas and expressions. The richness and variety of their French vocabulary and their ability to grasp and relate the meaning of short stories are at the same level as those of the French Controls.

French decoding skills. This capacity to grasp and use the meaning of spoken French is also evident in their performance on the tests of decoding skills (item 19). In this case the French they have to work with is not academic in content or form. Rather it is the spontaneous descriptive speech of French children when talking among themselves or of adult French speakers using everyday expressions. The fact that the Pilot Class scores as well as the French Controls in this task is noteworthy for two reasons: not only because the language used is nonacademic but also because the descriptions given require rapid mental processing of various alternatives.

French word associations. If we regard children's free associations as a linguistic expression of their trains of thought, then the Pilot and French Control groups have very similar networks of ideas when using French. The groups are alike in rapidity of associations, the number of idiosyncratic responses used, and the choice of paradigmatic-type responses. The only difference between the Experimentals and the Controls is in the Experimental group's tendency to give fewer transformational associations. Actually, we have noted this difference from grade I on, and we wonder whether it represents a distinctive mode of thought of native speakers of French, one that has not as yet been assimilated by the children in the Experimental program.[1] Overall, then, the Pilot Class shows no indication of retardation, slowness, or confusion in their French associations.

Arithmetic Competence

On tests of computational and problem-solving arithmetic, the Pilot Class performs at the same level as the English Controls, both groups scoring above the 80th percentile on nationwide norms (items 21 and 22). The Pilot and Follow-up Experimental Classes at grade II showed a similar capacity to utilize the skills and techniques acquired through French when tested in English. The children in the Experimental program not only appear able to assimilate mathematical notions through French, but also can keep pace with their English-speaking peers. This mathematical competence cannot be attributed to special training in mathematics nor to the text books used, since the Experimental children used French versions of the standard English texts.

Intelligence Measures

Three different measures of intellectual ability were used to assess the cumulative effects of the home-school language-switch program on the cognitive development of the Experimental children in grade III: a spring retest of the Progressive Matrices test, a retest with the Lorge-Thorndike scale, and a set of measures of "productive thinking" or "creativity" (items 23 and 28). As stressed earlier, the creativity as well as the intelligence measures are thought of as approximate indices only of very complex intellectual processes. Although reliable and valid, better indices will certainly become available as knowledge in this domain of psychology advances (see Cronbach, 1970).

With these measures as a barometer, the Pilot Experimental Class shows no signs of cognitive confusion or retardation on either the Matrices or the Lorge-Thorndike battery when compared to the English Controls; the overall means on the two tests are similar and are not statistically different from one another. On the vocabulary subtest of the Lorge-Thorndike battery, however, the Pilot Class mean is significantly below that of the Controls, reflecting an average difference of 1.5 vocabulary items. The items that posed problems for the Pilot Class, but not the Controls, were the following: a *tumbler* (a drinking utensil), *correspondence* (mail), a *vessel* (ship), *scurrying, collapsible,* and *an oxford* (shoe). No special attention is given to this difference because it is small and because on the Peabody Picture Vocabulary Test (item 8), a longer and

---

[1]Note that the English Controls use many fewer transformations than the French Controls, 1.98 percent vs 8.20 percent; this possible language difference merits special study.

more comprehensive test of English vocabulary, there was no significant difference between the Experimental and Control groups.

On the Lorge-Thorndike "not-belonging" subtest the mean for the Pilot Experimental Class is above that of the Controls just as it was for the Follow-up Experimental Class at the grade II level. Apparently the Experimental children reap some benefit on this type of measure.

The Experimental children perform particularly well on the creativity tests, especially those calling for a listing of "unusual uses." When functioning in French, their mean score on this measure is higher than that of the French Controls, and although the difference is not statistically reliable, it is nevertheless reassuring to realize that the Experimental children are not hampered linguistically in expressing original ideas in French. For example, when asked how one can use "une boîte de conserve," they are as able as the Controls to explain that one can "empêche une fenêtre de se fermer"; "on peut faire un pot de fleurs avec" or "on peut boire de l'eau dedans" and so forth. When functioning in English, the Experimental children score significantly higher than the English Controls on the English version of the "unusual uses" test. These differences favoring the Pilot Experimental Class are extremely important ones because they suggest that the bilingual experience may start to produce a particular type of intellectual advantage at about the grade III level. We will see if this apparent advantage holds up in later grades.

Foreign Language Sensitivity

Using the Russian Phoneme Discrimination test as an indicator of the children's sensitivity to foreign language sounds (item 29), we find a small difference favoring the Experimental children over "monolingual" Controls, but once again the difference is not statistically significant. If we review the yearly comparisons of errors made on this test starting with grade I, they take the following form:

Grade I	Experimental	Monolingual Controls
Pilot	19.60	15.51
Follow-up	14.21	16.98
Grade II		
Pilot	13.01	15.63
Follow-up	11.60	14.83
Grade III		
·Pilot	11.46	12.78

Note that in all cases except the grade I comparison for the Pilot Classes, the Experimentals make fewer errors in their discriminations than the Controls, but in no isolated instance is the comparison a reliable one. Thus we have no real evidence to suggest that the Experimental children are more skillful in discriminating foreign language sounds. This may be due, as mentioned earlier, to the fact that the "monolingual" controls have all lived in Montreal and likely have had some experience with a second language, either at school in the case of the English-Canadian children or in the community in the case of the French-Canadian children. Of course, substantial group differences may begin to show themselves at some future period in the program, say in grade V or VI, so we will reserve final judgment until that time.

Standings of the Experimental Classes on City-wide Norms

From the start of our investigation, we have had difficulty finding appropriate French Control Classes and in keeping contact with individual pupils in those classes finally chosen. This has been so for various reasons: the administration of French Catholic schools is completely separate from that of the English Protestant schools in Montreal; the pupils in the French Control Classes were separated at a very early age into technical or academic routes; and many children in the Control Classes have moved out of the province or to other neighborhoods. Whereas the French Control Classes have dwindled noticeably, we have had very few dropouts from the Experimental Classes for any reason. Because of this, we kept an eye open for a good opportunity to test the Experimental Classes against city-wide norms for French students, and with the generous cooperation of the Research Division of the Commission des Ecoles Catholiques de Montréal (C.E.C.M.), we were able to coordinate the administration of specially developed measures of achievement in French and mathematics (*Test de Rendement en Français* and *Test de Rendement en Calcul*) to the Pilot Experimental Class at the end of grade III and the Follow-up Class at the end of grade II, at the same time that all French-speaking children in the Montreal Catholic School System took the same tests. For comparison purposes, we also tested a new Experimental group of English Canadian pupils who had just finished grade I in the same experimental program as that followed by the Pilot and Follow-up Classes.

The C.E.C.M. tests are developed, pretested, and revised with care, and then administered in the fall of each year to all children in Montreal in regular classes (i.e., those of normal IQ or above) of the C.E.C.M. Although usually given in October, the tests cover the previous year's curriculum and each year a totally new set of tests is prepared in order to discourage teachers from preparing or coaching their pupils. As an example, the tests of French and mathematics given at the end of grade III (1969) are presented in Table 16. The norms cover approximately 15,000 children at each grade level, excluding any pupils attending special classes for slow learners.

The tests of *Rendement en Français* and *Rendement en Calcul* were both given to the Experimental Classes under the supervision of the school principal and the teachers, who followed carefully the prescribed instructions. However, because of scheduling difficulties, the tests were administered approximately three weeks after the date they were taken by the French pupils in the C.E.C.M. This delay may have constituted an advantage for the Experimental Classes, and the results must be interpreted in this light.

The results are presented in Table 17 where the Stanine scores and equivalent percentiles are given for each division of scores attained by the normative groups. The average scores for the Experimental Classes are inserted at the appropriate position. Considering the French examination first, note the progression from year to year, with the grade I Experimentals (a new class following the Follow-up group by a year) falling near the 60th percentile (Stanine 5), the grade II Experimentals at the 75th percentile range, and the grade III Experimentals above the 77th percentile range. These scores signify an extremely high overall performance. At the grade I level, the Experimentals, as a group, score higher than some 40 to 60 percent of the grade I children in French schools; the grade II Experimentals score better than 60 percent, and the grade III better than 77 percent of the French-speaking third-grade children in Montreal's schools. Keep in mind that this is an examination of achievement in French Language Arts developed for children whose native language is French.

On the mathmatics test, all three Experimental Classes fall near the 77th percentile range, meaning that from grade I on they perform, as a group, as well as or better than from 60 to 77 percent of the children in comparable classes in Montreal's French schools. This too is an impressive level of achievement which strengthens the argument made earlier that the children in the Experimental program have little difficulty comprehending and assimilating mathematical principles and techniques taught to them exclusively through the second language.

Results for the Follow-up Classes
at the End of Grade III (1970)

The findings to be discussed here are presented in Table 18, where the average scores for the Follow-up Classes are compared.

English Language Competence

The performance of the children on the various subtests of the *Metropolitan Achievement Test* (items 1-5 in Table 18, entered in Standard Score form) suggests that the bilingually instructed pupils' knowledge of English is equivalent to that of their English Control counterparts. At grade III the Follow-up Experimental Class performs as well as the English Controls on subtests of word knowledge, word discrimination, reading, spelling, and word usage. Only on the subtest dealing with English punctuation and capitalization (item 8) are they significantly below the English Controls, as was the case for the Pilot Experimental Class. Presumably there are differences in French and English styles of punctuation and capitalization that are not given special attention by the teachers in the experimental program.

Table 16

Test de Rendement en Français, End of Grade III (1969-70)

Lis attentivement le texte ci-dessous et réponds aux questions qui s'y rapportent (numéros 1 à 15).

Mon petit lapin.

Tous les ans, ma tante venait me voir et m'apportait quelque chose. Une fois, d'un air mystérieux, elle me dit: "Mets la main dans mon panier." Je croyais y trouver des fruits. Mais je sens un poil soyeux et quelque chose qui frémit. C'est un lapin! Je l'enlève et me voilà courant de tous côtés annoncer la bonne nouvelle.

C'est qu'il était beau, mon lapin, avec son nez rose et sa fourrure lustrée comme un miroir! Ses grandes oreilles nacrées et mobiles qu'il époussetait sans cesse, ses cabrioles pleines de fantaisies avaient, je dois l'avouer, une part de mon admiration.

Dès le point du jour, je m'échappais du lit pour revoir mon favori et le porter dans un plant de choux. Là, il mangeait gravement ses feuilles vertes, jetant sur moi de longs regards que je trouvais pleins de tendresse. Puis, il se dressait sur ses pattes de derrière, présentait au soleil son petit ventre blanc et lissait ses belles moustaches avec une dextérité merveilleuse.

D'après Michelet.

1. Combien de fois par année ma tante m'offrait-elle un cadeau?

    souvent; une fois par année; une fois par semaine; à mon anniversaire de naissance; une fois par mois.

2. A quel moment du jour suis-je allé rejoindre mon lapin?

    en soirée; l'après-midi; au lever; le midi; après la classe.

3. Qu'est-ce que mon lapin préférait manger?

    graines; viande; fruits; foin; légumes.

4. Dès le début de la journée, j'amenais mon lapin pour le faire ...

    courir; épousseter; jouer; manger; dresser.

5. Qu'est-ce que j'ai fait aussitôt mon lapin sorti du panier?

    je fais connaître l'événement à mon entourage; je le dépose dans sa cage; je cours lui donner à manger; je m'empresse de le caresser; je lui fais faire des cabrioles.

6. Quel autre titre pourrait-on donner à ce texte?

    un anniversaire de naissance; une surprise désagréable; un héritage; un cadeau vivant; un lapin bien élevé.

7. Quel mot veut dire à peu près la même chose que TROUVER?

    goûter; fouiller; apprendre; découvrir; suspendre.

8. Quel mot veut dire à peu près la même chose que ENLEVE?

    sors; dépose; enveloppe; cajole; examine.

9. Quels mots veulent dire à peu près la même chose que DE TOUS COTES?

    en avant; en vitesse; sans fin; nulle part; partout.

10. Quel mot veut dire à peu près la même chose que JETANT?

    retenant; attrapant; lançant; ménageant; contenant.

11. Quel mot veut dire à peu près la même chose que SE DRESSAIT?

    se couchait; se levait; se lançait; se sauvait; se baissait.

12. Quel mot veut dire à peu près la même cose que PRESENTAIT?

    léchait; séchait; exposait; tournait; consentait.

13. Quel mot veut dire le contraire de METS?

    baisse; enlève; joins; dépose; élève.

14. Quel mot veut dire le contraire de LUSTREE?

    peignée; noire; riche; terne; touffue.

15. Quel mot veut dire le contraire de MOBILES?

    ouvertes; tendres; inertes; pointues; longues.
    (*N.B.* Tu n'as pas à te servir du texte pour répondre aux questions suivantes)
    Complète chaque expression ci-dessous par le *bon mot*.

16. Doux comme un . . .   refrain; sifflet; agneau; remède; gâteau
17. Vif comme un . . .   poisson; orage; plongeon; moteur; policier
18. Orgueilleux comme un . . .   bouquet; paon; botaniste; honneur; ministre

    Sur chaque ligne ci-dessous, trouve un mot qui n'est pas de la même nature que les autres (qui n'est pas de la même sorte).

19.	décore	encore	picore	arbore	colore
20.	délicat	ingrat	immédiat	avocat	adéquat
21.	pastille	guenille	aiguille	coquille	gentille

    Que fait ou qu'indique chacun des adjectifs soulignés?

    1. qualité; 2. possession; 3. démontre; 4. nombre; 5. rang

22. L'ourse abrite *ses* petits en lieu sûr et part chercher de la nourriture.

23. Les meubles *anciens* sont recherchés par les collectionneurs.

24. A la récréation nous nous divisons en *deux* équipes de ballon.

A quel temps est employé chacun des verbes des phrases suivantes?

présent; imparfait; passé composé; futur; impératif

25. L'été dernier, nous sommes allés jusqu'en Gaspésie.

26. Personne ne doutait de l'honnêteté de cet homme.

27. Malgré la mer en furie, le paquebot arrivera à bon port.

Complète chaque phrase par le bon mot.

mais; met; tout; toux; tous.

28. Un bon sirop nous aidera à faire passer cette ___?___ tenace.

29. Ce chien aboie ___?___ il n'est pas méchant.

30. Malgré une invitation tardive, ___?___ sont venus à la fête.

Test de Rendement en Calcul, End of Grade III (1969-70)

1. 308 + 412 =   719;   712;   620;   710;   720.

2. 84 - 58 =   34;   16;   36;   26;   46.

3. Mon père me donne 2 pièces de 25¢, 4 pièces de 10¢ et 2 pièces de 5¢. Quelle somme d'argent m'a-t-il donnée?
20¢;   25¢; $1.00;   50¢;   75¢

4. Dans une classe, il y a 5 rangées de 6 pupitres chacune. Si 3 pupitres sont libres, combien y a-t-il d'élèves présents?
30;   22;   32;   27;   33.

5. Quel nombre compte 1 dizaine de plus que 180?
190;   280;   181;   290;   291.

6. 9 x 3 + 2 =   56;   29;   45;   54;   26.

7. J'ai enlevé 7 à un nombre et il est devenu 8. Quel était ce nombre?
1;   13;   14;   15;   16.

8. Combien y a-t-il d'unités dans 10 dizaines?
100;   10;   12;   120;   110.

9. Une livre de beurre coute 64¢. Quel est le prix d'une demi-livre?
$0.08; $0.32; $5.12; $0.09; $0.33.

10: J'ai 25¢. J'achète 4 crayons à 5¢ chacun. Combien me reste-t-il?
20¢;   30¢;   15¢;   10¢;   5¢.

11. Il me manque 2 pièces de 25¢ pour m'acheter une chemise de $3.00. Combien ai-je d'argent?
$3.50; $2.25; $2.75; $2.50; $3.25.

12. Marc a huit pièces de 5¢ et Louis cinq pièces de 10¢. Combien d'argent
    Louis a-t-il de plus que Marc?
    40¢;   50¢;   10¢;   15¢;   5¢.

13. Dans le nombre "12345", quel chiffre a le plus de valeur?
    1;   2;   3;   4;   5.

14. Je donne $2.00 à un marchand pour payer une commande de $0.88.
    Quelle somme me remettra-t-il?
    $0.12; $1.12; $2.12; $0.22; $1.22.

15. Ajoutez 1 dizaine et 2 centaines à "7810" et vous aurez . . .
    7822;   7831;   9010;   8020;   9110.

16. J'ai $4.47 et mon frère $5.15. Combien me manque-t-il d'argent pour
    en avoir autant que lui?
    $9.57; $1.78; $1.68; $0.78; $0.68.

17. J'avais $1.18. J'en ai dépensé la moitié. Combien me reste-t-il?
    $2.36;   64¢;   59¢;   57¢; $1.09.

18. Pour payer un crayon de 15¢ et un cahier de 20¢ je donne au marchand
    une pièce de 50¢. Combien me remettra-t-il?
    35¢;   15¢;   85¢;   30¢;   25¢.

19. Je dois attendre une heure avant de partir en voiture. Si 15 minutes se
    sont écoulées, combien me reste-t-il de temps à attendre?
    1h.15;   35 min.;   60 min.;   30 min.;   45 min.

20. Un père offre à son fils le choix entre 3 pièces de 25¢ ou 6 pièces de
    10¢. Combien le fils gagne-t-il de plus en choisissant les 3 pièces de 25¢?
    75¢;   60¢;   15¢; $1.35; $1.25.

21. Dans un panier de fruits il y a 3 fois plus d'oranges que de pommes.
    S'il y a 12 oranges, combien y a-t-il de pommes?
    18;   36;   3;   4;   15.

22. Danielle a 70 beignes à placer également dans 5 boîtes. Combien en
    placera-t-elle dans chacune?
    14;   18;   15;   13;   16.

23. Paul a 4 petites autos et Jean en a autant que lui plus 2. Combien ont-ils
    d'autos ensemble?
    16;   6;   8;   12;   10.

24. Il me faut placer également 150 volumes sur les 6 rayons d'une
    bibliothèque. Combien dois-je placer de volumes sur chaque rayon?
    26;   24;   25;   22;   28.

25. Pierre a $4.00 et Paul en a 3 fois plus. Combien de dollars les deux garçons ont-ils ensemble?

$12.00; $16.00; $7.00; $9.00; $18.00.

26. 1/8 de 48 =   384;   24;   16;   6;   36.

27. Maman achète pour 96¢ de sucre à 8¢ la livre. Combien en a-t-elle acheté de livres?

12;   13;   14;   15;   9.

28. Combien y a-t-il de demi-heures dans une journée?

12;   2;   48;   24;   36.

29. En 4 semaines, j'ai gagné 720 points. Combien ai-je gagné de points, en moyenne, par semaine?

130;   170;   190;   205;   180.

30. Un examen doit durer 1 heure. Après 1/4 d'heure, combien de minutes reste-t-il avant la fin de l'examen?

3/4;   30;   45;   35;   60.

Table 17

City-wide Norms for the Montreal French School System, 1969-70

Stanine	Cumulative Percentile	Français	Mathématiques	Français	Mathématiques	Français	Mathématiques
1	4	0 - 10	0 - 12	0 - 1	0	0 - 4	0 - 3
2	11	11 - 14	13 - 17	2 - 4	1 - 3	5 - 8	4 - 8
3	23	15 - 20	18 - 25	5 - 8	4 - 9	9 - 16	9 - 15
4	40	21 - 27	26 - 33	9 - 16	10 - 17	17 - 22	16 - 23
5	60	28 - 34[a]	34 - 42	17 - 24	18 - 27	23 - 30	24 - 32
6	77	35 - 41	43 - 49[a]	25 - 33[b]	28 - 35[b]	31 - 37[c]	33 - 40[c]
7	89	42 - 46	50 - 56	34 - 40	36 - 42	38 - 44	41 - 47
8	96	47 - 52	57 - 59	41 - 48	43 - 48	45 - 49	48 - 51
9	100	53 - 60	60 - 70	49 - 60	49 - 60	50 - 60	52 - 60

Mean Scores for the Experimental Classes: $\bar{X} = 31.00$ $\bar{X} = 44.00$ $\bar{X} = 27.59$ $\bar{X} = 33.39$ $\bar{X} = 37.22$ $\bar{X} = 35.92$

a) Placement of two new Experimental Classes as of the end of grade I, N = 52.

b) Placement of the Follow-up Experimental Class as of the end of grade II, N = 28.

c) Placement of the Pilot Experimental Class as of the end of grade III, N = 19.

Table 18

Test Results for the Follow-up Classes at the End of Grade III, 1970

Test Number and Name	Experimental Class		English Controls		French Controls		F Ratio	df
	Mean	Adjusted	Mean	Adjusted	Mean	Adjusted		
English Competence								
1. Word Knowledge (S.S.)	56.93	57.80	55.87	55.11	—	—	1.96	1,50
2. Word Discrimination (S.S.)	55.19	56.44	56.74	55.65	—	—	0.13	1,50
3. Reading (S.S.)	51.46	52.61	53.13	52.09	—	—	0.05	1,51
4. Spelling (S.S.)	54.79	56.32	59.23	57.84	—	—	0.42	1,51
5. Language Usage (S.S.)	58.96	58.65	59.65	59.92	—	—	0.15	1,50
6. Language Punctuation (S.S.)	46.48	48.10	54.84	53.43	—	—	5.94*	1,50
7. English Listening Comprehension	12.89	12.59	14.64	14.89	—	—	8.05**	1,53
8. Picture Vocabulary	49.20	48.98	48.69	48.90	—	—	0.00	1,54
9. *Speaking Skills in English: Story Invention*								
Linguistic Ratings								
Overall Expression	3.19	3.24	3.15	3.11	—	—	0.19	1,52
Grammar	3.22	3.38	3.09	2.96	—	—	1.93	1,52
Enunciation	2.85	2.97	2.88	2.78	—	—	0.38	1,52
Rhythm and Intonation	3.11	3.28	3.18	3.04	—	—	0.53	1,52
Word Counts								
Number of Words	128.19	127.46	133.09	133.69	—	—	0.16	1,52
Nouns (% of total)	0.19	0.19	0.22	0.21	—	—	4.49*	1,52
Different Nouns %	0.40	0.40	0.36	0.36	—	—	1.62	1,52
Adjectives %	0.09	0.06	0.09	0.11	—	—	2.30	1,52
Different Adjectives %	0.59	0.60	0.59	0.58	—	—	0.09	1,52
Verbs %	0.15	0.16	0.17	0.16	—	—	0.05	1,52
Different Verbs %	0.68	0.69	0.68	0.67	—	—	0.13	1,52

Table 18 (cont.)
Test Results for the Follow-up Classes at the End of Grade III, 1970

Test Number and Name	Experimental Class		English Controls		French Controls		F Ratio	df
	Mean	Adjusted	Mean	Adjusted	Mean	Adjusted		
10. *Decoding Skills in English*								
Children's Descriptions	11.21	9.01	7.88	9.81	—	—	0.03	1,52
Adults' Descriptions	7.29	7.35	7.25	7.19	—	—	0.09	1,52
French Competence								
11. French Listening Comprehension	11.19	11.32	—	—	15.19	14.96	20.23**	1,35
12. French Peabody	49.20	49.64	—	—	51.06	50.24	0.09	1,38
13. *Speaking Sk.'ls in French:*								
Story Invention								
Linguistic Ratings								
Overall Expression	3.36	3.36	—	—	4.20	4.22	4.25*	1,24
Grammar	3.05	3.00	—	—	4.20	4.30	10.28**	1,24
Enunciation	4.09	4.11	—	—	4.40	4.36	0.43	1,24
Liaison	4.73	4.78	—	—	4.00	3.88	4.08	1,24
Rhythm and Intonation	3.36	3.34	—	—	4.40	4.45	6.85*	1,24
Word Counts								
Total Words	86.07	86.04	—	—	146.22	146.32	3.17	1,29
Nouns %	0.16	0.16	—	—	0.17	0.17	0.57	1,29
Different Nouns %	0.76	0.76	—	—	0.73	0.72	0.38	1,29
Adjectives %	0.06	0.06	—	—	0.06	0.06	0.04	1,29
Different Adjectives %	0.67	0.67	—	—	0.63	0.63	0.13	1,29
Verbs %	0.17	0.17	—	—	0.19	0.18	1.47	1,29
Different Verbs %	0.69	0.69	—	—	0.63	0.63	1.04	1,29
14. *Decoding Skills in French*								
Children's Descriptions	5.66	5.74	—	—	7.69	7.54	10.89**	1,37
Adults' Descriptions	7.14	7.29	—	—	8.13	7.86	1.21	1,37

Test Number and Name	Experimental Class		English Controls		French Controls		F Ratio	df
	Mean	Adjusted	Mean	Adjusted	Mean	Adjusted		
Arithmetic Skills								
15. Arithmetic Computation (S.S.)	51.30	52.36	55.48	54.56	—	—	0.57	1,50
16. Arithmetic Problem Solving (S.S.)	53.63	54.65	54.71	53.82	—	—	0.13	1,50
IQ and Creativity								
17. Raven (English)	28.93	29.35	27.78	27.41	—	—	1.92	1,52
Raven (French)	28.93	29.12	—	—	30.19	29.85	0.28	1,36
18. *Lorge-Thorndike*								
Total	54.38	54.96	53.15	52.64	—	—	2.86	1,54
Vocabulary	19.97	20.00	18.94	18.91	—	—	2.76	1,54
Not-belonging	17.45	17.55	18.12	18.03	—	—	0.27	1,54
Go-together	16.97	17.41	16.09	15.70	—	—	4.56*	1,54
19. *Creativity*								
English Unusual Uses	4.56	5.09	6.33	5.90	—	—	0.75	1,52
English Consequences	5.93	6.33	7.64	7.31	—	—	1.51	1,52
French Unusual Uses	8.30	9.06	—	—	4.67	2.38	2.31	1,28
French Consequences	7.15	7.30	—	—	8.56	8.11	0.24	1,28

* $p < .05$
** $p < .01$

On the listening comprehension test (item 7), the Follow-up Experimental group falls significantly below the English Controls. There was no such difference with the grade III Pilot Classes, and we presume that the difference this year may simply be due to the lack of quiet testing rooms for the Experimental Classes. We will, of course, pay special attention to their performance on this measure at the grade IV level.

There was no significant difference in performance between the Experimental and English Control Classes on the *Peabody Picture Vocabulary Test* (item 8), indicating that the range of English vocabulary of the Experimental children has not been restricted by the language switch.

The spontaneous oral production of the children was measured with the *Story Invention* task (item 9). The linguist who analyzed the taped recordings found no differences between the Experimental and English Control Classes in overall expression, grammar, enunciation, or rhythm and intonation. Likewise, the formal word counts revealed only one statistically significant difference, out of the seven possible, between the two groups: the Experimental Class used 2 percent fewer nouns in their stories than did the Controls. Hence, the analysis of the formal word counts and the linguist's ratings replicate exactly the pattern of results found for the grade III Pilot Classes in their competence in English expression.

Furthermore, there were no significant differences between Experimental and Control children on either the children or adult forms of the *English Decoding* task (item 10). The fact that the Experimental children have no difficulty processing adults' or children's spontaneous speech lends credence to our argument that the trouble they had with the *Listening Comprehension* test may well have been simply a matter of poorer testing conditions.

French Language Competence

The performance of the Follow-up Experimental Class on the *Test de Rendement en Français* is of special interest because the comparison is made with city-wide norms for all grade III French-speaking pupils in Montreal who follow conventional French-Canadian educational programs. At the end of grade II, it will be recalled, the Experimental Pilot Class as a group scored above the 60th percentile on these norms, and it is of interest to note that the Follow-up Class also falls at Stanine 5, close to the 60th percentile, as shown in Table 19. We realized how impressive this performance was when we attempted to administer the same test to an English Control Class that had been following a conventional "French as a second language" program (FSL) from grade I on. As a class, they were unable to understand the instructions given in French or to work out the sample questions used as examples to introduce the test. This comparison is not intended as a criticism of existing FSL programs, for FSL specialists may have very different priorities in their aims and goals, but it is nevertheless the case that the Experimental children experienced no particular difficulties with this test.

On the test of *French Listening Comprehension* (Table 18, item 11), the Follow-up Experimental Class scored significantly lower than the French Controls. Since the Pilot Class at grade III was equivalent to the Controls on this test, we suspect that the difference noted here may also have been a function of the testing conditions which were ideal for the French Control pupils, but not for the Experimentals.

Quite unexpectedly, the Follow-up Experimental and French Control pupils have essentially similar scores on the French version of the *Peabody Picture Vocabulary Test* (item 12), indicating that the Experimental pupils have acquired a surprisingly complete vocabulary in French. This in fact is the first time we have seen the Experimentals "catch up" with the Controls on this measure, although the Pilot Experimental Class was close but reliably below the French Controls at the grade III level.

For the *Story Invention* task (item 13) there were no significant differences in the output of the Experimental and the French Control Classes on any of the formal word counts. The linguist who analyzed the tape recordings found the Follow-up and Pilot Experimental Classes very similar at grade III: they were both significantly poorer than the French Controls on grammar, rhythm and intonation, and overall expressive ability. Still they were judged to be at or above the average point on each index, and there were no significant differences between the Experimental and Control Classes in enunciation or use of liaison in French.

On the *Decoding* task (item 14) there was an important group difference: the Experimental children were as skilled as the French Controls when it came to decoding the descriptive speech of adults but were significantly poorer than the Controls when it came to decoding children's descriptions. Apparently the children have caught on to adult modes of verbal description, very likely due to the regular interaction with French teachers, whereas they seem now to show a deficit in decoding the descriptive speech of French-speaking children, possibly because of limited social interaction.

Arithmetic Competence

The Follow-up Experimental Class performed as well as the English Controls on both the *Computation* (item 15) and the *Problem Solving* (item 16) sections of the *Metropolitan Achievement Test*, replicating nicely the results obtained with the Pilot Classes at the grade III level. When interpreting this finding, one must keep in mind that the Experimental children have received all of their formal instruction in mathematics via French and in this instance were tested via English.

On the *Test de Rendement en Calcul* the Follow-up Experimental Class, as a group, fell near the 60th percentile (see Table 19), meaning that the class average is at the same level or higher than that of approximately 60 percent of French-speaking grade III youngsters in Montreal.

Intelligence and Creativity

The end-of-year results on the *Progressive Matrices* test (item 17) revealed no significant differences among the Experimental, English Control, and French Control Classes. Nor was there a significant difference between the Follow-up Experimental and English Control Classes on the *Lorge-Thorndike* total score (item 18). The Experimental pupils did, however, perform significantly better on the *Lorge-Thorndike* subtest dealing with the ability to choose items that "go together." Furthermore, the Experimental pupils performed at the same level as both the English and French Controls on the two measures of "Creativity" (item 19). As of the end of grade III, then, there is no evidence of *any* intellectual retardation or lag attributable to the Experimental pupils' intensive experience with a second language.

The Experimental Classes at the
Grade III Level: In Summary

Many noteworthy aspects of the Experimental children's performance have come to light in this analysis, and before these are summarized and integrated, the reader should keep in mind that from grade II on about 60 percent of the school program has been conducted in French and 40 percent in English, while in kindergarten and grade I the switch from home to school languages was about 90 percent complete. The Pilot Experimental Class, even more than the Follow-up, has also taken the full brunt of experimentation in the sense that the teachers of the Experimental children had no guidelines to follow and no materials or texts developed specifically for their purposes. When the Follow-up Classes moved up a year, the teachers at least had experience working out a program of their own.

What effect does such an educational program have on the Experimental children's progress in their home language when compared with Control children who attend a conventional English-language program through grade III? The answer is that they show no symptoms of retardation or negative transfer, and perform as well as the Controls on standard tests of English language competence. The only exception is some difficulty with English rules of punctuation. On tests of English word knowledge, word discrimination, and language usage, the Pilot and Follow-up Classes fall above the 80th percentile on national norms. Thus while performing as well as the Controls in English, they also meet very high national standards. Their reading ability in English is also comparable to that of the Controls, but in this case both groups score between the 55th and 65th percentiles, suggesting that Montreal's program of English

Table 19

City-wide Norms for the Montreal French School System, 1970-71

		End of Grade III Norms	
Stanine	Cumulative Percentile	Français	Mathématiques
1	4	0-8	0-5
2	11	9-13	6-10
3	23	14-19	11-17
4	40	20-29	18-26
5	60	30-37*	27-35*
6	77	38-44	36-44
7	89	45-49	45-51
8	96	50-55	52-57
9	100	56-60	58-68

*The mean scores for the Follow-up Experimental Class at the end of grade III:

Français: $\overline{X} = 34.17$, N = 27

Mathématiques: $\overline{X} = 33.43$, N = 27

Language Arts may place somewhat less emphasis on reading than would be expected from national norms.

The listening comprehension scores of the Pilot Experimental Class and their knowledge of concepts in English are also at the same level as those of the English Controls. The relatively poor showing of the Follow-up Experimental Class on listening comprehension, we suspect, may have been due simply to the poor noise control in the school where the Experimental Class was tested.

All signs are favorable also for their progress in English expressive skills. When asked to retell or invent short stories in English, both the Pilot and Follow-up Experimental Classes do so with as much comprehension as the Controls and with as good or better command of rhythm and intonation, enunciation, and overall expression. Their productions are as long and complex and their vocabulary as diverse as those of the Controls.

Their facility at decoding and utilizing the descriptive messages of English-speaking children and adults is also at the level of the Controls, and their word associations in English (tested only with the Pilot Classes at grade III) show as much maturity and appropriateness.

After three years in the program, how well do children progress in second-language competence when compared with children from French-speaking homes who follow a conventional program of French study? The answer is that they fare extremely well. For instance, as a group, their French listening comprehension score was not different from that of the French Controls, and their knowledge of complex French concepts showed a marked progress from grade II, although they are still reliably behind the Controls, but only by six or so vocabulary items. They scored reliably lower than the Controls on the 1968-69 version of the *Test de Rendement en Français*, but we believe that this was because the test called for a knowledge of grammatical nomenclature and stylistics the children had not yet been trained for. The Follow-up Experimental Class also scored reliably lower than the French Controls on listening comprehension, but this result too may have been due, in part at least, to the noisy testing conditions in the Experimental school.

The Follow-up Class scored at the same level as the French Controls on the Peabody Picture Vocabulary Test, which, incidentally, marks the first time that the Experimental children arrived at the same level as the native speakers on this measure of French vocabulary.

On city-wide norms for achievement in French we found that both the Pilot and Follow-up Experimental Classes scored at around the 60th percentile at the end of grade III, signifying that both classes performed as well or better, on the average, than 50 percent of Montreal's French-speaking children following conventional all-French programs.

The Experimental children's ability to produce the basic sound sequences of French is extremely good, as is their competence in enunciating and making appropriate liaisons in spoken French. Thus, they have achieved nativelike control over the distinctive sound units of French, but when retelling and inventing French stories, it becomes evident that the rhythm and intonation, and overall expression of both Pilot and Follow-up Experimental groups are not nativelike. By the end of grade III, then, they have not yet attained nativelike command of all aspects of the language. Yet, when *inventing* stories in French, the Pilot Experimental Class showed much better overall expression, enunciation, and rhythm and intonation than when simply *retelling* stories, a trend noted also with the Follow-up Experimental group at the grade II level.[2] Both sets of results suggest that these children are particularly motivated and clever in situations where they can express their own flow of ideas. In both cases though,

---

[2]The story retelling test was not used with the Follow-up Classes in grade III.

the verbal content of their French productions is as complex as that of the Controls and shows a similar degree of comprehension and vocabulary diversity. They make more errors than the French Controls, but these are mainly errors of gender and of contraction, not syntax-type mistakes.

The Pilot Class showed as much skill as the French Controls in decoding the spontaneous descriptive statements of French-speaking children and adults. Furthermore, their free associations in French are as rapid, mature, and appropriate as those of the Controls.[3] The Follow-up Experimental Class, on the other hand, were less skilled than the Controls at decoding descriptive statements made by children their own age. One might expect the Experimental children, with limited opportunities for interaction in French with peers, to have difficulties with children's images and descriptive styles. Interestingly enough, they had no difficulty, relative to the French Controls, in decoding adults' descriptions.

Although their progress in French is exceptionally good, especially when one considers their competence in English, there is still room for improvement in their French expressive skills. If a higher priority were given to the development of a nativelike command of the spoken language, then imaginative changes could be introduced into the present program at the early grades without hampering the progress the children make with the more receptive aspects of the language. For example, the "fun" subjects such as physical education, music, and art—conducted in English from grade I on—could become important practice periods for French expression. In other words, the teachers and administrators may have overlooked opportunities to compensate for the children's limited extracurricular experience in French.

How well do children following the program perform on tests of a nonlanguage subject such as mathematics? The answer is that they perform at the same high level as the English Controls (all groups scoring beyond the 80th percentile) in both computational and problem-solving arithmetic tests presented in English. We can be confident then that the Experimental pupils have been as able to grasp, assimilate, and utilize mathematical principles as the English Controls, and that they are able to transfer this knowledge, acquired exclusively through French, to English.

On the C.E.C.M. tests of *Rendement en Calcul,* a measure designed for French-speaking pupils following an exclusively French program of instruction,

---

[3] As noted in several earlier analyses, however, the French Controls make many more transformational associations than do the Experimental or the English Control Classes. This consistent contrast between the French and English languages is of theoretical interest, but actually incidental to the main trends that concern us here.

it is reassuring to find that the average scores of both Pilot and Follow-up Experimental Classes lie above the 60th percentile on the city-wide norms.[4]

Does a bilingual program of this sort develop a general sensitivity to foreign language sounds? The results of the *Russian Phoneme Discrimination* test provide no convincing evidence of any advantage going to the Experimental children. Although small differences favored the Experimental Classes at the end of each year except one, no single comparison was statistically reliable.

Apparently the development of skill with a new phonemic system does not automatically sensitize one to foreign sounds in general. Of course, the bilingual might find it easier than the monolingual to *learn* the sound system of new language by drawing on a broader range of phonemic controls, just as he may be able to transfer various strategies for learning vocabulary and grammar rules. The results of the repeated testing of phoneme discrimination, however, suggest that these other possibilities be examined carefully in follow-up research.

What effect does a bilingual program of this sort have on the measured intelligence of the children involved? There is no sign at the end of grade III of any intellectual deficit or retardation attributable to the bilingual experience. Retests using Raven's Progressive Matrices and Lorge-Thorndike tests of intelligence reveal that both the Pilot and Follow-up Experimental Classes are comparable to their respective Control groups. In fact, the Follow-up Experimental group is reliably ahead of the Controls on one subtest of the Lorge-Thorndike test. In terms of cognitive flexibility, the Pilot Experimental Class was more advanced than the English Controls in generating imaginative and unusual uses for everyday objects, although there was no comparable difference noted with the Follow-up Class. What is noteworthy is the fact that the Experimental children are able to perform at the same level as either the English or the French Control children on tests that call for imagination and productive thinking.

4The Pilot Class in fact scored even above the 75th percentile, but as mentioned earlier this might well be due to the advantage they had in taking the test about three weeks later in their school year than the pupils in the C.E.C.M.

Chapter Seven

The Pilot Class at Grade IV

As the Pilot Experimental Class started grade IV in the 1969-70 academic year, the St. Lambert Elementary School included numerous classes, ranging from kindergarten to grade IV, studying mainly through French. There were some conventionally instructed, all-English classes to be sure, but by this time there was a distinctive bilingual atmosphere in the school. Studying through French and speaking the language had become accepted norms of the school.

A joint committee of teachers, parents, administrators, and researchers had formulated the grade IV curriculum and helped to select appropriate texts. The committee's major concern was to insure that the experimental program would be comparable in content level to the normal grade IV English language program. The textbooks, workbooks, and other materials selected were those used widely by French-speaking students at the grade IV level in Quebec schools except for those of the English Language Arts course, which were standard materials for English-speaking grade IV students.

The grade IV Pilot Experimental Class was taught initially by a teacher from Belgium, but because of illness she was replaced for the last few months of the year by a male French-speaking teacher from North Africa.

Test Battery Used with the Grade IV Pilot Classes, Spring 1970

Except for the few major modifications listed below, the measures used at the end of grade IV were basically the same as those already described, with appropriate age adjustments.

1. For the English and French versions of the *Peabody Picture Vocabulary Test*, more difficult items, those from 60 to 136 in the series, were administered. The total possible score was 77.

2. The 1970 version of the *Test de Rendement en Français* (C.E.C.M.) was administered in November 1970 concurrent with its administration to all French-speaking children in Montreal. Although given during the first half of the students' fifth year of schooling, the test covered grade IV material. The nine subsections of the test dealt with the recognition of various parts of speech, grammatical analysis, appropriate usage, and so forth.

3. The 1970 version of the *Test de Rendement en Calcul* (C.E.C.M.) comprised thirty-five problems—presented as computational exercises or problems (given mainly in words) involving addition, subtraction, multiplication, division, set theory, basic geometric relationships, and so forth.

4. Because of the children's age, we switched to the standard form of Raven's *Progressive Matrices Test* (1958), and used sets B and C.

5. Similarly, the Level 3, Form A, Primary Battery of the *Lorge-Thorndike Intelligence Test* was used at the grade IV level. There are four parts to the test for this age group: sentence completion; recognizing which of five words is similar to a given set of three (e.g., rose, daisy, violet: red, garden, sweet, grow, lily); recognizing which of five words is most similar in meaning to a given word (e.g., land: ground, town, roof, river, grass); and arithmetic problem solving.

Results for the Grade IV Pilot Classes, 1970

The findings to be discussed here are presented in Table 20, where the mean scores of the Pilot Experimental Class are compared with the English and French Control Classes on the various tests administered at the end of grade IV.

English Language Competence

The results for the various subsections of the *Metropolitan Achievement* test (items 1-6, in Table 20) indicate that the Experimental pupils perform as well as the conventionally instructed English Controls on all subtests: Word Knowledge, Word Discrimination, Reading, Spelling, Usage, and Punctuation. They also perform at the same level as the English Controls on the *Listening Comprehension* test (item 7) and the *Peabody Picture Vocabulary Test* (item 8).

The spontaneous oral productions of the children when inventing stories (item 9) were analyzed in detail by a linguist, who found no differences between Experimental and Control pupils in terms of overall expression, grammatical usage, correctness, enunciation, or rhythm and intonation. Likewise, the formal word counts revealed only one statistically significant difference in the seven possible comparisons: the Experimental Class used a relatively smaller proportion of different verbs than did the English Controls. In general, however, the groups were similar in the proportion of nouns, adjectives, and verbs used in constructing their stories.

Table 20

Test Results for the Pilot Class at the End of Grade IV, 1970

Test Number and Name	Experimental Class		English Controls		French Controls		F Ratio	df
	Mean	Adjusted	Mean	Adjusted	Mean	Adjusted		
English Competence								
1. Word Knowledge (S.S.)	63.32	63.40	60.74	60.69	—	—	1.29	1,41
2. Word Discrimination (S.S.)	60.11	60.48	58.42	58.19	—	—	0.82	1,41
3. Reading (S.S.)	58.32	59.03	58.10	57.66	—	—	0.20	1,41
4. Spelling (S.S.)	61.53	61.39	61.61	61.70	—	—	0.02	1,41
5. Language Usage (S.S.)	63.68	63.88	64.48	64.36	—	—	0.04	1,41
6. Language Punctuation (S.S.)	54.26	54.71	57.48	57.21	—	—	0.87	1,41
7. English Listening Comprehension	15.10	15.30	15.22	15.09	—	—	0.05	1,43
8. Picture Vocabulary	36.55	36.93	34.19	33.95	—	—	2.22	1,43
9. *Speaking Skills in English: Story Invention*								
Linguistic Ratings								
Overall Expression	3.05	3.10	3.27	3.23	—	—	0.24	1,41
Grammar	3.30	3.35	3.43	3.40	—	—	0.03	1,41
Enunciation	3.00	3.07	3.03	2.99	—	—	0.08	1,41
Rhythm and Intonation	3.20	3.22	3.53	3.52	—	—	1.19	1,41
Word Counts								
Number of Words	213.70	227.62	199.61	189.66	—	—	0.26	1,39
Nouns (% of total)	0.20	0.20	0.20	0.20	—	—	0.22	1,39
Different Nouns %	0.34	0.34	0.37	0.37	—	—	1.52	1,39
Adjectives %	0.10	0.10	0.12	0.11	—	—	0.82	1,39
Different Adjectives %	0.56	0.57	0.56	0.56	—	—	0.07	1,39
Verbs %	0.16	0.16	0.17	0.17	—	—	0.13	1,39
Different Verbs %	0.61	0.59	0.66	0.68	—	—	5.80*	1,39

Table 20 (cont.)
Test Results for the Pilot Class at the End of Grade IV, 1970

Test Number and Name	Experimental Class		English Controls		French Controls		F Ratio	df
	Mean	Adjusted	Mean	Adjusted	Mean	Adjusted		
10. *Decoding Skills in English*								
Children's Descriptions	7.68	7.82	7.19	7.11	—	—	1.80	1,41
Adults' Descriptions	6.37	6.34	7.65	7.66	—	—	7.28**	1,41
French Competence								
11. French Listening Comprehension	13.65	13.91	—	—	15.64	15.28	1.20	1,25
12. French Peabody	38.30	38.87	—	—	46.79	45.97	3.84	1,25
13. *Speaking Skills in French:* Story Invention								
Linguistic Ratings								
Overall Expression	3.05	2.94	—	—	4.00	4.19	8.06**	1,22
Grammar	2.58	2.71	—	—	4.67	4.45	14.83**	1,22
Enunciation	3.84	3.97	—	—	4.92	4.71	4.59*	1,22
Liaison	4.37	4.30	—	—	5.00	5.11	6.69*	1,22
Rhythm and Intonation	3.37	3.42	—	—	4.92	4.84	16.37**	1,22
Word Counts								
Total Words	105.16	95.39	—	—	83.69	97.97	0.02	1,23
Nouns %	0.16	0.16	—	—	0.17	0.16	0.00	1,23
Different Nouns %	0.78	0.80	—	—	0.70	0.66	4.26*	1,23
Adjectives %	0.05	0.06	—	—	0.06	0.05	0.18	1,23
Different Adjectives %	0.62	0.64	—	—	0.71	0.69	0.18	1,23
Verbs %	0.16	0.16	—	—	0.19	0.19	6.89*	1,23
Different Verbs %	0.74	0.77	—	—	0.69	0.65	4.25*	1,23
14. *Decoding Skills in French*								
Children's Descriptions	6.21	6.36	—	—	9.00	8.80	8.64**	1,24
Adults' Descriptions	7.16	7.02	—	—	8.14	8.33	2.74	1,24

Test Number and Name	Experimental Class		English Controls		French Controls		F Ratio	df
	Mean	Adjusted	Mean	Adjusted	Mean	Adjusted		
Arithmetic Skills								
15. Arithmetic Computation (S.S.)	64.79	66.00	66.16	65.42	—	—	0.03	1,41
16. Arithmetic Problem Solving (S.S.)	61.16	61.99	60.84	60.33	—	—	0.34	1,41
IQ and Creativity								
17. Raven (English)	14.58	14.50	16.81	16.86	—	—	4.03*	1,41
Raven (French)	14.58	14.47	—	—	15.50	15.65	0.38	1,24
18. *Lorge-Thorndike*								
Total	61.89	63.32	56.83	55.89	—	—	2.48	1,39
Vocabulary	16.74	17.23	15.34	15.02	—	—	2.82	1,39
Not belonging	16.79	17.16	16.14	15.89	—	—	0.73	1,39
Mathematics	12.16	12.48	9.79	9.58	—	—	7.10*	1,39
Analogies	16.21	16.45	15.55	15.39	—	—	0.55	1,39
19. *Creativity*								
English Unusual Uses	6.95	7.60	7.71	7.25	—	—	0.05	1,39
English Consequences	7.35	7.74	8.79	8.51	—	—	0.50	1,39
French Unusual Uses	6.58	5.95	—	—	5.15	6.08	0.01	1,23
French Consequences	7.79	7.22	—	—	8.00	8.83	0.56	1,23

* $p < .05$
** $p < .01$

On the *English Decoding* task (item 10) the Experimental Class was at the same level as the English Controls when it was a case of decoding children's descriptions, but when dealing with adults' descriptions they were significantly poorer than the Controls. This outcome which remains to be replicated is interesting from one point of view: the Experimental children may be reflecting a relative lack of adult "teacher talk" in English, just as they appear to show a relative lack of "peer talk" in French. In any case, this finding indicates only a type of unfamiliarity with the English descriptive statements of adults, not a difficulty with English vocabulary or structure. The results of the listening comprehension and picture vocabulary tests reassure us on these grounds. In fact, the students' overall performance on all aspects of English language competence is very impressive since English has been a relatively silent language in their formal schooling.

French Language Competence

The standing of the Pilot Experimental Class on the *Test de Rendement en Français* is described in Table 21 where it is evident that they, as a class, perform better than approximately one-half of the French-speaking pupils at their grade level in the normative sample. Furthermore, there was no significant difference between the scores of the Experimental and French Control Classes on the test of *Listening Comprehension* (item 11 of Table 20). In addition, the Experimental Class was not significantly below the French Controls (as they had been in the earlier years) on the French version of the *Peabody Picture Vocabulary Test* (item 12). This finding is interesting because it suggests that the distributions of the scores in the Experimental and Control groups have started to overlap in this instance, thereby eliminating the significance of the difference between the mean scores. The fact remains, however, that the Experimental Class is still about seven items below the Controls on this test, as they have been since the earlier years ($\overline{X}_{Exp.}$ = 38.87, $\overline{X}_{French\ Control}$ = 45.97). Even so, the size of the Experimental pupils' repertoire of French concepts is extremely impressive when compared with the native speaker controls.

The linguist's ratings of the Experimental children's spontaneous oral productions in French (*Story Retelling*, item 13) indicated that they have not achieved perfectly nativelike competence in spoken French by the end of grade IV. The French Controls were rated significantly higher on each of the five indices: grammatical usage, overall expression, enunciation, liaison, and rhythm and intonation. Nevertheless, the Experimental Class, as a group, was placed at or above the neutral point (2.5-3.5) in competence for all indices, indicating that they have achieved a very good command of the French language in the eyes of a trained judge who used native speakers of French as his point of reference.

The results of the word count analyses showed no basic differences between the Experimental and French Control children. Their spontaneous productions

Table 21

City-wide Norms for the Montreal French School System, 1970-71

Stanine	Cumulative Percentile	End of Grade IV Norms	
		Français	Mathématiques
1	4	0-4	0-4
2	11	5-10	5-10
3	23	11-19	11-18
4	40	20-26	19-27
5	60	27-35*	28-36*
6	77	36-42	37-45
7	89	43-49	46-52
8	96	50-55	53-55
9	100	56-66	56-64

*The mean scores for the Pilot Experimental Class at the end of grade IV:

Français: $\overline{X} = 32.75, N = 20$

Mathématiques: $\overline{X} = 33.36, N = 19$

were similar in terms of length, percentage of nouns, percentage of adjectives, and variety of adjectives, but the Experimental Class did use a greater variety of nouns and verbs than the French Controls who, in turn, used a greater percentage of verbs. In summary, then, these findings suggest that the oral productions of the Experimental children, although recognizably nonnative, approximate very closely the spontaneous language of grade IV French children. The distinctive mark of the Experimental children's French is a tendency to avoid complex grammatical constructions in favor of simpler but nonetheless correct structures. They appear to understand every nuance of the teacher's spoken French, to read the language effortlessly, and to speak it—in their own style—naturally and spontaneously.

The Experimental class performed as well as the French Controls on the *French Decoding* task (item 14) when working with the descriptions of adults. They were, however, less able than the Controls to decode the spontaneous descriptive statements of French-speaking children. Given their relatively good performance on the *French Listening Comprehension* and *Peabody Picture Vocabulary Tests*, we see this difference as a reflection of their limited social interaction with French children their own age. They seem to have caught on to all aspects of French "teacher talk," however.

Arithmetic Competence

Arithmetic skills were assessed with two subtests of the Metropolitan Achievement Test, the Mathematics subsection of the Lorge-Thorndike Test, and the C.E.C.M.'s *Test de Rendement en Calcul*. First, there were no significant differences among groups on Computational Skills (item 15), or Problem Solving (item 16) as measured by the Metropolitan Test. This outcome is especially interesting because these tests are in English and the Experimental pupils have so far received all of their instruction in mathematics through French. Second, the Pilot Experimentals scored reliably better than the English Controls on the Mathematics section of the Lorge-Thorndike measure (item 18), also given entirely in English. Finally, on the *Test de Rendement en Calcul* (Table 21) they performed better than approximately 50 percent of the grade IV French pupils in Greater Montreal. There is no question then that the Experimental pupils are able to process mathematical notions with great skill in either English or French.

Intelligence and Creativity

All classes were administered the standard form of *Raven's Progressive Matrices* (item 17), similar in makeup to the colored form used previously, but more appropriate for use at the grade IV level. In this case, the Experimentals performed as well as the French Controls, but significantly lower than the English Controls. This difference between the Experimental and English Control children seems to us to be a chance affair, since in previous years the two groups were consistently similar in Raven's retest scores and since this year they scored at the same level on the Lorge-Thorndike Test (item 18). In fact, the Experimental pupils score generally higher on all subtests than the English Controls and significantly better on the mathematics section of the Lorge-Thorndike. Their relatively poor showing on the Raven test therefore must be seen in conjunction with their comparatively good performance on the Lorge-Thorndike test. We introduced the Lorge-Thorndike test from grade II on because it has both verbal and nonverbal subsections, and because the Raven test had been administered to all classes so often that its effectiveness as a measure of intellectual level or of change in level might be questioned.

To assure ourselves that this one difference favoring one of the Control groups was only a chance occurrence, we have looked into the results of the 1971 spring testing (the grade V level for the Pilot Classes and the grade IV for the Follow-up Classes) to see how the Experimental Classes compared on the Raven retests at that time. On this analysis we note that there is no significant difference among groups, the adjusted means scores were: Experimentals = 18.35; English Controls = 17.71; French Controls = 18.40; $F = 0.25$; 2,53 *df*. Nor is there any reliable difference for the Follow-up Classes at the end of grade IV: Experimentals = 16.77; English Controls = 16.55; French Controls = 18.92; $F = 1.50$; 2,64 *df*.

On the *Creativity* measures (item 19), there were also no significant group differences. That is, the Experimental pupils performed as well as the English Controls in English and the French Controls in French. We have already noted at the grade III level that the Experimental children scored reliably higher than the Controls on the tests of creativity, but since we have no replication of that tendency this year, we assume the advantage seen at grade III was either a chance occurrence or a transient phenomenon showing itself at a particular moment in the development of their bilingualism. This last possibility merits further investigation.

Sensitivity to Foreign Linguistic Sounds

In view of the results on the *Russian Phoneme Discrimination* test, which showed only slight differences favoring the Experimental Classes in sensitivity to the sounds of a totally foreign language, we tried to assess this ability more thoroughly in the 1970 end-of-year tests. The new procedure, described fully in an article by Davine, Tucker, and Lambert (1971) makes use of a broad range of phoneme sequences, some occurring at the start of both French and English words (e.g., /kl/ as in *clap* or *clef*); some found in French, but not in English words (e.g., /ps/ as in *psautier*); some found in English, but not French words (e.g., /sr/ as in shroud); and some occurring in neither English nor French words (e.g., /km/). If there were some advantage for bilinguals in learning the sound system of a totally foreign language, then we felt that this procedure should reveal it.

We compared the Experimental pupils and the monolingual youngsters in the French and English Control groups on their sensitivity to various combinations of these familiar and unfamiliar sounds. If the bilingual experience had created a generalized sensitivity to sounds occurring in foreign languages, the Experimental children should have shown an advantage in remembering and processing totally foreign initial sequences. There was, however, no such trend apparent in the results. Thus we feel confident in concluding that there appears to be no generalized phonemic sensitivity attributable to the Experimental program. The results of the Rabinovitch and Parver (1966) study remain a puzzle to us. Their subjects may have developed their bilinguality from early infancy on, or the advantage they describe may come in the teen years and later. Whatever the solution of that puzzle may be, we are now interested in determining if the bilingual experience heightens sensitivity to the syntactic or semantic systems of foreign languages. Our future research on this topic will follow these new directions.

Summary and Conclusions

After a five-year assessment period, what then can we conclude about the progress of the Experimental children in their two languages, their attempts to learn through a second language, and their overall intellectual and cognitive development? Their education has been characterized by a switch to French as the primary medium of instruction in kindergarten and grade I. Starting with grade II, English instruction was introduced through English Language Arts, but otherwise the main language of schooling was French. One can think of the program then as a type of "bilingual education" in the more conventional sense, although the major emphasis throughout has been clearly on French, one of the two major languages of the country but one that would likely be overlooked and bypassed in the home, school, and social environments of these young Canadians.

We have compared the performance of the Experimental children on a variety of tasks, using comparison groups or monolingually instructed French and English youngsters of the same intellectual capacity and the same social-class backgrounds as controls. In particular, we have tried to evaluate the impact of this novel educational experience on the development of skills in the children's home language, English; on the progress with French; on their competence in the nonlanguage subject matter, mathematics, taught via French; on their measured intelligence and creativity; and on their competence with the sound system of a completely novel foreign language.

After five years, we are satisfied that the Experimental program has resulted in no native language or subject matter (i.e., arithmetic) deficit or retardation of any sort, nor is there any cognitive retardation attributable to participation in the program. In fact, the Experimental pupils appear to be able to read, write, speak, understand, and use English as competently as youngsters instructed in the conventional manner via English. During the same period of time and with no apparent personal or academic costs, the children have developed a competence in reading, writing, speaking, and understanding French that English pupils following a traditional French-as-a-Second-Language program for the same number of years could never match. They have acquired a thorough mastery of the basic elements of French phonology, morphology, and syntax, and can speak and communicate in French without the inhibition or hesitation that so often characterizes the typical student of a foreign or second language. There is no question that given opportunities to use French in diverse social situations, the Experimental children, and others following them in the program, could become indistinguishable from native speakers of French in their oral expression, and at the same time they would profit fully from instruction presented in either of their languages. They could, in other words, easily become equally competent in all features of both languages.

We would not yet classify the Experimental children as "balanced" in their bilingual competence, even though such a goal is realistic and can be achieved, we believe, without incurring intellectual deficits or cognitive handicaps of any kind. It would, of course, be unreasonable to expect the school program, alone, to provide sufficiently varied conditions for the development of balanced expressive fluency. Since the Experimental children have their social interactions in a basically English milieu, the task of becoming "productively" bilingual becomes especially difficult. The natural limitations of this present program can help us gauge with more certainty how effective the same type of program would be in other regions of Canada or in other national settings where little contact with members of the second ethnolinguistic group would be possible, even though a desire to learn the other language is strong. In the Montreal area opportunities certainly do exist for assuring communicative competence in French outside of school. But parents must make their own decisions about whether to capitalize on these opportunities to enhance the French language experiences of their children. As we see it, then, this educational program has provided the children with all of the academic essentials needed to become balanced bilinguals, and this is an enormous step. Capitalizing on opportunities to interact with French-speaking children is, in main part, a parental matter. But, as we shall see in Chapter Nine, it happens to become a matter for children themselves to decide about, as well.

From the start of the project, we were convinced that the goal of bilingualism could be most efficiently attained if adequate attention were given to introducing in a sympathetic manner the other culture and its representatives and the fascinating contrasts this introduction provides, over and above those of a linguistic nature. With this aim in mind we have assessed the attitudinal changes that have taken place in the minds of children following this type of educational program. This topic is discussed in detail in the next chapter.

Chapter Eight

The Program's Effect on Pupils' Attitudes

Up to now, we have focused attention almost exclusively on the linguistic and cognitive impact of the program. Learning another language in this fashion is just as likely to have equally profound effects on the children's attitudes toward the people whose language they are mastering. In other words, much more goes on in language learning than simply acquiring skill in a new code (see Lambert and Gardner, 1972). Both directly and indirectly, children also learn a good deal about another people and another culture, and these interpersonal and cultural aspects of the language-learning process are of fundamental importance when trying to understand the program's overall effect on the children involved.

Earlier research has demonstrated how the attitudes and social motivation of the student of a second or foreign language can affect his rate and efficiency of learning. Much of this research has been conducted in the Montreal setting (Gardner, 1960; Gardner and Lambert, 1959) or in Ontario (Feenstra, 1968; Feenstra and Gardner, 1968) as well as in communities in the United States (Lambert, Gardner, Olton, and Tunstall, 1962), and one Asian setting (Santos, 1969; Lambert and Gardner, 1972). These studies showed how important the language learner's attitudes toward the "other" ethnolinguistic group can be in determining one's success in acquiring that group's language, quite independently of the student's linguistic aptitude or verbal intelligence. Thus, students with friendly and receptive attitudes toward the other group are more likely than those with suspicion or prejudice to make substantial progress in learning the other group's language, regardless of their language-learning aptitude.

In the present study, we push the same idea one step further by asking if the Experimental children's comprehensive, long-term experience with French will have affected their attitudes and outlook toward native speakers of the language they have learned so well. Before one can begin to answer this important question, it must be demonstrated as convincingly as possible that *parental* attitudes toward the other cultural group at the start of the program had not determined which children would be included in the experiment and which would not. Actually, we considered the matter of parental attitudes important enough to be included as one of the criteria, along with socioeconomic background and intelligence, for equating the Experimental and Control groups at the beginning of the project. We have already discussed the initial attitudes of parents in Chapter Two. For example, we found that the parents of pupils in the two experimental classes had essentially the same pattern of attitudes toward the French-Canadian people and their culture as the parents of children in the English Control groups. Hence we assume that there was no difference in family attitudes toward French people and the French culture at the start of the project. And it is from this uniform baseline that we examine what happens to children's attitudes toward the other ethnolinguistic group as they move through five years of the experimental program in comparison with the control groups who follow a conventional all-English school program.

The Children's Attitudes: The Pilot Classes at Grade II

Tables 22 and 23 summarize the patterns of attitudes of the Pilot Classes toward English Canadians and French Canadians at the end of grades II (Table 22) and III (Table 23). Attitudes towards self were measured by having the children describe themselves (the concept "me") on the same rating scales as used to describe the two major ethnic groups. These tables present mean scores for each of the Pilot Classes—the Experimental, the English Controls, and the French Controls—on each scale. The attitude profiles were compared and contrasted statistically with a two-way analysis of variance procedure that tests, first, whether the three groups of children differ significantly in the ratings assigned to English Canadians, French Canadians, or "me" (the Group or G effect); second, whether there are any common stereotypes of French or English peoples shared by all three groups of children (the Stereotype or S effect); and third, whether one group of children or another has a distinctive stereotype of English Canadians, French Canadians, or themselves (the G x S effect). We will consider here the differences or trends that turned out to be statistically significant.

Note first that for the characteristic *short . . . tall* in Table 22, only the group effect was significant, reflecting the fact that the French Control pupils restricted their ratings to the *shorter* end of the *short . . . tall* scale when describing English and French Canadians and themselves, while the Experimental

Table 22

Attitude Profiles of the Pilot Classes at Grade II, 1968

Characteristic	Significance Levels		Mean Scores for Ratings of:		
			English Canadians	French Canadians	Me
1. Short (1) – tall (7)	G effect at .01	Experimentals:	5.28	4.67	4.67
		English Controls:	3.84	3.12	3.97
		French Controls:	3.81	2.81	2.12
2. Bad (1) – good (7)	G effect at .05 G x S Interaction at .01	Experimentals:	5.39	4.67	5.11
		English Controls:	4.64	3.21	5.27
		French Controls:	4.50	5.67	5.14
3. Dumb (1) – smart (7)	S effect at .01 Interaction at .05	Experimentals:	4.89	4.67	5.33
		English Controls:	5.45	3.71	6.10
		French Controls:	4.73	5.80	6.00
4. Not nice (1) – nice (7)	G effect at .05 S effect at .05	Experimentals:	5.33	4.83	5.50
		English Controls:	4.56	3.37	5.12
		French Controls:	3.94	4.19	4.69
5. Not friendly (1) – friendly (7)	Interaction at .05	Experimentals:	5.33	5.00	5.50
		English Controls:	4.52	3.74	5.13
		French Controls:	4.12	5.37	5.06
6. Fat (1) – thin (7)	S effect at .01 Interaction at .05	Experimentals:	5.28	4.33	4.72
		English Controls:	4.22	3.66	4.88
		French Controls:	4.33	4.60	5.93
7. Slow (1) – fast (7)	Interaction at .05	Experimentals:	4.88	4.35	4.18
		English Controls:	4.36	3.55	4.82
		French Controls:	3.47	4.94	3.76

Characteristic	Significance Levels		Mean Scores for Ratings of:		
			English Canadians	French Canadians	Me
8. Little (1) – Big (7)	G effect at .01 Interaction at .01	Experimentals:	5.44	4.78	5.39
		English Controls:	4.39	3.55	4.90
		French Controls:	4.12	3.88	2.35
9. Not pretty (1) – pretty (7)	G effect at .01 Interaction at .05	Experimentals:	4.17	3.28	4.00
		English Controls:	4.87	4.29	5.74
		French Controls:	4.94	5.94	5.47

pupils more often used the *taller* end of the scale when making their judgments of height. Since the G x S interaction is not significant, no other comparisons on the *short . . . tall* scale are statistically different.

Several trends apparent in Table 22 call for special interest. First, with regard to the characteristic *good . . . bad*, the English and French Control children both see their own ethnic group as more *good* than the other group. This ethnocentric pattern resembles the rivalry typical of children who boast that "our" team is better than "yours." The trouble is that when ethnic groups are involved, this type of rivalry is far from being restricted to children. What is noteworthy in this case is the tendency for the Experimental children to be relatively more charitable in their ratings of French Canadians. That is, even though they also rate French Canadians as less *good* than English Canadians, in general they rate French Canadians much more favorably than do the English Control children. This more equitable outlook is evident also in the use of the *dumb . . . smart*, *not friendly . . . friendly*, and *slow . . . fast* scales where, in contrast, the English and French Control Classes emphasize differences between the two ethnic groups. These trends suggest to us that a more democratic and open-minded perception of the other ethnic group may derive from an immersion in a second language, coupled with protracted experiences with teachers who represent the other cultural group. The Experimental Class also makes more use of the *nice* end of the *not nice . . . nice* dimension when describing French Canadians. Still, they align themselves with the English Control Class when describing French Canadians as *fatter* than English Canadians. In sharp contrast, the French Controls emphasize the *thinness* and *smallness* of French Canadians, and particularly the *smallness* of themselves.

In one respect though, the Experimental children are less charitable than the English Controls: they feel French Canadians are less pretty than English Canadians. Note, however, that they also describe themselves relatively low in terms of prettiness, suggesting that this is not a particularly valued trait in their judgment. Whether this is the correct interpretation or not, it is clear that their self-views are less extreme than those of either the English or French Control groups on this trait.

Have the *self-conceptions* of children in the Experimental program been affected one way or the other by their experiences with another language and another culture? The evidence available at the end of grade II shows no signs of this sort. Relative to both Control Classes, the Experimentals see themselves as tallest, biggest, friendliest, and nicest. At the same time, they rate themselves as less thin, less pretty, and less extreme in goodness and smartness than do the two Control groups. The overall pattern of the Experimental children's attitudes, then, measured when they were still in small, neighborhood elementary school settings, was extremely fair and charitable: relative to the English and French Controls, they were less ethnocentric and biased toward their own ethnic group, although they had essentially healthy views of themselves as being particularly friendly, nice, tall, and big, but *not* extreme in smartness or goodness.

Attitudes of the Pilot Classes at Grade III

Do these generally favorable views of self and others change by the end of grade III? Remember that by grade III the Pilot Experimental Class had moved into a larger elementary school where several classes of French Canadian Protestant children of lower socioeconomic background followed their own separate educational program. For this reason it becomes difficult to isolate the effects of changes due to an extra year's schooling in the experimental program from changes attributable to that particular school and its special characteristics. The patterns described in Table 23 therefore may be due to either or both of these sources of influences.

In grade III the children were also asked to give their opinions of French people from France as a separate group. This addition, as will become evident, throws a new perspective on the development of the children's attitudes.

The ethnocentric trend noted in grade II appears again at III. For example, the French Control Class rates their own group (French Canadians) and the French from France as more *good* than English Canadians at the same time that the English Controls see both French Canadians and French French people as less *good* than their own group. The Pilot Experimentals likewise downgrade French Canadians and the French French, but again they are much less extreme than the English Controls in their ratings. The Experimental Class also shows an intermediary and less extreme outlook on the scales for *mean . . . kind, dumb . . . smart, sad . . . happy, slow . . . fast,* and *not handsome . . . handsome.* In each case the Pilot Experimentals in contrast to the English Controls have more temperate, less ethnocentric outlooks toward French people from Canada or France.

This more moderate ethnic outlook is of interest to us because it suggests that suspicion and distrust between groups may be reduced by this type of academic experience. Important as this trend is, the evidence is not fully convincing. For instance, the grade III French Controls who have *not* had corresponding academic experience with English also make very small differentiations between their own group, the French from France and the English Canadians. In other words, the French Control children also have a moderate outlook in the sense that they no longer display the strong ethnocentric comparisons they did at the grade II level. Nevertheless, the Experimentals and the French Controls both have more balanced outlooks when compared with the English Control children, who appear to remain as ethnocentric and suspicious at grade III as they were at II.

In certain other respects, the Experimental and English Control Classes have similar outlooks. Both see French Canadians as very *unfriendly* relative to

English Canadians, and both agree that the French from France are more friendly than French Canadians. The French Controls seem to view things quite differently: for them the English Canadians are the most unfriendly. Special research attention should be directed to this dimension and to its significance for grade III children. Reciprocated stereotypes of the sort seen here could seriously hamper between-group communication and understanding. We would like to know whether negative stereotypes typically start at this age level and whether they are reversible if opportunities for more social contact between groups are made available.

The Experimental and English Control groups also have a common view of the French from France as being *littler* than either the English or French Canadians. This, perhaps, has no special significance except that the opinion is widely held that European French people are on the average shorter or smaller than North Americans and it may or may not be true. What is more striking is the tendency for the Pilot French Control children at both grades II and III to see everyone and especially themselves as being *little*. What this peculiar self-conception means psychologically is a puzzle. It could simply be a matter of semantics: French children hear themselves referred to repeatedly as "les petits," not yet old enough or big enough to be considered as one of "les grands." On the other hand, it could have a deeper psychological significance.

In three instances, the grade III Pilot Experimental children make invidious distinctions between French Canadians and French people from France: French Canadians are seen as *dumber, meaner*, and *less friendly* than the French from France. These symptoms of denigration of local French people are worrisome and call for an explanation. It will be recalled that the various Experimental Classes were congregated into a large elementary school at the grade II level after having spent their kindergarten and first-grade years in special French classes in smaller neighborhood schools that were otherwise totally English-Canadian in makeup. The central school quickly developed a bilingual atmosphere not only because many Experimental Classes were by then being conducted in French, but also because several classes of French-Canadian children of the Protestant faith were attending the school and following their own separate program with their own cadre of teachers. There were, then, two aspects to the French atmosphere, one associated with the experiment itself, and the other with a somewhat strange subgroup of French-speaking youngsters who came mainly from socioeconomic backgrounds less advantaged than those of the Experimental children. In a short time, this segregated group of children had a reputation among administrators, staff, and other students of being academically inferior—which would be expected on socioeconomic grounds—and as the major source of discipline problems in the school. Even as they have been integrated into many of the Experimental Classes (other than the Pilot and Follow-up Classes), their reputation has not changed over time. The presence of this special subgroup and

Table 23

Attitude Profiles of the Pilot Classes at Grade III, 1969

Characteristic	Significance Levels		Mean Scores for Ratings of:			
			English Canadians	French Canadians	French from France	Me
1. Bad (1) – good (7)	G effect at .05	Experimentals:	4.68	3.77	3.82	5.14
	S effect at .01	English Controls:	4.81	2.22	3.19	4.93
	Interaction at .01	French Controls:	3.82	4.36	4.64	4.59
2. Dumb (1) – smart (7)	S effect at .01	Experimentals:	5.68	3.82	4.41	5.36
	Interaction at .01	English Controls:	5.90	3.55	3.90	5.83
		French Controls:	4.77	5.55	5.32	5.73
3. Not friendly (1) – friendly (7)	G effect at .05	Experimentals:	4.81	2.95	3.86	4.05
	S effect at .01	English Controls:	4.81	2.44	3.44	4.78
	Interaction at .01	French Controls:	3.73	4.82	4.82	4.86
4. Mean (1) – kind (7)	S effect at .01	Experimentals:	5.23	3.68	4.32	4.73
	Interaction at .05	English Controls:	4.55	3.03	3.07	4.93
		French Controls:	3.77	4.50	4.19	4.73
5. Slow (1) – fast (7)	G effect at .05	Experimentals:	4.14	4.05	3.82	4.36
	S effect at .01	English Controls:	4.66	2.86	2.48	5.00
	Interaction at .01	French Controls:	3.82	4.50	4.55	5.00
6. Little (1) – big (7)	G effect at .01	Experimentals:	4.29	4.43	3.57	3.86
		English Controls:	4.93	4.21	3.43	4.46
		French Controls:	3.67	3.56	3.17	3.22
7. Sad (1) – happy (7)	G effect at .05	Experimentals:	4.86	4.45	3.86	5.14
	S effect at .01	English Controls:	4.72	3.28	3.00	5.10
		French Controls:	4.64	4.91	4.27	5.00
8. Not handsome (1) – handsome (7)	G effect at .01	Experimentals:	5.00	4.36	3.82	3.77
	Interaction at .01	English Controls:	4.40	2.14	3.00	4.25
		French Controls:	4.00	4.52	4.81	4.71

the reputation they have had from the start could be significant in interpreting certain features of the attitudes of the Experimental children. For instance, they might think of French Canadians as dumb, relatively, if they were to draw only on their impressions of French Canadian youngsters in their school. In the same way, they might have the idea that French Canadians are meaner and less friendly. This line of speculation does not, of course, rule out an alternative interpretation, namely that the children are simply reflecting in their attitudes the tensions that exist between English- and French-speaking Canadians in the Montreal community (see Lambert, 1967; Lambert, 1971). It seems unlikely the teachers involved in the experiment have fostered such stereotypes. The Pilot Experimental Class had a teacher from France for their kindergarten year, but their teachers in grades I to III have all been French-Canadian, and each was admired and respected. Whatever the basic causes, this distinction drawn between French Canadians and French people from France may most profitably be regarded as a symptom of a need for more contact with and information about French Canada and its people.

Although it is difficult to eliminate stubborn and unfair stereotypes, they can best be modified in the early years of life, and active efforts to counteract such views should be introduced as early as possible into programs such as this. For instance, in grades V and VI the Experimental children will be introduced to Canadian history, and this could be an important occasion to help develop a more balanced and fairer view of Canada and its people by exposing the children to *two* versions of history, one presenting the French-Canadian perspective, taught by a French-Canadian teacher, and the other the English-Canadian point of view. To select and use exclusively one version of Canada's history prejudices the children from the start. Perhaps one of the most valuable lessons the children can learn is that history can very easily be biased and selective.

There is one other important theme apparent in Table 23, one that touches on the Experimental children's self-conceptions. In some respects, they differ from those in the English and French Control groups in that they rate themselves very high on the *good* and *happy* traits, but relatively low on the *friendly, fast, handsome,* and *kind* traits. What is striking about the last four characteristics is that, as self-ratings, they appear to be compromises between the ratings assigned to English Canadians and those assigned to people from France. This suggests that the Experimental children may locate themselves psychologically with reference to two cultural groups, the English-Canadian community, represented by their home life, and the French community (especially the European-French community) introduced to them through schooling. Compromises of this sort are especially clear in their ratings of *smartness* and *friendliness* (Table 23). For *handsomeness*, however, they rate themselves much closer to French people from France than to English Canadians. In contrast, the English and French Control children rate themselves very much as they rate their own membership groups, but never with reference to the other ethnic group. This may mean that the Experimental children's self-concepts are being modified and tempered by their experiences at school, that they are becoming *both* English Canadian and French in selected ways. We see nothing disconcerting in these trends because the Experimental children generally have a very healthy view of themselves.

Attitudes of the Follow-up Classes at Grade II

The reliability of these results must of course be checked with the Follow-up Classes. However, there have been substantive differences in the experiences of the Pilot and Follow-up Experimental Classes that could have influenced their ethnic attitudes differentially. For instance, those in the Follow-up Class moved into the larger elementary school one year earlier in their schooling, and they have had only teachers from Europe (France or Belgium) from kindergarten through grade II. Do they, then, have a different pattern of attitudes from the Pilot Experimentals? The information as of the end of grade II is given in Table 24. Note first that only four comparisons are statistically significant, and only two of these involve significant interactions. Nevertheless, a fairly clear set of comparisons emerge. On the *bad . . . good* dimension, the Experimental children see French Canadians as least *good* and the French French as most *good*, whereas the English Control do not rate any of the three ethnic groups very high on the *good* dimension. For the trait *smartness*, the Experimental children also downgrade French Canadians, comparatively, at the same time that they rate the French French at the same high level as they view their own ethnic group. They also view the French from France as more *friendly* and *prettier* than either the English or French Canadians. In contrast, the English Control children rate English Canadians highest on all four traits and yet they do not exaggerate distinctions between their own group and the others as the Pilot English Control Class did at grade II. The French Control children rank their own ethnic group highest on *goodness* and *smartness* but second to the French French on *friendliness* and *prettiness*. In general, then, the Follow-up Experimentals appear to have developed an attraction for French people from France who are seen either as equivalent to their own group in certain respects (*goodness* and *intelligence*) or somewhat more favorably than their own group in other respects (*friendliness* and *prettiness*).

These findings suggest that important nonethnocentric attitudes are being fostered in the course of the experimental program, but again it seems that the charity they have for French people is selectively directed toward the French from France. It is the Experimental children in particular, who, while expressing very favorable views of French people from France, see French Canadians as particularly *bad* and *dumb* even though essentially similar in *friendliness* and *prettiness* to English Canadians.

Table 24

Attitude Profiles of Follow-up Classes at Grade II, 1969

Characteristic	Significance Levels		English Canadians	Mean Scores for Ratings of: French Canadians	French from France	Me
1. Bad (1) – good (7)	G effect at .05 S effect at .01	Experimentals: English Controls: French Controls:	4.44 3.90 3.93	3.11 3.43 5.07	4.56 3.69 4.57	4.89 4.98 5.43
2. Dumb (1) – smart (7)	S effect at .01 Interaction at .01	Experimentals: English Controls: French Controls:	5.25 5.40 4.07	3.83 4.27 5.53	5.33 4.83 5.33	6.17 5.94 6.33
3. Not friendly (1) – friendly (7)	S effect at .01 Interaction at .05	Experimentals: English Controls: French Controls:	3.89 4.13 3.38	3.69 3.32 4.77	4.28 3.66 5.15	4.58 5.17 5.54
4. Not pretty (1) – pretty (7)	G effect at .05 S effect at .01	Experimentals: English Controls: French Controls:	4.86 4.85 5.23	4.74 3.96 5.47	5.54 4.52 5.65	5.63 5.74 5.94

With regard to their self-conceptions, the Follow-up Experimentals, relative to the other groups of children, see themselves as least *good*, least *friendly*, and least *pretty* (although in each case their ratings still fall on the positive side of the scales) and intermediate in *smartness*. Since all the groups tend to rate "me" more favorably than they rate their own ethnic group, it is difficult to determine in this case if the Experimental children's ratings reflect a perceptual similarity between themselves and the French French (as appears to be the case for *friendliness* and *prettiness*) or whether they too simply rate "me" more favorably than they do any ethnic group.

We have already seen that the parents of those in the Experimental Classes wanted their children to learn French in order to meet a new group of people, to come to understand a different way of life, and to develop new friendships. However they seemed reluctant to have their children identify with the other group to the extent of "thinking and behaving as French people do." Our analysis of the children's attitudes and self-conceptions, however, suggests that something very much like identification and emulation may be taking place as a consequence of the home-school language-switch program. Except for certain biased and nasty views of French Canadians, the changes, in general, are charitable and democratic ones. But the major point is that changes do take place, signifying that becoming bilingual very likely involves more than merely mastering the linguistic code of a foreign people. Attitude changes and identification with members of the other group are also very likely to take place.

Attitudes of the Follow-up Classes at Grade III

At the end of their third year in the program (the spring of 1970), the attitudes of the children in the Follow-up Classes were assessed again, this time with the set of bipolar rating scales listed in Table 25. Consider first their self-ratings (i.e., their profiles of ratings for the concept "me"). All three groups have a generally favorable view of themselves as being intelligent, strong, friendly, affectionate, industrious, kind, happy, humble, self-confident, pleasant, calm, and not overly talkative. There is a significant difference among groups on only one trait—good looks—and it is the French Control pupils who view themselves as less good-looking relative to the views the Experimentals and English Controls have of themselves. Still, the overall similarity of profiles for the three groups of children lends strong support to the notion that this type of intensive learning through the medium of a second language does not affect pupils' self-images in any discernable way.

The similarity of self-views also serves as a convenient base line to examine each group's perceptions of the English Canadians, the French Canadians and the European French. First, there is no consensus of views of English Canadians. In fact, there are significant group differences on most of the rating scales (see Table 26), owing largely to the distinctive views held by the French Control

Table 25

Grade III Follow-up Pupils' Self-views

| | Mean Ratings Given By: | | | | |
Trait	Experi-mentals	English Controls	French Controls	F	df
1. intelligent (7) . . . stupid (1)	6.47	6.48	6.00	0.90	2,75
2. strong (7) . . . weak (1)	6.30	5.77	5.82	0.87	2,75
3. friendly (7) . . . unfriendly (1)	6.50	6.65	5.76	2.74	2,75
4. affectionate (7) . . . unaffectionate (1)	5.83	5.48	6.24	0.83	2,75
5. industrious (7) . . . lazy (1)	5.83	6.13	5.82	0.28	2,75
6. kind (7) . . . mean (1)	6.13	6.58	6.35	1.32	2,75
7. happy (7) . . . sad (1)	6.50	6.52	5.94	1.43	2,75
8. humble (7) . . . proud (1)	5.37	4.32	5.47	1.86	2,75
9. possesses self-confidence (7) . . . lacks self-confidence (1)	5.47	5.19	5.53	0.21	2,75
10. good looking (7) . . . ugly (1)	6.40	6.35	5.41	3.14*	2,75
11. pleasant (7) . . . unpleasant (1)	6.00	6.58	6.18	1.64	2,75
12. calm (7) . . . emotional (1)	5.80	5.52	6.12	0.54	2,75
13. talkative (7) . . . nontalkative (1)	4.50	4.55	3.29	1.55	2,75

* p <.05

pupils. Relative to the Experimentals and the English Controls, the Follow-up French Controls perceive English Canadians as more stupid, unaffectionate, mean, unpleasant, lazy, ugly, emotional, and less strong, less friendly, and less happy. In contrast, the Experimentals have a particularly favorable view of English Canadians, their own ethnolinguistic group.

Similarly, the three groups of children differ in their attitudes toward French Canadians. Note in Table 27 that the French Control pupils view French Canadians more favorably than either the Experimentals or English Controls, seeing them as more intelligent, strong, friendly, affectionate, industrious, kind, happy, humble, self-confident, good-looking, pleasant, and calm, but less talkative. In each case, the comparison is statistically significant.

Table 26

Grade III Follow-up Pupils' Attitudes toward "English Canadians"

Trait	Experimentals	English Controls	French Controls	F	df
		Mean Ratings Given By:			
1. intelligent (7) . . . stupid (1)	6.03	5.64 —— 3.94		10.84**	2,77
2. strong (7) . . . weak (1)	5.77	5.24	4.47	3.79*	2,77
3. friendly (7) . . . unfriendly (1)	6.27	5.42 —— 4.24		9.79**	2,77
4. affectionate (7) . . . unaffectionate (1)	5.53	5.39 ——3.18		10.08**	2,77
5. industrious (7) . . . lazy (1)	5.63	5.64 —— 3.94		5.37**	2,77
6. kind (7) . . . mean (1)	6.33	5.82 —— 3.88		13.80**	2,77
7. happy (7) . . . sad (1)	5.80	6.00 ——4.88		3.30	2,77
8. humble (7) . . . proud (1)	5.57	4.73	4.29	2.52	2,77
9. possesses self-confidence (7) . . . lacks self-confidence (1)	4.67	4.79	4.29	0.33	2,77
10. good-looking (7) . . . ugly (1)	5.83	5.67 —— 3.94		7.23**	2,77
11. pleasant (7) . . . unpleasant (1)	5.77	5.58 —— 2.24		35.73**	2,77
12. calm (7) . . . emotional (1)	5.27	4.67	3.24	5.83**	2,77
13. talkative (7) . . . nontalkative (1)	5.63	5.39	5.65	0.18	2,77

* p <.05

** p <.01

As for European-French people (Table 28), all three groups of pupils have essentially the same attitude profile, and in general the mean ratings fall near the neutral point of each scale. In other words, they all see the European French as neither intelligent nor stupid, neither strong nor weak, and so forth.

In summary, then, the three groups of children present very similar attitudes toward European-French people and essentially similar self-views. it is their attitudes of English and French Canadians that diverge in interesting ways.

Table 27

Grade III Follow-up Pupils' Attitudes toward "French Canadians"

		Mean Ratings Given By:				
	Trait	Experi-mentals	English Controls	French Controls	F	df
1.	intelligent (7) ... stupid (1)	3.07	3.00 —— 6.18		19.01**	2,77
2.	strong (7) ... weak (1)	3.03	3.24 —— 5.65		10.90**	2,77
3.	friendly (7) ... unfriendly (1)	3.40	3.85	5.29	4.36*	2,77
4.	affectionate (7) ... unaffectionate (1)	3.90	3.82 —— 5.59		4.30*	2,77
5.	industrious (7) ... lazy (1)	3.17	2.97 —— 5.65		12.33**	2,77
6.	kind (7) ... mean (1)	4.37	3.45 —— 6.12		12.32**	2,77
7.	happy (7) ... sad (1)	4.23	4.06 —— 5.82		4.76*	2,77
8.	humble (7) ... proud (1)	3.67	3.94 —— 5.47		4.81*	2,77
9.	possesses self-confidence (7) ... lacks self-confidence (1)	4.10	4.52	5.65	3.75*	2,77
10.	good-looking (7) ... ugly (1)	3.83	4.00 —— 6.00		6.80*	2,77
11.	pleasant (7) ... unpleasant (1)	3.57	3.82 —— 6.18		10.05**	2,77
12.	calm (7) ... emotional (1)	3.20	3.15 —— 5.82		10.98**	2,77
13.	talkative (7) ... nontalkative (1)	4.67	5.24 —— 3.12		5.03*	2,77

* p <.05

** p <.01

Attitudes of the Pilot Classes at Grade IV

The attitudes of the Pilot Classes at the grade IV level were assessed in the same fashion as that just described for the Follow-ups: they gave their personal feelings toward English Canadians, French Canadians, European-French people, and themselves (i.e., the concept of "myself"), using a series of adjectival rating scales. Considering first their self-descriptions (Table 29), the three groups of

Table 28

Grade III Follow-up Pupils' Attitudes toward "European-French People"

	Trait	Experi-mentals	English Controls	French Controls	F	df
		Mean Ratings Given By:				
1.	intelligent (7) . . . stupid (1)	3.80	4.58	4.76	1.74	2,77
2.	strong (7) . . . weak (1)	4.10	4.82	4.53	1.18	2,77
3.	friendly (7) . . . unfriendly (1)	4.87	5.00	4.88	0.04	2,77
4.	affectionate (7) . . . unaffectionate (1)	4.17	4.58	5.06	1.07	2,77
5.	industrious (7) . . . lazy (1)	3.77	4.85	4.18	2.00	2,77
6.	kind (7) . . . mean (1)	4.03	5.09	4.88	2.01	2,77
7.	happy (7) . . . sad (1)	4.57	5.36	4.35	1.79	2,77
8.	humble (7) . . . proud (1)	4.17	4.12	3.65	0.33	2,77
9.	possesses self-confidence (7) . . . lacks self-confidence (1)	3.80	4.94	4.71	2.88	2,77
10.	good-looking (7) . . . ugly (1)	4.07	4.97	3.82	2.29	2,77
11.	pleasant (7) . . . unpleasant (1)	4.27	5.42	4.47	2.88	2,77
12.	calm (7) . . . emotional (1)	3.97	4.48	4.06	0.57	2,77
13.	talkative (7) . . . nontalkative (1)	4.13	5.18 —— 3.88		3.27*	2,77

* $p < .05$

pupils had essentially similar patterns of ratings. They all saw themselves as. relatively intelligent, strong, friendly, affectionate, industrious, kind, happy, humble, self-confident, good-looking, pleasant, and calm. On one trait only was there a difference, and in this instance the French Controls, relative to the two English-Canadian groups, rated themselves as less talkative. The major finding, however, is that all three groups have basically similar views of themselves, healthy and optimistic ones at that. Thus the egos of the bilingually instructed pupils have apparently not been disturbed in any discernable way as a result of their particular educational experience.

Table 29

Grade IV Pilot Pupils' Self-views

		Mean Ratings Given By:			
Trait	Experi-mentals	English Controls	French Controls	F	df
1. intelligent (7) . . . stupid (1)	6.55	5.94	6.33	1.18	2,63
2. strong (7) . . . weak (1)	6.00	5.65	5.47	0.38	2,63
3. friendly (7) . . . unfriendly (1)	6.55	6.35	5.87	1.13	2,63
4. affectionate (7) . . . unaffectionate (1)	6.00	6.16	5.53	0.80	2,63
5. industrious (7) . . . lazy (1)	5.70	5.81	6.07	0.17	2,63
6. kind (7) . . . mean (1)	6.60	6.13	6.13	0.76	2,63
7. happy (7) . . . sad (1)	6.15	6.35	6.73	0.72	2,63
8. humble (7) . . . proud (1)	5.65	4.29	5.80	2.94	2,63
9. possesses self-confidence (7) . . . lacks self-confidence (1)	5.70	5.71	5.27	0.32	2,63
10. good-looking (7) . . . ugly (1)	6.55	6.06	6.07	0.68	2,63
11. pleasant (7) . . . unpleasant (1)	6.35	5.90	5.73	0.75	2,63
12. calm (7) . . . emotional (1)	5.65	5.29	4.93	0.40	2,63
13. talkative (7) . . . nontalkative (1)	4.70	4.35 ⎿_____ 2.53 ⏌		4.11*	2,63

* p <.05

All three groups also have a very similar and favorable conception of English Canadians (Table 30). The Experimental, English Control, and the French Control Classes each describe English Canadians as essentially intelligent, strong, friendly, affectionate, industrious, kind, happy, humble, self-confident, pleasant, and calm. Significant differences turned up for two traits only (*good-looking . . . ugly* and *talkative . . . nontalkative*), and on these the French Controls, relative to the Experimental and English Control pupils, rate English Canadians as less good-looking and less talkative.

Table 30

Grade IV Pilot Pupils' Attitudes toward "English Canadians"

Trait	Mean Ratings Given By:			F	df
	Experi- mentals	English Controls	French Controls		
1. intelligent (7)... stupid (1)	5.70	5.68	5.07	0.72	2,63
2. strong (7)... weak (1)	5.50	5.32	4.73	1.00	2,63
3. friendly (7)... unfriendly (1)	5.90	5.45	4.87	1.77	2,63
4. affectionate (7)... unaffectionate (1)	5.40	5.29	4.40	1.78	2,63
5. industrious (7)... lazy (1)	5.10	5.35	4.80	0.39	2,63
6. kind (7)... mean (1)	5.60	5.48	5.40	0.09	2,63
7. happy (7)... sad (1)	5.95	5.39	5.40	0.83	2,63
8. humble (7)... proud (1)	5.00	4.90	5.00	0.02	2,63
9. possesses self-confidence (7)... lacks self-confidence (1)	4.60	4.74	4.73	0.04	2,63
10. good-looking (7)... ugly (1)	6.35	6.00 —————— 4.07		13.06**	2,63
11. pleasant (7)... unpleasant (1)	5.90	5.19	4.87	1.33	2,63
12. calm (7)... emotional (1)	4.60	4.68	4.20	0.30	2,63
13. talkative (7)... nontalkative (1)	5.40	5.58 —————— 3.60		5.47**	2,63

** p <.01

There are important attitude changes reflected here especially for the case of the Pilot French Control group. Comparing their attitudes at grades III and IV, it seems these children have developed, or at least give an expression of, a much more favorable view of English Canadians, especially in terms of kindness and friendliness. It will be interesting to see whether a similar improvement appears with the Follow-up Classes at the end of grade IV.

As in grade III, the grade IV pupils again differ markedly in their perceptions of French Canadians (Table 31); in fact, statistically significant group differences

Table 31

Grade IV Pilot Pupils' Attitudes toward "French Canadians"

	Mean Ratings Given By:				
Trait	Experi-mentals	English Controls	French Controls	F	df
1. intelligent (7)... stupid (1)	2.50	3.87	5.47	9.37**	2,63
2. strong (7)... weak (1)	3.50	3.45 ——6.00		9.25**	2,63
3. friendly (7)... unfriendly (1)	2.65	3.13 ——5.87		12.76**	2,63
4. affectionate (7)... unaffectionate (1)	3.15	3.74	4.87	3.10	2,63
5. industrious (7)... lazy (1)	2.65	3.42 —— 6.07		16.76**	2,63
6. kind (7)... mean (1)	3.55	3.48 ——5.47		5.63**	2,63
7. happy (7)... sad (1)	3.80	3.61 ——5.80		6.40**	2,63
8. humble (7)... proud (1)	3.25	4.19	5.60	5.65**	2,63
9. possesses self-confidence (7)... lacks self-confidence (1)	3.50	4.39	5.60	5.09**	2,63
10. good-looking (7)... ugly (1)	3.30	3.39 ——5.93		9.00**	2,63
11. pleasant (7)... unpleasant (1)	3.50	3.71 —— 5.87		6.81**	2,63
12. calm (7)... emotional (1)	2.95	3.52 ——5.27		6.61**	2,63
13. talkative (7)... nontalkative (1)	4.90	4.90	3.87	1.05	2,63

** $p < .01$

were found for eleven of the thirteen traits. The French Controls consistently rated French Canadians more favorably than did either the English Controls or the Experimentals. Both the English Controls and the Experimentals were caustic in their reactions, describing French Canadians as relatively stupid, weak, unfriendly, lazy, mean, sad, proud, nonconfident, ugly, unpleasant, and emotional. There were no significant group differences for the traits *affectionate . . . not affectionate* and *talkative . . . nontalkative,* the ratings in these two cases being essentially neutral.

Table 32

Grade IV Pilot Pupils' Attitudes toward "European-French People"

		Mean Ratings Given By				
	Trait	Experi-mentals	English Controls	French Controls	F	df
1.	intelligent (7) ... stupid (1)	3.60	4.13	4.27	0.54	2,63
2.	strong (7) ... weak (1)	4.40	3.87	4.67	0.81	2,63
3.	friendly (7) ... unfriendly (1)	4.25	4.06	4.80	0.65	2,63
4.	affectionate (7) ... unaffectionate (1)	4.65	4.13	4.87	0.90	2,63
5.	industrious (7) ... lazy (1)	3.85	3.74	4.60	0.92	2,63
6.	kind (7) ... mean (1)	4.30	3.94 ——	5.80	5.00**	2,63
7.	happy (7) ... sad (1)	4.55	4.26	4.87	0.51	2,63
8.	humble (7) ... proud (1)	3.95	4.84	4.87	1.53	2,63
9.	possesses self-confidence (7) ... lacks self-confidence (1)	4.25	4.42	4.53	0.12	2,63
10.	good-looking (7) ... ugly (1)	4.10	4.19	4.93	0.90	2,63
11.	pleasant (7) ... unpleasant (1)	4.60	4.29	4.93	0.67	2,63
12.	calm (7) ... emotional (1)	4.30	4.23	4.67	0.27	2,63
13.	talkative (7) ... nontalkative (1)	4.60	4.42	3.33	1.74	2,63

** $p < .01$

The reactions of all three groups to European-French people are remarkably similar (Table 32), although in general they rate European-French people in a neutral or slightly positive fashion on the various traits. The only significant group difference was due to the French Controls, who, in comparison to the English Controls, considered the European French to be especially kind.

The Children's Attitudes: Summary and Conclusions

Several important summary statements can be made about the changes in the children's attitudes. After grade II, there is no further indication of a moderation in the attitudes of the pupils in the Experimental Classes toward French people. Instead at both grade III and IV levels, we find that their attitude profiles are substantially similar to those of the English Control Classes. The pattern of moderation in the attitudes of the Experimental children in the earlier grades was a statistically reliable one (see Reynolds, Wargny, and Lambert, 1970), and the different pattern noted beyond grade II suggests to us that changes taking place within the youngsters themselves and in their social environment may have contributed to the year-to-year variations.

What might these changes be? Our answers to this question are, of course, speculations only, but they express our hunches and tentative interpretations. First, the patterns noted for both the Pilot and Follow-up Experimental groups in the 1970 testing can be looked on as "perfectly normal" reactions of nine- or ten-year-olds. Their attitudes, in other words, are much like those of English-speaking pupils attending conventional school programs, in the sense that their conceptions of themselves are very favorable and show no signs of ambiguity, and their views of their "own" ethnolinguistic group reflect as much pride as do those of the English Control children. Likewise their attitudes toward French-Canadian and European-French people are essentially the same as those of the English Control pupils. It is difficult from these data to suggest that because of their French-oriented academic training, they are socially lost and in search of an identity.

What seems to us a more plausible interpretation of the state of mind of third and fourth grade Experimental children is that they are anxious to remain close to the norms of their own peer group with regard to feelings toward own-group and other-groups. For example, they may be concerned about appearing too "French" in outlook, and as a consequence give no special place to French people when questioned about their attitudes. Many very recent events suggest that there may well have been stronger social pressures to pay attention to the peer-group attitudinal norm in 1970 than there had been previously. In the 1970 testings, we found the Experimental and English Control groups at both grade levels expressing a generally neutral to slightly favorable attitude toward European French, but relatively negative opinions about French Canadians. Unfavorable views of French Canadians have been found consistently in earlier research on the attitudes of adults in the Quebec setting (see Lambert, 1967; Lambert, Frankel, and Tucker, 1966), but because they show themselves at this young age and appear slightly exaggerated for the Experimental Pilot Class, they call for special comment.

First, it should be emphasized that the educational aim of the program is to develop competence in both Canadian and European forms of French by having teachers from Europe as well as from Canada, and by making certain that the texts used present *both* cultural centers of French in a very favorable light. The relatively unfavorable attitudes toward French Canadians noted in 1970 were more likely due to factors other than biases of teachers, text materials, or the like. In our opinion, the salient factors were the Experimental children's experience with unrepresentative samples of French-Canadian young people attending their school, and the current tensions between English- and French-speaking residents of the greater Montreal community.

As mentioned, the children in the Experimental Classes attended school with French-Canadian Protestant youngsters who come from lower social-class homes in most cases. As a group, they have a generally lower level of school achievement, and have developed a reputation among the English-speaking administration, staff, and students of being academically and culturally behind, and difficult to discipline. If these were the only or the major proportion of French-Canadian young people with whom the Experimental children came into contact, their experiences would obviously be limited to an unrepresentative sample of French Canadians, a sample that could easily bias the children's attitudes. If we assume that this bias did play a role in the formation of the Experimental children's attitudes, there are still no simple solutions to the problems that follow from it. For example, we discouraged the mixing of French Protestant pupils in either the Pilot or Follow-up Classes because we did not want the Experimental Classes to have an advantage over the Controls of being able to use French with native speakers at school. Had the classes been mixed, the consequences on the children's attitudes and stereotypes might have been worse. Getting to know others through regular face-to-face contact need not generate respect and affection (see Jones and Lambert, 1967), especially when there is a strong likelihood that negative stereotypes about the intelligence of French Canadians could, with a biased sample, actually be confirmed through personal experience. This, of course, is a major social problem today for all members of underprivileged groups, and practical solutions have yet to be worked out.

But there are other factors very likely involved in the shaping of the attitudes of the children in the Experimental program. The tension between English and French Canadians in Montreal has become progressively more hostile over the past ten years (see Lambert, 1970), and one can expect that the suspicions which adults have of the other ethnic group will filter down to children. Many recent incidents have contributed to the English Canadians' suspicions and fear of French Canadians. Bombs have been placed in mailboxes, homes, and businesses in the English-speaking areas of the city; louder and more hostile demands for French unilingualism have become common, and were especially prominent in the political campaigns of all provincial parties in the spring election of 1970; demands and demonstrations have been made to make McGill, a major English-language university, into a French-language institution; the provincial government is now reluctant to allow immigrant families to have their children schooled in English; and French, it is said, must become the language of work throughout the province. These isolated issues became integrated into a political movement in 1970 and the further tension it generated most certainly would have touched the lives of the English-Canadian children in our study.

Social tension, of course, is a reliable characteristic of settings where people urgently need programs of mutual understanding such as the one described here. For us, it is reassuring to realize that the children in our experiment are able to progress so well in learning the other group's language in spite of the tense social climate. In our view, these children have been given the opportunity to become as French and as Québecois as any French-speaking youngster, and, at the same time, as English Canadian in language and outlook as any English-speaking youngster.

For many residents of the province, the future of the French language in Quebec and in Canada is a matter of the greatest importance, even though the outlook is not always encouraging. One of the disillusioned is V. Prince, a French-Canadian editorialist, who recently summed up his views as follows:

> Avec l'industrialisation, l'urbanisation, la télévision, la communication par satellites, aucune minorité ne peut vivre isolée comme autrefois, à moins de se cantonner dans les reserves. Il lui faut, si elle veut préserver son identité, se doter de moyens bien supérieurs à ceux dont elle disposait jusqu'ici.
>
> Est-il encore possible de renverser la vapeur? Les froides statistiques démographiques apportent une réponse nettement négative. Mais ces statistiques ne tiennent pas complètement compte de l'élément humain. Il y a, par exemple, dans diverses régions du pays, un facteur nouveau depuis quelques années: l'éveil de la jeunesse. Ceci se vérifie, notamment, au Manitoba, en Ontario et au Nouveau-Brunswick. Les jeunes, plus scolarisés, ne laissent plus aux élites traditionelles le soin de défendre seules la cause du français. Ils bousculent même leurs aînés. Robert Maheu a tenu compte dans ses projections, de l'adoucissement récent des lois scolaires de plusieurs provinces. Nous nous demandons pourtant s'il en a suffisamment soupesé les conséquences.
>
> Il y a aussi un autre phénomène qui n'est peut-être pas aussi important mais qu'il est probablement à propos de souligner quand même: l'intérêt plus marqué d'un certain nombre d'anglophones pour le français. Plusieurs d'entre eux s'efforcent d'apprendre la seconde langue officielle du pays.[1]

As we see it, few other groups of anglophones, if any, will have shown as much interest in Quebec and in Canada as the children and the parents

---

[1]V. Prince, "L'avenir du français au Canada et au Québec," *Le Devoir*, 30 décembre 1970, p. A-15.

involved in this experiment. The children have become fully competent in French with little apparent effort, personal sacrifice, or loss of identity. In fact, at the grade III and IV levels they appear almost stubbornly like the English and French Control children in their self-views and social attitudes. But since we are convinced that the goal of biculturalism or other-culture sensitivity must be linked to the goal of bilingualism, we believe that the Experimental pupils during the next few years can easily develop a sensitivity and positive outlook toward members of both of Canada's major ethnolinguistic groups, in spite of the social tensions in the community. This type of attitude change will probably not result from the children's school experience only. More likely it will be an offshoot of the experiences made possible by the educational program. With their highly developed language skills, the pupils should by now be able to seek out and come into contact with an increasingly diverse sample of both English and French Canadians and this should broaden their sociocultural perspectives. In the next chapter we turn directly to the Pilot and Follow-up pupils at the end of their fifth and fourth years, respectively, to see what *they* think about the program and the influence it has had on them.

Chapter Nine

Pupils' Own Views of the Program

By now we have looked at the effects of the home-school language-switch program from a variety of points of view—how it affects the children's cognitive and linguistic development, their attitudes, and so forth. However, we have not yet examined the program's overall impact from the viewpoints of the pupils involved, which could very well be the most important and most interesting slant of all. The following questions prompted this phase of the investigation: Do the children involved in the experiment feel that they are making real progress in French? That is, do they feel that French has become a functional language for them? If they do, to what uses have they been able to put the language? For instance, have they been able to penetrate the social borders of the surrounding French-speaking society? Do they feel that they have had an overdose of French? In other words, has their intensive experience with French been a burden so that now they are eager to drop out of the program and return to the conventional English-language educational stream?

To assess the children's personal views of such matters, we devised a "Pupils' Opinions" questionnaire and administered it to the Pilot and Follow-up Classes in the spring of 1971, that is, near the end of grades V and IV, respectively. The questionnaire was worded to be equally appropriate for the children in the grade V and IV English Control Classes, who, it will be recalled, have studied "French as a Second Language" from grade I on. Thus, by using a common set of questions, we were able to compare the impressions of both the Experimental and English Control children concerning the French training they have received so far.

The children completed the questionnaire during a regular class period at school. In Table 33 we summarize the children's responses to each of the questions asked them. The Chi-square (X^2) statistic was used to test the significance of the differences between the responses of the Experimental and English Control children.

Table 33

Pupils' Opinions of Elementary School French Programs

[Instructions accompanying each questionnaire:] Some schools in the greater Montreal area have programs of French for pupils in kindergarten and elementary classes. You are one of those who have started French early. Now we want to know how far along in French you think you are, and how well you can speak and understand the language.

The questions to follow are simple ones, but there are no right or wrong answers to them. We want you to read each question carefully, and when you are sure that you understand it, answer it as well as you can. We want to have your own personal answers because pupils' opinions about the French program in your school are the most important of all. If you don't understand a question, just raise your hand.

First, how well can you speak French? Better than English or worse? Put an X in the space below that says how well you can speak French compared to English. [The entries below are percentages. The X^2 values and the significance levels are given at the right; n.s. means not significant; * = $p < .05$, ** = $p < .01$, and *** = $p < .001$].

1. In *speaking*, I am:

	much better in French than in English	a little better in French than in English	about as good in French as in English	a little better in English than in French	much better in English than in French	X^2
Experimental Grade IV	5	10	29	35	13	28.94***
English Control Grade IV	0	0	0	36	65	
Experimental Grade V	0	12	24	60	4	37.41***
English Control Grade V	0	0	8	4	88	

Table 33 (cont.)
Pupils' Opinions of Elementary School French Programs

2. In *understanding* spoken French, I am:

	much better in French than in English	a little better in French than in English	about as good in French as in English	a little better in English than in French	much better in English than in French	X^2
Experimental Grade IV	5	10	43	30	13	17.80**
English Control Grade IV	0	0	13	44	44	
Experimental Grade V	4	17	50	25	4	25.30***
English Control Grade V	0	0	7	37	56	

3. In *reading*, I am:

	much better in French than in English	a little better in French than in English	about as good in French as in English	a little better in English than in French	much better in English than in French	X^2
Experimental Grade IV	0	18	48	28	8	18.38**
English Control Grade IV	0	0	28	25	47	
Experimental Grade V	4	12	48	28	8	30.76***
English Control Grade V	0	0	4	15	81	

4. In *writing*, I am:

	much better in French than in English	a little better in French than in English	about as good in French as in English	a little better in English than in French	much better in English than in French	X^2
Experimental Grade IV	10	10	50	23	8	22.27***
English Control Grade IV	0	0	32	13	55	
Experimental Grade V	4	32	36	28	0	28.94***
English Control Grade V	0	4	7	22	67	

Next, we want to know how you have been able to use your French outside of school.

5. How often do you watch French T.V. programs?

	I only watch French programs	I watch more in French than in English	I watch some in French and some in English	I watch more in English than in French	I only watch English programs	X^2
Experimental Grade IV	0	3	33	53	13	1.25 n.s.
English Control Grade IV	0	3	22	56	19	
Experimental Grade V	0	0	20	68	12	2.27 n.s.
English Control Grade V	4	0	19	54	23	

6. How well do you understand radio and T.V. programs in French?

	I understand every word	I can't follow everything, but I do get most of it	I can only get the general idea, not many of the words	X^2
Experimental Grade IV	10	73	18	11.01**
English Control Grade IV	0	48	52	
Experimental Grade V	8	92	0	27.25***
English Control Grade V	0	31	69	

7. How often do you see French movies, either on T.V. or in a cinema?

In the past year, about how many French movies have you seen (outside of school)?

Experimental Grade IV	2.38
English Control Grade IV	5.88
Experimental Grade V	2.52
English Control Grade V	4.11

In the past year, about how many English movies have you seen (outside of school)?

Experimental Grade IV	19.68
English Control Grade IV	32.85
Experimental Grade V	18.76
English Control Grade V	34.22

Table 33 (cont.)

Pupils' Opinions of Elementary School French Programs

8. How well do you understand French movies?

	I understand every word	I can't follow everything, but I do get most of it	I can only get the general idea, not many of the words	X^2
Experimental Grade IV	11	69	20	19.26***
English Control Grade IV	0	28	72	
Experimental Grade V	4	84	12	18.41***
English Control Grade V	0	30	70	

9. How good are you as a translator from *French to English?*

	I can translate everything	I can translate most things	I can translate some things, but not that many	I can hardly translate anything	I can't translate anything at all	X^2
Experimental Grade IV	8	65	25	3	0	27.83***
English Control Grade IV	0	13	59	25	3	
Experimental Grade V	4	92	4	0	0	27.24***
English Control Grade V	4	22	44	26	4	

10. How often have you had an occasion to be the translator for your family?

	I've had many occasions	I've had some occasions	I've had only a few occasions	I've had hardly any occasions	I've had no occasions at all	X^2
Experimental Grade IV	40	23	13	18	8	20.88***
English Control Grade IV	0	19	19	28	34	
Experimental Grade V	36	44	12	4	4	26.39***
English Control Grade V	4	7	22	33	33	

11. Do you think you could now teach your brothers or your sisters to speak and to understand French?

	Yes, I could be a very good teacher	Yes, I could teach them quite a lot	Yes, I could teach them a little	No, I couldn't teach them at all	X^2
Experimental Grade IV	16	59	24	5	26.72***
English Control Grade IV	0	13	53	34	
Experimental Grade V	4	46	46	4	10.58**
English Control Grade V	0	15	50	35	

12. How often have you tried to be the French "teacher" in your family?

	They ask me to teach them very often	They ask me to teach them sometimes, but not very often	They only ask me what certain words mean	They never ask me to help them in French at all	X^2
Experimental Grade IV	5	30	48	18	12.41***
English Control Grade IV	0	9	38	53	
Experimental Grade V	8	32	56	4	15.99**
English Control Grade V	0	7	44	48	

13. During the past year, how often have you spoken French at home with your parents or your brothers and sisters?

	I speak French with them as often as I speak English	I speak French with them a little bit each day	I hardly ever speak French with them	I never speak French with them	X^2
Experimental Grade IV	10	50	38	3	12.25**
English Control Grade IV	0	25	56	19	
Experimental Grade V	0	64	32	4	14.72**
English Control Grade V	0	15	56	30	

Table 33 (cont.)
Pupils' Opinions of Elementary School French Programs

14. Have you ever been asked by a French-speaking person to translate from *French to English?*
If yes, does it happen often?

	Yes	No	Very Often	Only Once in a While	X^2
Experimental Grade IV	65	35	28	72	3.17 n.s.
English Control Grade IV	33	67	0	100	
Experimental Grade V	72	28	22	78	
English Control Grade V	41	59	20	80	0.02 n.s.

15. When you talk with your classmates (who know French as well as you do), which language do you use when you meet after school or on the way home, or even in class when the teacher can't hear?

	Always French	Most of the time French	Sometimes English sometimes French	Most of the time English	Always English	X^2
Experimental Grade IV	0	0	40	28	33	11.73*
English Control Grade IV	0	0	10	19	71	
Experimental Grade V	0	0	32	56	12	22.61***
English Control Grade V	0	0	7	15	78	

16. Do you think any of your family members (your mother, father, sisters, or brothers) would make fun of you if they heard you speaking French?

	Yes	No	X^2
Experimental Grade IV	13	88	0.22 n.s.
English Control Grade IV	9	91	
Experimental Grade V	16	84	1.36 n.s.
English Control Grade V	30	70	

17. Do you think any of *your friends* would make fun of you if they heard you speaking French?

	Yes	No	X^2
Experimental Grade IV	15	85	0.48 n.s.
English Control Grade IV	21	79	
Experimental Grade V	24	76	0.29 n.s.
English Control Grade V	31	69	

18a. Now that you are learning to speak and understand French, have you met any French-speaking young people in your neighborhood?

	Yes	No	X^2	How Many?
Experimental Grade IV	90	10	1.78 n.s.	6.08
English Control Grade IV	79	21		5.93
Experimental Grade V	96	4	6.64*	7.45
English Control Grade V	68	32		8.79

18b. If yes, which language do you speak together?

	Almost always French	Sometimes French, sometimes English	Almost always English	X^2
Experimental Grade IV	53	39	8	3.29 n.s.
English Control Grade IV	31	62	8	
Experimental Grade V	63	38	0	15.00***
English Control Grade V	13	50	38	

Table 33 (cont.)

Pupils' Opinions of Elementary School French Programs

19a. Now that you are learning to speak and understand French, have you met any French-speaking young people at camp, or on summer visits?

	Yes	No	X^2	How Many?
Experimental Grade IV	38	63	1.47 n.s.	2.40
English Control Grade IV	24	76		.89
Experimental Grade V	42	54	0.00 n.s.	2.00
English Control Grade V	44	56		3.95

19b. If yes, which language do you speak together?

	Almost always French	Sometimes French, sometimes English	X^2	Almost always English	X^2
Experimental Grade IV	53	33		13	2.39 n.s.
English Control Grade IV	25	36		36	
Experimental Grade V	50	50		0	3.54 n.s.
English Control Grade V	11	67		22	

20. Have you made any *very good friends* who are French-speaking?

	Yes	No	X^2	How Many?
Experimental Grade IV	85	15	9.63**	3.00
English Control Grade IV	52	48		2.00
Experimental Grade V	88	12	7.96*	3.14
English Control Grade V	52	48		3.40

21. Would you rather have English-speaking or French-speaking friends?

	I would rather have English-speaking friends than French-speaking ones	I would like to have some English-speaking and some French-speaking friends	I would rather have French-speaking friends than English-speaking ones	X^2
Experimental Grade IV	20	78	3	5.78 n.s.
English Control Grade IV	43	50	6	
Experimental Grade V	0	100	0	13.49**
English Control Grade V	38	58	4	

22. Suppose you met a French-speaking boy (or girl) at a skating rink, would you speak to him (or her) first or wait for him to speak to you first?

	I'd speak to him (or her) first	I'm not sure what I'd do	I wouldn't speak to him (or her) unless he spoke first	X^2
Experimental Grade IV	38	55	8	3.18 n.s.
English Control Grade IV	24	56	21	
Experimental Grade V	36	56	8	2.54 n.s.
English Control Grade V	19	62	19	

Table 33 (cont.)
Pupils' Opinions of Elementary School French Programs

23. If you were playing with an English-speaking friend, and a French-speaking boy (or girl) wanted to play with you, would you invite him (or her) to play too?

	Yes, I'd invite him (or her) to join us	I'm not sure what I'd do	I wouldn't invite him (or her) to join us	X^2
Experimental Grade IV	75	23	3	2.03 n.s.
English Control Grade IV	59	38	3	
Experimental Grade V	72	28	0	6.42*
English Control Grade V	41	48	11	

24. Would you like to play with more French-speaking children if you had the chance?

	Yes, I would very much	I'm not sure	No, I'd rather play with only English-speaking children	X^2
Experimental Grade IV	23	68	10	3.00 n.s.
English Control Grade IV	22	53	25	
Experimental Grade V	48	52	0	6.29*
English Control Grade V	23	62	15	

25. What would your mother say if you brought a French-speaking friend home to play?

	She'd be very happy	I'm not sure what she'd say	I don't think she would like it	X^2
Experimental Grade IV	78	23	0	2.75 n.s.
English Control Grade IV	59	41	0	
Experimental Grade V	84	16	0	4.51 n.s.
English Control Grade V	65	19	15	

26. Do you speak or hear French often during vacation times, like at camp or when you travel?

	Yes, nearly all the time	Sometimes, but not often	Hardly ever	No, it's always English	X^2
Experimental Grade IV	23	43	28	8	1.71 n.s.
English Control Grade IV	16	45	23	16	
Experimental Grade V	12	52	36	0	9.19*
English Control Grade V	4	32	36	28	

27. Now that you have learned French at school, do you know how French-Canadian people think and feel about things?

	I know very well how French-Canadian people think and feel	I know a little about how French-Canadian people think and feel	I don't know how French-Canadian people think and feel at all	X^2
Experimental Grade IV	15	62	23	1.47 n.s.
English Control Grade IV	9	75	16	
Experimental Grade V	8	68	24	4.58 n.s.
English Control Grade V	12	38	50	

28. Do you know how French people from France think and feel about things?

	I know very well how French people from France think and feel	I know a little about how French people from France think and feel	I don't know how French people from France think and feel at all	X^2
Experimental Grade IV	13	49	38	1.30 n.s.
English Control Grade IV	6	45	48	
Experimental Grade V	0	48	52	5.99*
English Control Grade V	8	19	73	

Table 33 (cont.)
Pupils' Opinions of Elementary School French Programs

29. Now that you have learned French at school, how do French-Canadian people seem to you?

	They are *very different* from English-Canadian people	They are *similar* to English-Canadians in some ways, different in others	They are *very much like* English-Canadians	X^2
Experimental Grade IV	21	24	55	5.03 n.s.
English Control Grade IV	19	48	32	
Experimental Grade V	24	48	28	2.34 n.s.
English Control Grade V	12	42	46	

30. How do French people from France seem to you?

	They are *very different* from English-Canadian people	They are *similar* to English-Canadians in some ways, different in others	They are *very much like* English-Canadians	X^2
Experimental Grade IV	21	51	28	4.66 n.s.
English Control Grade IV	42	45	13	
Experimental Grade V	42	54	4	8.24*
English Control Grade V	36	28	36	

31. Since you have been learning about French people at school, do you like *French-Canadians* more now than you did before?

	I like them more now than I did before	I like them about the same as before	I don't like them as much now	X^2
Experimental Grade IV	58	38	5	0.96 n.s.
English Control Grade IV	48	48	3	
Experimental Grade V	64	32	4	13.30**

32. Since you have been learning about French people at school, do you like *French people from France* more now than you did before?

	I like them more now than I did before	I like them about the same as before	I don't like them as much now	X²
Experimental Grade IV	51	49	0	4.56 n.s.
English Control Grade IV	36	55	9	
Experimental Grade V	30	65	4	6.91*
English Control Grade V	4	85	11	

33. Suppose you happened to be born into a French-Canadian family, would you be just as happy to be a French-Canadian as an English-Canadian person?

	Just as happy to be French-Canadian	More happy to be English-Canadian	More happy to be French-Canadian	X²
Experimental Grade IV	69	28	3	2.98 n.s.
English Control Grade IV	52	39	10	
Experimental Grade V	84	16	0	8.08*
English Control Grade V	48	41	11	

34. Suppose you happened to be born in France, would you be just as happy to be French (from France) as an English-Canadian person?

	Just as happy to be French (from France)	More happy to be English-Canadian	More happy to be French (from France)	X²
Experimental Grade IV	67	33	0	0.22 n.s.
English Control Grade IV	61	39	0	
Experimental Grade V	62	33	4	2.18 n.s.
English Control Grade V	42	54	4	

Table 33 (cont.)

Pupils' Opinions of Elementary School French Programs

35. After studying French for several years, some children seem to change their personalities while others seem to stay the same. How about you? Do you think you have become less English-Canadian in your thoughts and feelings; or do you see yourself now as being both English- *and* French-Canadian, or as more English-Canadian?

I think I am: More English-Canadian than I would have been without the French schooling	Somewhat less English-Canadian	Both English and French	More French than English	X^2
Experimental Grade IV	27	5	65	3	12.22**
English Control Grade IV	52	21	27	0	
Experimental Grade V	13	21	66	0	14.97**
English Control Grade V	52	35	13	0	

36. Do you enjoy studying French the way you do at your school?

	I enjoy it very much	Some of it is good, some not so good	Most of it is not so good	X^2
Experimental Grade IV	45	43	13	7.06*
English Control Grade IV	18	52	30	
Experimental Grade V	52	48	0	15.95***
English Control Grade V	16	40	44	

37. Would you rather go to an all-English school?

	Yes, I would very much	I'm not too sure	I enjoy school as it is	X^2
Experimental Grade IV	3	23	75	17.11***
English Control Grade IV	31	38	31	
Experimental Grade V	4	28	68	13.46**
English Control Grade V	46	27	27	

38. In your opinion, is too much time spent on French?

	Too much time is spent on French	Just about the right amount of time is spent on French	Not enough time is spent on French	X^2
Experimental Grade IV	15	75	10	2.04 n.s.
English Control Grade IV	16	63	22	
Experimental Grade V	0	80	20	11.94**
English Control Grade V	26	37	37	

39. Do you want to continue learning French?

	Yes, I want to very much	I'd like to continue but put less time into French	I really don't want to learn French anymore	X^2
Experimental Grade IV	70	28	3	3.33 n.s.
English Control Grade IV	55	33	12	
Experimental Grade V	84	16	0	12.84**
English Control Grade V	37	44	19	

Table 33 (cont.)

Pupils' Opinions of Elementary School French Programs

40. Do you think you are behind in English compared to children at other schools who don't study French?

	Yes, I'm definitely behind in English	I may be a bit behind, but not very much	I don't think I'm behind in English at all	I may be ahead in English	X^2
Experimental Grade IV	13	36	38	13	8.22*
English Control Grade IV	9	9	61	21	
Experimental Grade V	4	36	52	8	2.38 n.s.
English Control Grade V	7	19	59	15	

Competence in the Language

The first four questions dealt with the children's personal estimates of their competence in speaking, understanding, reading, and writing French. The group comparisons at both grade levels are very impressive. For example, 44 percent of the Experimental grade IV pupils (the Follow-up group) say that they *speak* French about as well as or better than they speak English. None of the grade IV English Controls, in contrast, feel they have achieved such a degree of competence. At the grade V level, 36 percent of the Experimental Pilot Class, but only 8 percent of the English Control Class, feel they have attained that degree of competence. With regard to *understanding* spoken French, 60 to 70 percent of the two Experimental groups believe they are as good or better in French than in English compared with 7 to 13 percent of the Control children. In *reading* ability, 50 to 60 percent of the Experimental pupils report they are as good or better in reading French than English while only 4 to 28 percent of the Control groups claim this degree of competence. With regard to *writing* skills, over 70 percent of the Experimental children feel they can write as well or better in French than English compared to 31 and 7 percent for the Control groups.

In interpreting these differences, one should keep in mind that the children in the Experimental Classes have performed each year at very high levels of skill on objective tests of English competence. We presume then that the large proportion of pupils who report that they have equivalent French skills are using their English competence as a point of comparison. Still one should also ask whether the pupils themselves *feel* that they are behind in any way in their development of equivalent skills in English. Question 42 bears directly on this issue. When asked if they think they are behind in English compared with children at other schools who do not study via French, the grade IV Experimentals show a greater tendency than the Controls to feel "a bit" behind (36 to 9 percent), whereas the Control pupils are more convinced that they are not behind at all (38 to 61 percent). However, this tendency has diminished by grade V in the sense that 36 percent of the Experimentals feel they may be a bit behind compared with 19 percent for the Controls, while over 50 percent of both groups at grade V do not believe they are behind in English at all. Thus, the Experimental children may have the impression at the end of grade IV that they had to pay a small price in English for their competence in French, but this impression becomes negligible by the end of grade V.

Use of French outside School

French movies and T.V. Although the Experimental groups appear justifiably confident in their French competence, we felt it important to explore the uses they make of the language. Do they, for instance, watch French TV programs more often than the Control children? Question 5 indicates that both groups at both grade levels watch somewhat more English than French TV. However, their comprehension of French (Q. 6) is, in their estimation, very good compared with that of the Controls. They report understanding most of what is said, whereas the Control pupils say they can only get the general idea of the programs. This ability to apply their French competence is evident also in their comprehension of French movies (Q. 8). At both grade levels, their personal estimates of their comprehension of French far surpasses those of the Controls. Movie watching—either English or French—however, is apparently not a major pastime of the Experimental children (Q. 7). In fact, the Experimental pupils estimate that they have seen only half as many movies in the past year as the Controls. This could have several meanings, one possibility worth pursuing being the idea that the language-switch program diminishes the more passive, spectator-type activities of youngsters.

Translating and teaching. Several questions (9 through 14) focused on the children's competence and experience in translating from French to English and in tutoring or teaching the language. When asked how good they were at translating (Q. 9), the Experimental pupils at both grade levels express much more confidence than the Controls. By grade V, for example, over 90 percent say they can translate "most things." Furthermore, they report they are very frequently called on to be the translator for the family (Q. 10). This suggests that many more occasions present themselves to those who attain an advanced degree of second-language competence. For instance, they are called on much more often by French-speaking people to translate (Q. 14). Apparently, then, they become recognized as valuable linguistic mediators by both English-speaking and French-speaking people in their community. In other words, once the children reach a certain point in the development of bilingual skills, the occasions to further develop their competence seem to snowball. The Control children apparently have not developed their competence sufficiently to experience the snowball effect.

The Experimental children's confidence in their ability to tutor or "teach" family members in French is also much greater than that of the Controls (Q. 11). Over 50 percent of the Experimentals at both grade levels feel they could teach "quite a lot" of French compared with only 15 percent of the Controls. The Experimentals also report having many more requests from family members for help with French (Q. 12) and more occasions to speak French within the family (Q. 13). They apparently become disseminators of French and language resource people for those around them.

With classmates and with French-speaking children. When asked about their use of French with classmates at the same stage of development as themselves (Q. 15), the Experimental pupils mention that they sometimes use French and sometimes English. Although they report using French much more often than the Control Classes do, it is still only a "sometimes" affair. This finding is of interest because the teachers at the grade IV and V levels have mentioned that the children in the Experimental Classes now use French less often among themselves than they did in earlier grades, whereas they spontaneously and consistently use French with the grade IV and V teachers. When asked by one of the teachers to discuss this tendency, the children explained, with no hesitation, that they did not want to use the language in any artificial or "phoney" way; they looked on their classmates as part of their English-speaking world whereas the teacher represented their French world. They seemed to enjoy both worlds, but wanted to be natural in the choice of language of communication.

The same idea is represented in their reactions to Question 19, where about 25 percent of the grade V Experimental pupils feel that their English-speaking friends would take it as unnatural and inappropriate to communicate among themselves in French. In this regard, they are similar to the English Control children, 31 percent of whom have the same feeling about speaking French with English-speaking friends.

When it comes to communicating with French-speaking youngsters, note in Question 20 that the children in the Experimental Classes at both grade levels are more likely than the Controls to meet French-speaking children. Both Experimentals and Controls who do meet French-speaking children report making contact with a sizable group, about six to eight individuals. Of special interest is the finding that more of the Experimental than the Control children say they use French when communicating with their new French-speaking acquaintances. In fact, over 60 percent of the grade V Experimentals say they "almost always" use French, compared with only 13 percent of the English Controls. When asked about meeting French-speaking young people in other than neighborhood settings (e.g., at summer camps and so forth), the same pattern emerges: the Experimental children, who meet about the same number of people as the English Controls (Q. 21a), are much more likely to use French with French-speaking acquaintances (Q. 21b). The advantage in making social contacts with French speakers, then, seems to show itself in the larger number of neighborhood encounters enjoyed by the Experimental children and in their willingness and capacity to use French when communicating with French acquaintances.

Friendships. Have the children in the Experimental program developed more and closer friendships with French-speaking children? Compared with the English Control Classes, a larger proportion of them say they have made "very good friends" with French youngsters (85 to 52 percent, for the Experimental and English Controls, respectively), even though the average number of new friends made is essentially the same for both groups (Q. 22). There are also important group differences in the proportion of French-speaking friends the children would *like* to have. Those in the Experimental Classes express a definite desire to have both French *and* English friendships in comparison with the Controls, who show a much stronger desire to have English-speaking rather than French-speaking friends (Q. 23). This pattern of results, however, does not suggest that the Experimentals are overly eager to develop social contacts with French-speaking rather than English-speaking youngsters. Instead, they seem to be interested in developing a genuinely balanced repertoire of friendships. For example, when asked in Question 26 if they would like to play with more French-speaking children, both Experimental and English Control groups emphasize that they are *not sure* (over 50 percent of the respondents reacted in this way), even though the grade V Experimentals do show a greater eagerness to play "with more French-speaking" youngsters than do the Controls (48 to 23 percent).

The children in the Experimental Classes apparently receive more parental encouragement than the Controls for establishing contacts with French children (Q. 27), and this factor may, along with their sense of competence in the language, account for their greater interest and willingness to initiate social contacts with French-speaking youngsters (see Q. 24 and 25). When asked if they would make the initial overture to a French-speaking child their own age whom they might encounter at a skating rink, the Experimental children are somewhat more ready than the English Controls to start up a conversation (Q. 24), but this trend is not statistically significant. They are, however, more likely to invite a French-speaking youngster to join in an ongoing activity than the English Controls (Q. 25). These results suggest that the development of high-level skill in a second language facilitates spontaneous social contact with members of the other linguistic community.

Knowledge about and Attitudes toward French People

What influences, if any, do the different types of French programs have on children's knowledge about French people and on their attitudes toward the French? From one point of view this becomes the most important question to ask about a program of foreign-language study, because changes in attitudes or in ethnocentric outlooks have far greater social significance than the simple mastery of a new language. The children's responses to questions 29 through 36 provide us with a fascinating set of answers to this basic question.

First, in Question 29 the children were asked if, as a consequence of their study of French, they understood better how French Canadian people "think and feel about things." At the grade IV and V levels both the Experimental and the English Control children emphasize that they "know a little" about how French Canadian people think and feel; but relatively few take extreme positions (i.e. few say they know a "good deal" about French Canadians' thoughts and feelings and few say they know "hardly anything"). When asked the same question about French people from France (Q. 30), a noticeable grade level difference in response pattern appears: the grade IV children in both Experimental and Control groups say they know little or nothing about the thoughts and feelings of the European French, while at grade V, the Experimental children show relatively more confidence than the Controls in their knowledge about French people. Still, here again, hardly any confess to being experts in any sense.

The experimental program has not had the effect of making French people seem similar to the children's own ethnic group. If anything, it has highlighted the differences of French people. When asked if French-Canadian people seem similar to English Canadians (Q. 31), the older Experimental children are relatively conservative; to them, French Canadians are similar in some ways but different in others. The grade IV Experimentals are somewhat more likely to see French Canadians as similar. French people from France (Q. 32) are more often seen as different, but the grade IV Experimentals still are relatively more prone than the grade V Experimentals to see them as being similar in selected ways. The grade V Experimentals are much more likely than the Controls to view the French from France as being different from English Canadians.

Although the French are seen as different, the Experimental children nonetheless believe that their attitudes toward French people have become more favorable as a consequence of their language program. When asked if their liking of French people has changed (Q. 33 and 34), the grade V Experimental children say they like French people (both French Canadian and European French) more now than before they began their study of French, whereas the English Controls express the view that there has been no essential change in their feelings toward French people.

A similar trend of improved attitudes is apparent in the reactions of the grade V Experimental Class to Question 35. In this case, they were asked how they would feel if they happened to be born into a French-Canadian family, and a much greater proportion of the older Experimental children say they would be "just as happy" to be French Canadian as English Canadian (84 percent of the Experimental children express this feeling compared to 48 percent of the Controls). With regard to being French from France (Q. 36), there are no Experimental-Control group differences at either grade level. Still over 60 percent of the Experimentals say they would be just as happy to be European French as English Canadian. These findings suggest then that an important amelioration of attitude and outlook toward French people has taken place, especially toward French Canadians.

Self-views

A major concern of certain parents and educators from the start was that the children in the language-switch program might lose their English Canadian identity and sense of allegiance. As planners of the study, we did not anticipate this eventuality, because we felt that the program offered the children every possible chance to retain full contact with family and normal peer groups while opening a new dimension to their personalities, one we saw as appropriate and desirable for Canadians. In other words, we had confidence that the children could develop a psychologically comfortable dual identity—a feeling of being both English and French in makeup—without psychological conflict. The children's responses to Question 37 bear directly on this matter. Both groups of children in the Experimental Classes see themselves as becoming both English *and* French to a much greater degree (65 versus 20 percent) than do the Control groups, who instead see themselves as becoming more English-Canadian as a consequence of their own experience with French at school. These marked differences are very encouraging from our point of view, and because they have a potentially tremendous social significance, this matter of dual identity should be examined in much greater detail in follow-up research.

Children's Personal Evaluations of the French Programs

Do the comparison groups differ in their enjoyment of the study of French? Realizing that the Experimental groups have taken the language-switch option and the Control groups a conventional FSL option, their reactions to Question 38 are interesting. Both the grade IV and V Experimental groups express a much greater degree of enjoyment in their mode of studying French; in fact, between 45 to 52 percent say they "very much" enjoy studying French their way in contrast to 16 to 18 percent of the Controls. The Controls actually find most of their French study "not so good" (30 to 40 percent versus 0 to 13 percent for the Experimentals). To Question 39, the Experimentals clearly express their enjoyment of school *as it is* (68 to 75 percent in contrast to 27 to 31 percent for the Controls); and they show no interest, compared to the Controls, in going to an all-English school. To Question 40, the Experimental children feel that about the right amount of time is spent on French, neither too much nor too little. This contrast is especially sharp in the grade V group comparisons. Furthermore, in their answers to Question 41, the Experimental Classes show more eagerness to continue learning French (70 to 84 percent versus 37 to 55 for the Controls). In contrast, the Controls apparently want to reduce the time spent on French or to discontinue French study entirely. The Experimental children's satisfaction with their mode of French study and their eagerness to continue is, it seems to us, a very impressive endorsement of the whole scheme.

Summary

By the end of grades IV and V the children in the Experimental Classes have become sufficiently skilled in the French language to be able to communicate comfortably with French-speaking people and establish satisfying friendships with them. Compared with the English Control children, they have developed their French language competence to the point that they are able to enter French-Canadian spheres of social activities and establish satisfying relationships. They have also come to appreciate French people and French ways of life and now consider themselves to be both English- *and* French-Canadian in makeup. Moreover, they are extremely satisfied with the French program offered them, and reject the idea of transferring to a conventional English program. In contrast, the Controls, who have had hardly any French training, relatively speaking, other than the standard FSL program, feel they have had *too much* French, and are much more favorable to the idea of transferring to an all-English school program. Too little French turns out to be too much for them, while a great deal of French has, it would seem, merely whetted the appetites of the Experimental children.

Chapter Ten

The Bilingual Education of Children: In Perspective

This book tells the story of a longitudinal investigation of two groups of English-Canadian children whose elementary schooling was conducted exclusively in French in kindergarten and in the first grade and, from grades II through IV, mainly in French, except for two half-hour daily periods of English Language Arts. In telling the story, we have given attention to the working hypotheses that oriented the study and the measurement techniques used to assess the program's impact on the cognitive and attitudinal development of the children involved. We felt the details were appropriate because the project should have universal significance since its central theme, the bilingual education of children, is a major concern of minority groups in all countries of the world and an educational issue of first priority for citizens in most developing nations.

A group of parents concerned about the ineffectiveness of prevalent methods of foreign-language teaching were instrumental in stimulating a community-wide interest in the project because it promised to be a better alternative. They were particularly impressed with recent attempts to teach advanced ideas in science and mathematics in the elementary grades and wondered why a foreign or second language could not be taught equally effectively. As residents of a multicultural and multilingual society, they also realized that they and their children were part of a much larger experiment in democratic coexistence, one that requires people of different cultures and languages to develop mutual understanding and respect. An essential first step for them as residents of Quebec was to learn the other major linguistic group's language thoroughly. As developed, the program, referred to as a home-school language switch, may well serve as a model for other bicultural or multicultural communities and for essentially monocultural settings where a serious desire exists to develop a high level of competence in a second or foreign language. A fundamentally new educational issue is introduced here: rather than estimating how many years of schooling should be provided to develop some unspecified degree of achievement in a second or foreign language, the educator in this case asks how one goes about developing complete bilingual competence in both the home and the school languages.

Our plan called for a detailed study of the linguistic, cognitive, and attitudinal development of children in a Pilot and a Follow-up Experimental Class in comparison with control classes of children carefully matched for measured intelligence and social-class backgrounds following conventional English-Canadian or French-Canadian academic programs. The Experimental and English Control Classes were also comparable in terms of parental attitudes toward the French-Canadian people and culture. Moreover, all of the parents were equally motivated to have their children learn French. If given the opportunity, the large majority of the English Control parents would likely have placed their children in the experimental program. We had decided in advance, however, to limit the project to two experimental classes only.

The major questions that guided us in planning the investigation are given below together with a brief review of the main findings at the end of grade IV. With these as a background, we shall then try to put the project itself in perspective and discuss its significance.

What effect does such an educational program, extended through grade IV, have on the Experimental children's progress in home-language skills? The overall answer is that they are doing just as well as the English Controls at the end of grade IV, showing no symptoms of retardation or negative transfer. On tests of English word knowledge, word discrimination, and language usage, the Experimental Pilot Class, as a group, falls above the 80th percentile on national norms as do the Controls. This indicates that those in the experimental program do as well as the Controls, with both groups performing at a very high level of achievement in terms of national norms. Their reading ability, listening comprehension, and knowledge of concepts in English are all at the same level as those of the English Controls.

All signs are favorable also as to their progress in English expressive skills. They retell and invent short stories in English with as much comprehension and with at least as good command of rhythm, intonation, enunciation, and overall expression as the Controls. Their spontaneous productions are as long and complex and their vocabulary as rich and diverse.

Their facility at decoding and utilizing spontaneous descriptive instructions given by English-speaking children and adults is also at the same level as that of the Controls, and their word associations in English show as much maturity, naturalness, and spontaneity. At certain grade levels they were also reliably faster than the Controls in producing associations in English, indicating that they had no difficulty processing English.

How well do children progress in developing second-language skills under such a scheme? The answer is that they fare extremely well when compared with children from French-speaking homes who follow a normal French program of study. Their French listening comprehension scores from grade II on in general were comparable to those of the Controls, and their knowledge of complex French concepts is remarkably advanced. In fact, at the grade IV level, they score at the same level as the French Controls on a test of vocabulary. From grade I on, they have mastered the distinctive phonemes of French, and demonstrate a nativelike command of the language when reading in French. However, when asked to retell or invent short French stories, the linguists who rated their oral proficiency found that their rhythm, intonation, and overall expression in French was clearly not equivalent to that of the French Controls, even at grade IV. On the other hand, their expression, enunciation, and rhythm and intonation are noticeably better when they invent stories of their own than when they retell someone else's stories, suggesting that they are particularly motivated and clever when permitted to express their own flow of ideas with their own choice of expressions. Although they are not yet as fluent as the Controls, the verbal content of their productions in French is as long and complex, the vocabulary is as diverse, and they show a similar degree of comprehension of the themes or plots. They make more errors in their French productions, especially errors of gender and contraction. Their free associations in French are as rapid, mature, and appropriate as those of the Controls, and they show nativelike skill in decoding spontaneous descriptions produced by French-speaking adults or by children their own age. In grade IV, however, they were not as able as the French Controls to decode the descriptive speech of children even though they were still as proficient as the Controls at decoding adult descriptions.

Striking as their progress in French is, they could very likely be brought even closer to nativelike competence in the spoken aspects of the language, if this were considered important. But if one were to stress nativelike expression with drilling and laboratory techniques, one might jeopardize the high level of competence already attained in the more receptive skills of French and the ability to use the language as a medium of learning. Even so, changes could be introduced easily into the program to provide more opportunities for expression by, for example, teaching physical education, music, and plastic arts (subjects that lend themselves naturally to social communication) in French. Teachers could also direct more attention to the content and fluency of the child's speech in French without neglecting form, structure, and style. Of course, means could be found to foster interaction with French children outside school, which would be the most natural way to enhance expressive competence.

How well do children following this program assimilate a nonlanguage subject such as mathematics? The answer is that on tests of computational and problem-solving arithmetic, they perform at the same high level as the controls—both groups scoring beyond the 80th percentile on national norms. One can be confident, then, that the children have been as able as the French Control groups to grasp, assimilate, and utilize mathematical principles taught through French exclusively and that they have transfered this knowledge to English.

What effect does a bilingual program such as this, extended through grade IV, have on the measured intelligence of the children involved? There are *no* signs at the end of grade IV of any intellectual deficit or retardation attributable to the bilingual experience, judging from yearly retestings with standard measures of intelligence, nor is there any symptom of their being handicapped on measures of creative thinking. In fact, the Experimental children are either at the same level, or, in the earlier years, slightly advanced, in their capacity to generate imaginative and unusual uses for everyday objects, whether tested in English or French.

As the children in the program develop bilingual skills, do they show simultaneously a generalized sensitivity for the sounds of a totally foreign language? Most of us have heard that becoming bilingual makes learning other languages easier. We examined one aspect of this attractive idea from the first grade on by comparing the children in the Experimental Class and the monolinguals in the Control Classes on their abilities to discriminate the phonemes of Russian, a language totally foreign to all those included in the analysis. By grade IV, we have uncovered no evidence that the bilingual children have more sensitivity to foreign language sounds than the monolinguals. This outcome suggests that we should now shift attention to other factors that may differentiate the bilingual from the monolingual when learning a new language. For example, the bilingual learning a third language might be sensitized to *grammatical* similarities and contrasts and show an advantage over the monolingual in the mastery of this aspect. Or a more efficient manner of linking novel symbols to referents might show itself in an advantage with vocabulary development. Research, then, should be directed in these or other directions to test further the possibility of a bilingual advantage.

What effect does the home-school language switch have on the children's self-concepts and their attitudes toward French people in general? At the grade II and III levels the attitudes of the children in the Experimental Classes were much fairer and more charitable than those of the English and French Control children. On standard measures of social attitudes, they were less ethnocentric and less biased toward their own ethnic group than were the Controls. At the same time, they had healthy views of themselves. This pattern was statistically significant and clear enough to be taken as an indication that suspicion and distrust between groups may be effectively reduced by means of this particular academic experience.

However, when retested in the spring of 1970, we found both the grade IV and III level Experimental groups essentially similar to the English Controls in their attitudes: neutral to slightly favorable toward European-French people, relatively hostile toward French Canadians, and clearly favorable to their own group. We are not certain what could have caused this change, but our speculations are that three factors likely played a role: 1) the French-Canadian demands for separatism and the accompanying hostility toward English Canadians which were intense at that time; 2) the children's contact with French-Canadian Protestant children in their school who come from relatively lower social-class backgrounds and who are academically poorer and less docile; and 3) their wanting to be like others in their peer group and not too "French" in outlook.

It was important therefore to test the children again in 1971 after the social nightmare of the 1970 kidnappings and the menacing demands for secession were quelled, at least temporarily. Thus, in the spring of 1971 when the Pilot Classes were in grade V and the Follow-ups in grade IV, the children were asked, through a comprehensive, interview-type questionnaire, for their attitudes toward French Canadians and toward the European French. At this time, we find that the Experimental children have unmistakably more favorable attitudes toward French Canadians and European-French people than do the English Controls; the Experimentals also give various signs that they are much more closely identified with French people and the French way of life. After five years in the program, then, we were delighted to see that the children had broadened and liberalized their perceptions of the other ethnic group to the point that they, relative to the English Controls, thought of themselves as being *both* English- and French-Canadian in outlook. We consider this outcome to be at least as important as the mastery of the other group's language.

There was no evidence at any point that the children's self-concepts were confused or different, relative to the Controls; at all grade levels the Experimental children described themselves in optimistic and healthy terms.

What does an educational experience of this sort mean to the children involved? As the Experimental children completed grades V and IV respectively, they were asked to give their own opinions and evaluations of the program and its impact on their lives. As it turned out this was the most revealing and reassuring phase of the whole investigation to date. Compared to the English Controls who have followed a conventional FSL program since kindergarten, the Experimentals show complete confidence in their second-language ability to the extent that they feel they can use it naturally in communication with French-speaking youngsters, with whom they are able to establish satisfying friendships. They have, in other words, become competent enough in French to break through the language and cultural shell that isolates the English- and French-Canadian communities, and they have learned to appreciate French-speaking people and their ways of life to the extent that they tend to think of themselves as being both English- and French-Canadian in makeup. They are also extremely pleased with the program, making it clear that they want neither to switch out of it nor to interrupt their continuing progress in French. The contrast with the Control children who have had only FSL experience is striking; in degree of competence in French, in the social utility of the language, in attitude changes, and in motivation to continue with French, the Experimental children are a group apart.

The Program's Effects on Those Involved

As we reflect on the project itself and the bilingual development of the children who have been in it for a five-year period, our thoughts, as psychologists, turn to certain processes that seem to run their course in the minds not only of the children involved, but also in the minds of their parents, their teachers, and various community leaders who, from the sidelines, have watched this program grow and expand. It is to these "goings on" that we now turn our attention briefly with the purpose of explaining how the program functioned and what psychological significance it had for all involved.

The Program's Effects on the Children

What goes on in the minds of children during the course of their participation in the program? We see two types of processes of special interest; one cognitive, the other attitudinal. Four of the many cognitive happenings, discussed in earlier chapters, stand out as promising theoretical leads that could, with careful follow-up study, have relevance for language pedagogy and for educational practices in general. At the moment, however, our comprehension of them is vague and fragmentary, and they should be taken only as hypotheses for further study.

Cognitive Processes

Incipient contrastive linguistics. From kindergarten on, the children who switch languages for schooling get caught up in a process of comparing and contrasting two linguistic codes, one learned from infancy, and a new one that surrounds them from the very first day of school. We think the process may start as a type of translation game in which the youngsters construct personalized glossaries to link the new sounds and expressions they hear with everyday things and events they have already labeled in their home language. But as they begin translating and realizing that "Bonjour, mes enfants" probably is another way of saying "Good morning, boys and girls," they also learn that in other contexts "bon" and "jour" pull apart and take on the equivalent functions of "good" and "day." Then the comparison and contrast of codes starts to become more systematic as the children notice salient differences in word order ("mains sales" which differs from "dirty hands"), of gender ("le tableau noir" and "la porte," which differ from "*the* blackboard" and "*the* door"), and the like. The comparison process apparently is encouraged as much by similarities as it is by contrasts, for the children seem as delighted with other-code equivalents for terms they already knew (e.g., *silence* in French = *silence* in English) as they are with novel and unfamiliar contrasts (*sensible* in French = *sensible* in English). It is our impression that comparing languages is a very interesting process for the children, and that this children's version of contrastive linguistics helps them immeasurably to build vocabulary and to comprehend complex linguistic functions. Our inferences for the existence of this process, sketchy as they are, come from observations of the children and from analyses of their performance on English tests of vocabulary. For example, it became apparent that the children understood certain concepts in English that they would likely only have learned about through French, not only concepts with cognates in English (e.g., *canine*) but also those without (e.g., *gable*). Our hunch is that they searched out the English equivalent of each new French concept as it developed, so that learning the meaning of the French word *canine* made the English equivalent easy, whereas learning what the French word *pignon* means led them on a search for the English gloss *gable*.

Linguistic "detective" skills. Another recurring process experienced by the children was, we believe, the early development of a linguistic "detective" capacity, that is, an attentive, patient, inductive concern with words, meanings, and linguistic regularities. Our inferences in this case were based on the children's better-than-expected scores on tests of French word discrimination, listening comprehension, and decoding. Their precocious skill in linking spoken French words with appropriate written words (as measured in the word discrimination test), and their remarkable capacity to understand and react appropriately to French speech (as seen in the decoding task) suggests that this process, like the preceding one, developed spontaneously and served as a source of interest and motivation.

The transfer of skills across languages. A third process that we felt was operating is usually referred to as a "transfer" of skills from one language to the other. We refer here to the higher-order skills of reading and calculating, which were developed exclusively through the medium of French and yet seemed to be equally well and almost simultaneously developed in English. In fact, we wonder whether in these cases there actually was a transfer of any sort or whether some more abstract form of learning took place that was quite independent of the language of training. These developments took place so rapidly that we had little time to take notice of them. It seemed to us that all of a sudden the children could read in English and demonstrate their arithmetic achievement in that language. This process, which occurs rapidly and essentially without deliberation, is amenable to research, especially now that we know about when to expect its occurrence. In fact, research on reading and calculating in a weaker language may throw more light on the independent roles played by language and thought in the child's cognitive development than would be possible with monolingual children learning through their only language.

This line of reasoning leads to the writings of L. S. Vygotsky, the Russian psychologist whose research and discussions on thought and language have been a great source of intellectual enrichment for us. Vygotsky draws an important distinction between what he calls "spontaneous" or familiar, everyday concepts and "scientific" or school-learned concepts. In his research with primary school children, he asked them to complete sentences that were purposely left incomplete after words such as "because" or "although." Spontaneous concepts, those dealing with familiar, everyday situations, were worked into sentences like "The boy fell off his bicycle because ... " and scientific concepts, those developed in formal schoollike settings, were placed in sentences like "Economic planning is possible in the USSR because ... " Vygotsky found that the "scientific" concepts were mastered and understood *earlier* than the spontaneous ones. For example, eight-year-olds were able to use concepts such as "because" appropriately enough in spontaneous conversations, but in more formal testing situations, they made errors of the sort "The boy fell off his bicycle because *he was taken to the hospital.*" The fact that they made more errors with familiar, everyday concepts than with scientific ones, such as "If a ball rolls off a table, it will fall downward because *of the force of gravitation*" is fascinating. Vygotsky's central point is that the youngster "lacks the awareness of" everyday concepts and thus is unable to work with them in an adaptable, flexible manner. He argues that children are more adaptable in their use of scientific concepts because a teacher has brought them more into consciousness through explanations, examples, questioning, and corrections. It is because these concepts have been developed through instruction and painstaking collaboration with a tutor that the child can make more intelligent use of them. Once a number of scientific concepts are mastered, the awareness accompanying their development spreads to everyday concepts, so that by age ten children were found to use both types intelligently. But the development of scientific concepts led the way.

It is at the next step in his argument that our research makes direct contact with Vygotsky:

The influence of scientific concepts on the mental development of the child is analogous to the effect of learning a foreign language, a process which is conscious and deliberate from the start. In one's native language, the primitive aspects of speech are acquired before the more complex ones. The latter presuppose some awareness of phonetic, grammatical, and syntactic forms. With a foreign language, the higher forms develop before spontaneous fluent speech . . . The child's strong points in a foreign language are his weak points in his native language, and vice versa. In his own language, the child conjugates and declines correctly, but without realizing it. He cannot tell the gender, the case, or the tense of the word he is using. In a foreign language, he distinguishes between masculine and feminine gender and is conscious of grammatical forms from the beginning . . . The child can transfer to a new language the system of meanings he already possesses on his own. The reverse is also true—a foreign language facilitates mastering the higher forms of the native language. The child learns to see his language as one particular system among many, to view its phenomena under more general categories, and this leads to awareness of his linguistic operations. Goethe said with truth that "he who knows no foreign language does not truly know his own." (Vygotsky, 1962, pp. 109-110.)

It is certain then that Vygotsky would not have been at all surprised by the two-way bilingual relay of concepts and linguistic principles that we have caught glimpses of from the grade I level on. Nor would he have been surprised to learn that the Experimental children have maintained full capacity in English language skills or in mathematics or reading. He would probably expect an intellectual advantage to show itself as the children approach bilingual balance. He might even endorse a slight paraphrase of Goethe's idea, that one who does not know another *people* well does not truly know his own. That is to say, he might have expected important changes to take place in the children's attitudes toward their own and the other enthnolinguistic groups.

The written language as a frame of reference. The fourth example concerns the strategies that Experimental children use to develop expressive competence in French. We noted that they had mastered the distinctive phonemes of French very early in the program and this suggested that their attention was drawn to the ways novel sound units of French are produced. It was evident too that they were able to read and recite in French with almost flawless command from the first grade on. When it came to retelling a story heard for the first time, however, they seemed to deviate noticeably from the nativelike command of the language they had when reading, reciting, or even when creating or inventing a story in their own words. Piecing these parts together as best we can, we come to the conclusion that the French written word plays a central role in the children's development of expressive competence in the language. The written form of French seems to become a dependable frame of reference which helps to concretize the free-floating sounds and words of the language. It is used by the teacher as the core material which is turned to for oral reading experiences, for practicing proper intonation and rhythm with the teacher being the model and the corrector of errors, and for dictée. In one sense, then, the children's mental schemata for proper speech likely derive from the teacher-controlled reading exercises, and these schemata are drawn on when the child is free to construct his own modes of expressing ideas in French. Actually his "own" ways of expressing himself in French may in a large part be the mental regeneration of the teacher's modes of expression, and in this sense the teacher becomes a clearer link with the written word than some stranger whose distinctive style of expression the child is asked to copy in the story retelling procedure. The major point is that the written form of the second language may be of prime importance not only in giving substance to vocabulary but also in schematizing appropriate modes of expression. Today's emphasis on audio-lingualism and audio-visualism may have diverted children's experiences too far away from reading and writing and the advantages they can provide.

Attitudinal Processes

Within the first two weeks of the kindergarten year, the children in the experiment appear to adjust to the use of a peculiar language as the medium of communication between the teacher and themselves. Neither the language nor the teacher are any longer strange. The teacher's naturally supportive and understanding attitude toward the children makes their contact with a French-speaking person a positive and friendly one from the start. One gets the impression from visiting the classes that being French adds to the teacher's charm, making her and the business of being in a French class something special in the eyes of the children. Much the same as they learn about their own language through comparisons and contrasts with another language, children seem to learn a good deal about their own group and others through contrasts and comparisons of ethnic groups (cf. Lambert and Klineberg, 1967). The comparisons afforded by the experimental program are typically sympathetic and favorable. From this start, the children's attitudes toward French people and French ways of life are shaped continuously through teacher-pupil interaction and by the feelings of accomplishment in learning the other group's language that begin to show themselves very early in the program. The peculiarities of the setting in which this experiment was conducted introduced the children to an unrepresentative group of French-Canadian pupils who, because of their generally lower social status, had developed a reputation for being less clever and less disciplined. But by grade V, other forces seem to have counteracted the unfavorable impressions these youngsters have of French Canadians as a group: for example, the teacher influence was a contant factor throughout; moreover, the experimental children apparently developed sufficient competence with French to permit them to enter French-Canadian social spheres and establish satisfying friendships on their own. In other words, by grade V they seem to have encountered a fairer sampling of French-Canadian people because of their language competence.

The attitude profiles of the Experimental children by the fifth grade indicate that important affective changes have occurred during the course of the project. The children state that they enjoy the form of education they are receiving and want to stay with it; their feelings toward French people have become decidedly more favorable; and they now think of themselves as being both French- and English-Canadian in personal makeup. It is this apparent identification with French people—those from Canada and those from Europe—that raises the question of biculturalism. Has the program made the children more bicultural? It is difficult to answer this question because the meaning of bicultural is so vague. It is certain that the children now feel they can be at ease in both French- and English-Canadian social settings, and that they are becoming both French and English in certain regards; but not becoming less English as a consequence. It is certain too they have learned important contrasts in ways of behaving. For example, they have learned that in classes with European-French teachers they should stand when a visitor enters while they need not stand in classes that are conducted by English-Canadian or French-Canadian teachers. We wonder how much more there is to being bicultural beyond knowing thoroughly the languages involved, feeling personally aligned with both groups, and knowing how to behave in the two atmospheres. Are there any deeper personal aspects to cultural differences? That is, does culture actually affect personality all that much or is it perhaps a more superficial and thinner wrapping than many social scientists have suggested? In a recent attempt to examine cultural contrasts of English and French Canadians, for example, Lambert (1970) was struck more by cross-cultural similarities of behaviors, attitudes, and values than by differences; a similar conclusion is suggested in a recent paper by Cole and Bruner (1971). In other words, perhaps through ethnic group comparisons, the children in the experiment may be learning that young people are basically pretty similar regardless of the language they speak.

Not many people have opportunities to develop this important notion, but one who, through his own extraordinary experiences, seems to be able to see through the filter of culture is Thor Heyerdahl, the leader of the Kon Tiki and Ra expeditions. For example, in his log book on board Ra II he wrote:

I could not have had better companions. The multinational teamwork is perfect and a real comfort . . . It is remarkable to learn that our small, short-lasting problems never come from racial, national, political, or religious difference, but solely from individual quirks, such as if one is making a mess when another wants order, or someone wants to rest while another feels he should finish an important job. Man is man wherever you find him; I feel he cannot be divided or united according to height, color, or pencil lines on a map (Heyerdahl, 1971, p. 44).

The Program's Effects on Parents

The parents who pioneered the experiment were called on to show additional resolution at various points in its development. In most cases, the parents were not able to monitor their children's schooling nor to help them with their work in French. Instead they had to rely on the school authorities to oversee the program and insure, in some way, that nothing would go wrong. They could, however, form opinions about the methods of teaching, and perhaps because of their concern and the passive role they had to play in their children's education, some expressed worries of various sorts: that the children were not being taught to read in English, that the teachers were overemphasizing discipline in the classroom, that the mathematics training seemed old-fashioned and rigid, that the children were asked to do too much memorizing, and so forth. But they stayed with it and, even when perplexed and uncertain, remained supportive and reassuring with their children. Many factors contributed to the parents' resolve: they had a personally important goal in mind and were committed to it publicly since they had enrolled their children in the program; the children, curiously enough, seemed content and even interested in school, and were clearly developing competence in the second language; and the research team presented yearly reports and group discussions of how the children seemed to be doing. Some mothers showed chagrin at the fact that their children were "wild about" their teacher, and in certain cases we felt that their feelings were more intense than those normally experienced by most mothers as they learn to share their child's affections, for in this instance the other woman was French-speaking. But these overreactions were not numerous and they disappeared from view within the first two years.

The parents' willingness to stay with the experiment has been unmistakable if we take the number of dropouts as an index. Not only have very few dropped out, but some who moved out of the area have tried to drive their children long distances to keep them in. Another index is their eagerness to help other parents keep the program as active and energetic as it was when their children were starting out. For instance, at a recent large gathering in the school district, we were impressed to hear the parents of the Pilot and Follow-up children, now in grades VI and V, insisting that plans be started immediately for a fully bilingual high school and junior college program. In an open discussion, there were nothing but favorable or enthusiastic reactions heard about the program, and we were unable to learn of one dissatisfied parent. At that meeting, however, there were many parents whose children had not been in the program; and they wanted to explore various compensatory alternatives, such as switching to French as the sole medium of instruction in one or more of the advanced grades.

We have seen that the parental attitudes at the start of the project were basically friendly and favorable ones. They wanted their children to learn French for essentially integrative reasons—getting to know the other ethnic group and their distinctive ways—but they did not want them to go so far as to think and feel like French Canadians, in other words. to lose their English-Canadian identity. How will they interpret the attitudes of their children who by grade V come to think of themselves as being both English- and French-Canadian in disposition and outlook? Some may see this as a worrisome sign of identity loss, but we believe they will come to interpret their children's enjoyment in having both English- and French-Canadian friends and both types of outlooks as a valuable addition, not a subtraction or cancellation of identities. As we see it, the children are acquiring a second social overcoat which seems to increase their interest in dressing up and reduces the wear and tear placed on either coat alone. Our guess is that the children are beginning to convince any worried parents that the experience is, in fact, enriching and worthwhile.

Of course, the parents cannot share fully their children's experience or their development of a dual identity. Nevertheless, in the few noticeable cases where the divergence of views between parents and children has become very apparent, even those parents give the impression that they are pleased that their children are being prepared to take their place in a new type of multilanguage and multicultural society and help shape its development. As parents, they can easily take pride in the fact that they have gone out of their way to help in this special type of preparation.

The Program's Impact on Teachers

It seems clear then that both the parents and the pupils themselves prefer the home-school language-switch program to traditional instruction where French is taught as a second language. One wonders though what opinions teachers have of the program, not only those participating in the experiment, but also others outside who are nonetheless affected by the rapid expansion of this new type of education.

In our informal contacts, we have found two distinctive reactions among the English-Canadian teachers in charge of the English Language Arts program. Some are amazed and delighted with the children's competence in all aspects of English, while others seem to expect the children to be disastrously retarded and go out of their way to search for deficiencies of one sort or another. Recently, Campbell, Tucker, and Taylor (1971) examined the opinions of English-speaking and French-speaking teachers toward the traditional program of English language instruction with French as a second language in contrast to the St. Lambert-type language-switch program. It was found in that investigation that both French and English teachers feel that the traditional program provides English-speaking children with a firm grounding in English language arts, but not in French. They also felt that there was good coverage of content subjects as well as the development of a sensitivity to their own, but not the other group's, cultural heritage. The home-school language-switch idea was viewed favorably by Francophone teachers in general, but not by Anglophone teachers, who, in spite of the apparent success of the plan, apparently regard this type of program as a threat to their job security. This reaction by Anglophone teachers calls for very thorough follow-up study. Their resentment could jeopardize the development of similar programs in other settings, and if they see no chance of playing an equivalent role in French-Canadian schools, they could leave the teaching profession permanently.

If language-switch programs prove themselves in other schools and over a longer span of years, more parents will demand this type of opportunity for their children. Then presumably teacher training colleges will recognize that there is less need for monolingual Anglophone teachers and adjust their enrollment quotas and training programs accordingly. In time, too, the French-Canadian school systems may try similar projects and request the services of English-Canadian teachers.

The Program's Effects on Community Leaders

What goes on in the minds of community leaders who have watched from a distance the development and expansion of a program initiated by a small group of parents and school officials in the community? From a sociological perspective, the project has tipped off balance a smoothly functioning community, and one can be certain that various corrective adjustments will be set in action. Mrs. Melikoff's fascinating analysis of the reactions of members of the local school board and those they represent brings to light the strains placed on the social system (see Appendix A). The concerns of the community leaders are real ones, to be sure. Over the past few years in the Province of Quebec, plans have been formulated by the political party in office to abolish the existing school systems, thereby eradicating the present separate Catholic and Protestant school commissions and leaving in limbo the jurisdiction of English-language education. These changes have provoked anxieties in the English-Canadian communities. On one side there are those who believe that the English-speaking minority should have faith in the goodwill of those making the decisions, while others worry about having too much trust in French-Canadian politicians and educators who, the counterargument runs, have not had a monopoly on constructive, innovative changes in education in the past. The sceptics also underscore the fact that the present project was an English-Canadian idea, stemming from English-speaking parents and principals with absolutely no encouragement or advice from the Provincial Ministry of Education, made up mainly of French-speaking educators. They talk instead in terms of the linguistic rights of English-speaking Canadians.

For many, then, the success of the program plays into the hands of political leaders, especially those with separatist tendencies who can use it as a demonstration that a French education does not appear to hurt English-speaking children in the least. Thus some see the program as a scheme to make French the "working language" of the Province at the expense of the English-Canadian educational system. Although we see no need for concern about the vitality of the English language in the Province or about bilingualism eroding the English-Canadian culture, we as researchers are nevertheless sensitive to any political influences that would affect the *voluntary* nature of the program. It has been this very precious feature that has enabled parents and their children to decide whether to enroll or continue in the program or not. There is no question in our minds that a program of this sort will be successful *only* if those involved want it to be and are given opportunities from the start to have a hand in shaping it.

The debate is a lively one and without doubt it will continue, especially since more than thirty-five French-speaking teachers have already been hired by the South Shore Protestant Regional School Commission alone, and some ten to twelve more are added each year. The question now is whether power figures in the English-speaking community will make a move to limit or stop the program, or whether parents, children, school authorities, and teachers will be successful in their demand that the program continue and expand.

The Program in Perspective

Although the educational plan described here seems remarkably effective in this Canadian setting, it is not proposed as a universal solution for all communities or nations planning programs of bilingual education. Instead we have in mind a much more general guiding principle: in any community where there is a serious widespread desire or need for a bilingual or multilingual citizenry, priority for early schooling should be given to the language or languages least likely to be developed otherwise, that is, the languages most likely to be neglected. When applied to bilingual settings, this principle calls for the establishment of two elementary school streams, one conducted in language A and one in language B, with two groups of teachers who either are or who function as though they were monolinguals in one of the languages. If A is the more prestigious language, then native speakers of A would start their schooling in language B, and after functional bilingualism is attained, continue their schooling in both languages. Depending on the sociocultural setting, various options are open to the linguistic minority group: 1) prekindergarten or very early schooling, with half-day instruction in language B and half-day in A; 2) schooling in language B only until reading and writing skills are certified, then introducing instruction via A; or 3) a completely bilingual program based on two monolingually organized educational structures which allow children to move back and forth from one language of instruction to the other. Rather than teaching language A and B as languages, emphasis would be shifted from a linguistic focus to one where languages are thought of primarily as vehicles for developing competence in academic subject matters, including various forms of creative work.

The province of Quebec provides a convenient illustrative example. Here the French Canadians—one of the ethnic minority groups of the nation, but a clear majority in the Province—have a popular political movement underway based in part on a philosophy of making French the "working language" of the Province and in part on a plan to separate the Province politically from the rest of Canada. For English-speaking Canadians who see the value and importance of keeping two or more national languages, the home-school language switch described in this book is an appropriate policy, since French for them would otherwise be bypassed, except for conventional second-language training programs that have not produced the required proficiency, and since it is certain that the use of English will continue because of the English nature of the rest of Canada and the proximity and influence of the United States. French Canadians, however, have reason to fear a loss of their language, faced as they are with the universal importance of English and the relatively low status attached to minority languages in North America. French Canadians also may denigrate their own distinctive dialect of French because it differs from the European version that has gained such high status throughout the world. A French to English version of the home-school switch would worry them, as it would any North American minority group, because they believe that English would easily swamp French. Many have a sense of inferiority about their home language and for them training in "school" French, not English is a requisite. They, in fact, often hear exhortations to abandon their own variety of French for the standard form (see d'Anglejan, 1971) without considering the interesting alternative of developing and maintaining both styles. For French Canadians, then, a valuable alternative would be to start prekindergarten training at age four with half of the school day conducted in French and half in English (cf., Tucker, Otanes, and Sibayan, 1970). The classes would be taught by two different teachers presenting themselves as monolinguals. Starting in grade I, two separate academic offerings could be instituted, one fully French, the other fully English, with options for each student to move from one to the other for one or more content subjects until both languages are developed to equivalent degrees. Such a program could also integrate French- and English-Canadian children who so far have remained essentially strangers to one another because of separate schools based on religion and language.

In the Canadian setting, however, political decisions could have consequences that work against such a principle. For instance, a widespread movement toward unilingualism and separatism in the French Canadian society could postpone the thorough mastery of English beyond the receptive early years, and all the advantages of being bilingual could easily pass from French Canadians to English Canadians. As we have seen, it is the English Canadians who now have the opportunity, in home-school language-switch programs, to become fully proficient in French *and* English.

APPENDIX A

PARENTS AS CHANGE AGENTS IN EDUCATION:
THE ST. LAMBERT EXPERIMENT[1]

The school's role may be seen historically as an extension of the parents' role as educators. The parents delegate this role for various reasons, such as not feeling qualified to teach their children what they must know to function in society or to develop their individual capacities. With the growing complexity of society over the years, this delegation of responsibility becomes more and more understandable. Since in democratic societies such as ours, the schools have been primarily financed by the parents, and since the administration of the schools has mostly been in the hands of parents' representatives (the school boards), what is taught in the schools can generally be said to represent what the parents wish their children to be taught, perhaps with some time lag.

Parents have generally abdicated any direct control of school programs, either because they were generally satisfied or because, as stated above, they felt unqualified, or simply because they felt helpless to make changes. Since changes usually come about very slowly, parents whose ideas are ahead or different from those of the majority have traditionally banded together to form private schools, if they were in a financial position to do so, or else have tried to make up what they felt was missing in their children's education through private lessons or other means.

-----

[1]Mrs. Olga Melikoff is currently completing her M.A. in second language teaching at the Université de Montréal. She was one of the founding members of the parents' group which initiated the St. Lambert experiment. She has served as a Commissioner of the South Shore Protestant Regional School Board (1964-67), and as chairman of the French Committee of the South Shore Protestant Regional School Board (1967-70). Mrs. Melikoff has been chairman of the St. Lambert Bilingual School Study Group since 1966. She is the mother of three children, the youngest of whom is a member of the Pilot Class at St. Lambert Elementary School.

What happens when a group of parents not only want change but are determined to effect this change within the public school system, despite the opposition of a large segment of the community, as well as of school board members, school administrators, and teachers? What would be their methods to bring about change, and would they have any hope of success?

In this paper we shall examine what a group of parents of the City of St. Lambert, Quebec, were able to accomplish in the field of educational change in the matter of a few years and the conditions that prompted the innovation. The parents spearheaded a radical change in second-language teaching which not only caught on in this Montreal South Shore area, but is serving as a model in nearby Montreal and in schools far removed from this location.

The parents' activities may be roughly divided into three periods:

(1) 1963-1965—preparing the groundwork and developing certain skills in research and communication;
(2) 1965-1967—playing a supportive role in the implementation of the program;
(3) 1967 to the present—helping to institutionalize the experiment.

We shall examine each stage of the development of the program as seen through the eyes of a parent very much involved in all three periods.

1963-65—Preparing the Groundwork

Birth of the St. Lambert Protestant Parents for Bilingual Education

On October 30, 1963, a group of twelve parents met to discuss what they considered a lamentable situation in the local school system. Children were graduating from English Protestant schools in this province with little more knowledge of French than their parents had had, despite claims that the programs had been considerably improved over the years. Their knowledge was not perceptibly superior to that of graduates from the English provinces of Canada and was not sufficient to enable the students to communicate with their French-Canadian neighbors. The parents felt their children were being shortchanged and should have the opportunity to become "bilingual" within the school system, since it was so difficult to achieve this skill outside of school. The day of the French maid or French tutor was gone and, at any rate, it never did solve the problem for the large majority. St. Lambert was in 1963 approximately 50 percent French, 50 percent English. It seemed inconceivable to the parents that the children of the two ethnic groups should remain "incommunicado" forever because of language differences. Both groups did cooperate in certain community endeavors such as children's sports programs; yet if there was no tension between the groups, there was also very little communication. The parents decided to organize themselves to do something about this language problem.

Parents' Motivation

Some members of the group had generally more "instrumental" reasons for wishing their children to be bilingual. They wished the continuing progress and success of their children in a province progressively becoming more dominated by the French fact. Others considered bilingualism a personal asset for cultural, intellectual, and social reasons—the so-called "integrative" motivation. All were concerned with French-English relations in the province, at a time when these were not yet making the headlines.

It was basically a calm period for English Quebecers, and they were watching with favor the "quiet revolution" going on in the French sector. The reforms in education were looked upon with particular interest and satisfaction. This small group of St. Lambert parents represented those who were generally interested in educational issues and perhaps looked at them from a more critical point of view than average.

In a province where schools were divided along confessional lines—Catholic and Protestant (or non-Catholic)—several of these Protestant parents had put their children in French Catholic schools or even in the academically weaker French Protestant classes to give them a chance to become fluent in the second language. The former practice had proven successful for some parents, but never had wide appeal because of the question of religious instruction in the schools. However, this source of bilingual training was gradually being closed down to all Protestants in St. Lambert because of a condition of overcrowding within the Catholic system. This forced the keenest proponents of bilingual education to turn to their own system for a solution. Their experience in the St. Lambert Catholic schools, which happened to be among the best in the province, disposed them favorably to French education, a veritable unknown to the average English-speaking Quebecer. Hence we see that some of the parents in the group had already crossed the linguistic and cultural line and did not find it threatening, as far as educational options go.

Parents' Initial Program

At their first meeting the group elected officers and outlined its goals. These were to give the children early training in the second language before stereotypes and prejudices had a chance to form, and to take advantage of the young child's apparent ease in language learning. It was also felt that a second language would make the rather lean program of the early years more challenging for the average child. The method for attaining these goals would be to institute kindergarten and the first three grades entirely in French within the English Protestant system. Three years of French was considered a minimum on the basis of the experience of parents who had had their children in French schools.

From a tactical point of view, it was decided that the first move would be for two parents to visit the supervisor of the Chambly County Protestant Central School Board, under whose jurisdiction St. Lambert Protestant schools fell. Another member, remembering that she had heard Dr. W. E. Lambert of McGill University speak on bilingualism, was to get in touch with him for possible support. Little did the parents know at this time, what the consequences of these modest overtures would be.

First Approach to Board

The first visit to the Supervisor was encouraging. He stated that if enough children could be found to form one French kindergarten class of twenty children, consideration would be given to the request. He did express doubt, however, that twenty children could be found. Would the board assist the group in finding the names of eligible parents from the tax rolls? No, he said, this would not be possible. This first negative answer gave the first hint of many more to come.

Using a variety of methods, the group made up a list of parents and mailed out a rather Madison Avenue sheet requesting parents to sign up their children if they were in sympathy with a four-year French program (kindergarten and first three grades). The response was quick and overwhelmingly in favor of the proposal. Over the next two months, over one hundred families returned the sheets, listing the names of several hundred children ranging in age from one to nine years. Rather than referring to the number of families, the more impressive figure of 240 parents was always used when stating the number of original supporters of the proposal.

With this information in hand, the group approached the St. Lambert School Board, where a confused and self-conscious group of commissioners hastened to state that they did not handle educational policy. They referred the parents to the Chambly County Board, on which they were represented by two out of five members.

Request to the Chambly County Protestant Central School Board

The Central Board was the result of the centralization policy of the fifties that united the boards of St. Lambert and five other South Shore communities. There were doubts expressed whether centralization benefited St. Lambert as much as it did the other areas; but in the case of the proposal for bilingual education, the fact of centralization may well have been an asset. The conservative St. Lambert members and the Board chairman, from a similar type of community, were immediately negative to the proposal. The other areas, perhaps to get even with St. Lambert, towards whom they had feelings of jealousy, or possibly because they felt a greater personal need for bilingualism in their own lives and communities, were more favorably disposed. A fair amount of animosity was evident at this and subsequent meetings, animosity between Board members themselves and toward the parents, who were threatening the long-held view of the superior quality of education being offered by the English school system.

The Board decided that a committee of two—the Supervisor and a St. Lambert member—would seek the advice of experts and report on the feasibility and desirability of putting the parents' proposal into effect. The committee of two carefully drafted a questionnaire, which they would not show the parents and which was found later to misrepresent their proposal to a certain extent, and mailed it to twenty "experts" on the teaching of French. These experts were mainly supervisors of French as a second language in schools in and around Montreal, at Macdonald College, the teacher-training college of McGill University, and a few private schools.

Becoming "Experts"

The parents' group immediately realized that they must become "experts" too, if they were going to be able to argue their case. They visited Dr. Lambert of McGill, who was interested in their proposal, though he thought that French schooling would be a better choice for the parents than an experiment in an English milieu. They contacted Dr. Wilder Penfield and received fatherly and encouraging advice from him. The group insisted that in the name of fairness, these two men should be sent the Board's questionnaire, and this concession was made. When the results were finally tallied, the St. Lambert member announced that only two of the experts were totally in favor of the proposal. These two were Dr. Lambert and Dr. Penfield! Though others found some parts of the program commendable, they would not endorse it for the public school system. Some thought it would be all right for pupils of superior intelligence; all thought it would affect the children's development in the mother tongue. With these findings, the Board found the support it was looking for and dismissed the parents' request. In the meantime three of the parents had written up in some detail the essence of their proposal in the form of a brief.

The first of the writers based her arguments on the observable increase of need for the English to know French in Montreal; the other two writers based their arguments largely on the UNESCO Report on the teaching of second languages published in 1962, a report that described new approaches to language learning all over the world and cautiously endorsed second-language learning at an early age. This document became the group's bible. It was felt that most of the models discussed did not go far enough to assure the level of bilingualism desired. The essence of the problem was how to increase the number of contact hours in French to attain fluency without sacrificing subject matter. The solution appeared to be sufficient exposure in the early grades to permit the teaching of any subject in either language in the higher grades.

It was felt that the skills required in learning to read and write were sufficiently similar in concept in both languages, so that learning them in French was essentially the same experience as learning them in English. Hence there was little or no hesitation in recommending French reading and writing before reading and writing in the mother tongue.

A second-language experience especially designed for the English-speaking child with his English-speaking peers was considered a less stressful situation than placing him in a milieu designed for French children, in other words, than in placing him in a French school. What might be lost in proficiency would be gained in self-confidence. Another consideration discussed at some length in the brief was the assumption that young children have certain advantages over older children and adults in learning another language. Not to be carried away by theories and to find out what really goes on in a classroom, the parents began at this time to visit or correspond with schools that gave nonconventional language instruction.

The brief was written that first winter and circulated to about fifty experts of the parents' choosing, as well as to the Board members. It was given favorable publicity in *The Montreal Star* and elsewhere. A *Star* editorial of January 29, 1964, said of the proposal: "It is a revolutionary proposal, but if Quebec is to be bilingual, as so many now agree that it should be, some revolutionary steps will have to be taken in the schools." Many encouraging letters were received. The Board, though highly embarrassed by the response, would not consider changing its stand. It even chose to ignore the parents' counterarguments and criticisms of the Board's questionnaire and left the parents' letters unanswered.

Nature of Parents' Group

As a result of this treatment the group became a more cohesive and determined body. The nucleus of about twenty members met frequently during the following year. Each new member went through a process of unburdening himself by describing his own experiences with trying to learn French and by citing examples of his friends and neighbors. Old members heard them out and then patiently explained the alternatives that had faced the group and how the program had been reached by concensus through a process of eliminating conventional approaches of improving second-language teaching. It was a type of sensitivity training, though not consciously so, and contributed to a feeling of solidarity and respect among the members. Though only eight people did most of the actual work, the efforts of the whole group at this stage were essential. Mutual reinforcement gave the members the courage and the will to continue against rather overwhelming odds. For most, this was a first experience with community action, and they found it unusually stimulating and often nerve-racking. The specter of two hundred parents kept the administrators and board members uneasy too, and it was known that some of them were having severe nervous reactions to the group's forceful approach.

Parents' Language Classes

Despite the Board's rejection of the proposal, the parents had no thought of abandoning their project. Instead they came up with the idea of sponsoring language classes for the children of St. Lambert to make up for what they were not getting in school and to demonstrate the method that the group favored—immersion in a "language bath." The bath was to be provided by one French teacher immersing ten to fifteen students. Three summer and two winter sessions were subsequently held, with the parents carrying the full load, both financially and pedagogically. At first they rented space in church halls and then from the Catholic school commissioners, who seemed favorably impressed with the parents' desire to have their children learn French. Later they were able to rent rooms in one of the St. Lambert Protestant schools. This was a small step toward getting "a foot in the door." The language sessions were generally successful, and when the children returned to their school classes, the French supervisor admitted that they had benefited and were ahead of their classmates in oral expression. However, all the parents' calculations and efforts showed that extracurricular French could only amount to a fraction of the time and effectiveness that was possible if the children's school experience was in French.

Local Political Action

Since the St. Lambert Board, acting through their Central Board representatives, had been instrumental in turning down the parents' proposal, it was decided to unbalance the composition of the Board in favor of the project. At first, the parents decided to put up two candidates for the two vacancies coming up in June 1964. On learning this, the Board members proposed a deal whereby they would put up one candidate and would not oppose a candidate of the parents' choice. There had been no school board elections in St. Lambert for years; members traditionally chose their own successors when one wanted to get off the Board. There was a smugness that had developed over the years, perhaps from a lack of issues, in what was essentially a self-satisfied community. The idea of exposing and fighting a radical proposal and thereby polarizing the electorate did not appear to be to the liking of the Board members. The group decided to go along with their proposal, thus guaranteeing themselves at least one seat. A member of the parents' group was thus elected by acclamation and served a three-year term.

The three-year period was characterized by a number of personnel changes, owing to the transition from centralization to a larger regrouping of boards called "regionalization." This transition, with its attendant confusion, often made the parents' task more difficult. It was necessary to explain the proposal over and over again to new personnel. At the same time, it favored the parents in that new appointees did not know what their predecessors had agreed to. A director-general, known to be against the proposal, was brought in from outside the area, and a number of leading administrators were bypassed in promotions to new posts. This resulted in a group of them leaving the area in dissatisfaction.

Acceptance of an Experimental Class

In the unsettled climate of the winter 1964-65, the parents staged some well-attended public meetings under the sponsorship of the Home and School Association. One parent wrote a series of articles on the advantages of early bilingualism in the local press. The French supervisor, who had recently visited the Toronto French School and the classes sponsored by the parents, declared at a Home and School meeting that he thought the early immersion method was undoubtedly extremely effective. He said that he personally did not have any objection to trying out an experiment at the kindergarten level.

By that spring, the St. Lambert Board had become accustomed to the idea of an experiment, and its representatives on the Central Board would no longer oppose it. The composition of the Central Board had that year undergone the usual minor changes. When faced by the favorable publicity of the parents' classes in the local press, and by the persistence of the parents who attended Board meetings regularly, the Central Board relented. They agreed to set up one experimental kindergarten for the fall of 1965.

The parents felt that the Board members accepted the proposal, not through any conviction of their own, but because the pressures on them were more than they could resist. Besides, kindergarten was not a legal requirement at that time, and hence could not be considered a serious commitment. Though not done in the spirit the parents would have liked, the passage of a resolution creating this class was nevertheless a first and most important victory for the parents' group.

Although enough children for two classes applied, permission was granted for one class only. This was only "half" a kindergarten class, as usually defined. Some of the parents who had been most active almost missed enrolling their children, and a substantial number of parents were disappointed. Registration opened one spring day at 1 PM, and by 1:05 PM the quota of twenty-six children was reached.

1965-67—Playing a Supportive Role

Responsibility of Parents

Now the parents' group felt the full weight of responsibility for the success of the Experimental Class. They felt compelled to play a leading role in setting it up. They could hardly leave it in the hands of reluctant administrators who did not know exactly what was expected of them. It was an awkward, unprecedented role for parents, and understandably the administration felt threatened by it. However, there was not much choice for the parents' group. They found the teacher, one whom they had hired themselves for their winter classes, spent hours during the year encouraging her and the skeptical principal of the school selected for the experiment. As an English reading specialist, the principal was fearful for the children's English development. What would happen to children who did not have the usual reading-readiness preparation in English of the other kindergarten children? Of course the problem would be even greater in grade I, when they would miss all the English Language Arts program. On the other hand, she wished the parents luck and did hope the experiment would be successful.

Without leadership from within, the parents' group took further initiatives. They arranged meetings with the parents, since not all were as confident as the members of the organizing group. After all, the experiment was radical for English-speaking parents in this country. They watched their children for signs of emotional strain or deterioration in mother-tongue development. By Christmas time, most were relieved to find the children absorbing with apparent ease a language which they themselves had failed to master. The young scholars even appeared happy. The teacher was particularly gifted in art, and artistic expression helped the children adjust to the inevitable linguistic frustration of the early months. It took a certain amount of courage for parents to put their children in the program, especially when the school authorities took the approach—"You asked for it; if it doesn't work, it's not our fault." Their attitude was justified, considering the circumstances described above.

With the launching of the first kindergarten, the parents' group felt that their major objective had been attained. Over the next few months they decided to phase themselves out of existence by handing over the remaining "watchdog" functions to a smaller group. This smaller group would be asked to see that the experiment was given a fair chance to succeed and to grow in accordance with the parents' objectives.

The St. Lambert Bilingual School Study Group

The smaller group elected to carry on consisted of two members of the original St. Lambert Protestant Parents, two members of the St. Lambert Home and School Association (both active members of the former group as well), and one member from the St. Francis (English Catholic) Parent Teachers' Association. This group took the name of the St. Lambert Bilingual School Study Group and was active till 1970. During this five-year period, it added one member and received diminished support from another. This latter member was a business man who found it difficult to attend the extensive daytime meetings of the group. The new member was an English consultant of the South Shore Board whose special concern, as the experiment progressed, was the quality of the English instruction given the Experimental Classes.

The Study Group turned out to be far more than a watchdog; its essential role was to hold the experiment together when it was in danger of collapsing, as it was on a regular basis. At the same time, it evolved into a position where it was able to extend its influence to a study of the whole problem of second-language teaching on the South Shore. Monies remaining from the St. Lambert Protestant Parents were passed on to the new group for incidental costs such as printing and mailing, and to finance a trip to Toronto for two members in the following year. The remaining amount of $200 was donated for French library books for the bilingual classes.

Though the larger parent group was no longer active, the administrators and Board were never sure of this, and when dealing with the Study Group felt that they were dealing with the original two hundred parents. In a way this was true, for whenever trouble brewed, formerly active members were called on to lend support by appearing at Board meetings, by serving on a telephone committee, or whatever was required.

The Second Brief

The first thing that the Study Group tried to do was to establish a firmer community base for the experiment and to have the experiment officially recognized by the Department of Education in Quebec. It was felt that these two measures would help to ensure the survival of the experiment. The first proved easier to attain than the second.

A brief was prepared, dated December 1965, and submitted to the Minister of Education, Mr. Paul Gérin Lajoie. In this brief, the Study Group enlarged and reworked some of its original ideas. In particular, it suggested the introduction of the mother tongue at the grade II level, instead of the grade IV level as in the first brief. This was thought a better way of satisfying the Board and members of the community who were not favorable to the original program. It would also be less threatening for the English teachers in the employ of the Board. From the children's point of view it was considered that it would be to their advantage to grow in both languages simultaneously by minimizing any loss of early experience with formal English. In a more ambitious vein than hitherto contemplated, it was suggested that the experiment cross religious and linguistic lines in the community, inasmuch as some interest was being shown by English Catholics. It was felt that the experiment would be particularly meaningful if French Canadians took part.

In addition to the Minister, the brief was sent to all Board members and a list of about fifty other persons. These included the local member of Parliament, the late Mr. Pierre Laporte; the Royal Commission of Bilingualism and Biculturalism, a federal commission studying the position of Canada's two official languages throughout the country; the head of the Superior Council of

Education of Quebec; the heads of teaching colleges; Dr. Penfield and Dr. Lambert of McGill; and a host of others.

Reception to the brief was highly favorable—good wishes flooded in from many sources, except from the Ministry. The only word from them was an acknowledgment from the Minister's administrative secretary, indicating that the brief would be brought to the Minister's attention without delay. But it is debatable whether he ever saw it.

At a public meeting a few years later, one of the Study Group members heard the Minister discuss a bilingual experiment in some community other than St. Lambert. When the member questioned him and mentioned the brief sent to him, he merely looked puzzled. He did not appear to have heard of the project, or else had confused St. Lambert with some other community.

Despite lack of official recognition, the brief produced a number of good results. First of all, it received the endorsement of several local organizations interested in education, such as the South Shore University Women's Club, whose names were appended to the brief. The Catholic School commission was also interested in the proposal. Several meetings were held between the Catholic Commissioners and the Study Group, but in the end they felt overextended in experiments and did not want to embark on another. Also, they had the possibility within their own system of changing children from the French to the English stream and vice versa, a practice they were not entirely happy about because of some failures. They had also had some outstanding successes among children who had made switches, including the children of one of the Commissioners herself. Though they refused to take part in the experiment, they did promise to cooperate whenever needed, and subsequently did so. They allowed a class in one of their schools to become the Control Group in the evaluation program that started the following year and offered help to teachers on programs and techniques. However, this offer was only rarely accepted.

Problems of Continuing Project

As the kindergarten year reached the midyear mark, the Board would make no commitment on continuing it into grade I. The second brief produced a mixed reaction among the members. Regionalization was now in progress and the Board's responsibilities had increased considerably. The parents kept in constant touch by attending meetings and writing letters. These efforts were not completely successful and individual Board members began raising a series of objections to continuing the experiment. Some of the objections were of a practical nature—costs, teachers, texts—others were emotional. Some Board members saw the experiment as "selling out" to the French Canadians, as a threat to English education in the Province. They did not say so directly, but the list of objections was so extensive that it was evident to the Study Group that they were just a smoke screen for concealing deeply felt emotions.

The Study Group did not attempt to fight the issue on emotional grounds, but concentrated on refuting the practical objections one at a time. They promised to find the teachers, choose the textbooks, and evolve suitable programs. They assured the Board that the experiment would cost nothing except the initial one of replacing books. (This proved a slight exaggeration, though remarkably little additional expense, apart from increased transportation costs, ever resulted.) The Board's most serious objection was that they would be held responsible in the event the experiment was a failure. They felt that the parents could hold them liable if their children were not able to function normally in English at a later date, or if their education were held back in some way or another.

Calling on McGill University

This final objection was a critical one to solve. Fortunately the Study Group knew where to turn. They visited Dr. Lambert at McGill and without any difficulty persuaded him to become involved in an evaluation program. Dr. Lambert, whose studies on bilingualism were already extensive, was interested in this potentially wide area of experimentation. His participation would be edifying both to himself and to McGill, and it would remove some of the onus of responsibility from the Board. After some awkward overtures, Dr. Lambert and the Board were brought together by the Study Group. His services were gratefully accepted by the Board. With this major objection overcome, the Board agreed to carry on the experiment into grade I and to open up an additional two kindergartens in St. Lambert in the fall of 1966.

Certain problems were to arise in regard to Dr. Lambert's collaboration, since all ramifications were not immediately visualized. Was he being employed by the Board, did he have the right to publish the results on his own, would his evaluation be the sole evaluation or should the Board make its own evaluations too? Would the Board be expected to advance any money toward the evaluation of one community's experiment? In the first year of testing, over $4,000 was spent, the funds coming mainly from the Canada Council. Nothing was spent by the Board. In subsequent years, the Department of Education agreed to contribute a small share of the expenses. Often their payments arrived late, and the Board would advance money, but not without much soul-searching and hesitation. Dr. Lambert was offered money by various American interests, in the course of the next few years, but felt that in a matter of such concern to education in Quebec, the Department of Education should invest research funds.

Launching of Grade I

Thus in its final days, the Chambly County Board agreed to permit the continuation of the experiment and the inclusion of two follow-up kindergartens. The really compromising step had been taken, and the new South

Shore Protestant Regional School Board, successor of the Chambly Board, inherited this dubious stepchild. Approximately two-thirds of the eligible five-year-olds in St. Lambert enrolled in the new option.

Again the Study Group had to provide leadership to the infant experiment. Not one of the administrators of the new Board wholeheartedly backed the program. The new Director of Elementary Education would not recommend it to any parents, though a few years later he helped set up a similar program in an area under the jurisdiction of another board. The new French consultant, brought in from outside the region, admitted skepticism. A first-grade program was put together in a very offhand fashion; two administrators claimed it took them a couple of hours to complete. The Study Group members did what they could to prevent an unsuitable program from being adopted, and changes were incorporated before the school year began.

Two Study Group members and the newly-hired teacher attended a course in new methods of teaching French reading during the summer. They also contacted the Montreal Catholic School Commission, the St. Lambert Catholic School Commission, and the Toronto French School to seek guidelines, which they in turn strongly recommended to the Board, with varying degrees of success. They helped find the grade I teacher, a French Canadian, and spent a lot of time encouraging her at the beginning of the year.

With the teacher and the school principal, two Study Group members visited the Toronto French School. This school was two or three years ahead of the St. Lambert experiment in offering a program in bilingual education, somewhat along the lines of that recommended by the parents for St. Lambert. When conceiving their program, the parents were not aware of the Toronto initiative, but were to become indebted to that school for inspiration and advice.

Comparison with Toronto French School

The program offered in Toronto was more ambitious than that advocated by the St. Lambert parents as far as actual curriculum content. In Toronto, their goal was to prepare their pupils for both the French baccalauréat as well as the Ontario high school leaving certificate. They also offered enrichment, such as the teaching of Russian in grade III and other courses in advance of the usual curriculum. Some selection of pupils was made in Toronto and fees eliminated others. In St. Lambert the parents wanted to make the possibility of bilingual education open to children of any intellectual capacity and at public expense. Though the parents felt that enrichment was desirable, they did not want to mix their goals. A revision of the school's offerings could be left to others or to another time. They wanted the "normal" education, with one exception—it should lead to bilingualism by the end of elementary school, with no deficit in the mother tongue. It was hoped that the testing program would ascertain if these goals were being reached.

Study Group and Dr. Lambert Linked by Common Concerns

Many problems plagued the infant experiment. The grade I teacher fell ill in the month of March and was replaced by a teacher with a more traditional background. Some of the children were upset by the change and, for the first time, were complaining about going to school. What may have been considered a normal reaction to school in the monolingual program, was viewed with alarm in the experiment. One or two parents removed their children at the end of the year for a variety of reasons, but the mortality rate was and continued to be very low over the following years. Transfer of families away from St. Lambert was the prime reason for withdrawing from the program.

Administration of the project continued to be weak. At the beginning of grade II, when the teacher who was hired did not turn up, a totally unqualified teacher was hired in her place, much to the consternation of the Study Group and Dr. Lambert. This type of situation helped to bring Dr. Lambert and the Study Group closer together, for both were generally in agreement over how things should or should not be done. Dr. Lambert became involved in the Study Group's problems, even though they were not technically part of his mandate. For example, he was instrumental in finding teachers and advising parents who were worried about possible ill effects of the program on their child, because of this or that perceptual or intellectual difficulty.

Each year the Study Group brought the parents together to hear Dr. Lambert's evaluations. Every result was carefully analyzed and measures were suggested to counteract this or that possible ill effect. Besides testing the Pilot Class, Dr. Lambert extended his evaluation to the Follow-up Class, using the same control groups—Rabeau School in St. Lambert for French Controls, and Roslyn School of Westmount and a twin class in St. Lambert as English Controls. The results of the testing supported the parents significantly in their continuing struggle to develop and institutionalize the program.

Period from 1967 to the Present

Institutionalization of the Bilingual Program

After a three-year term of office on the St. Lambert Board, the parent member withdrew her candidature in favor of another member of the original parents' group. Again this nomination went unchallenged. A second Board replacement was also supported by the parents' group; hence a firm foothold was established on the local Board. Subsequently the former member became a member of the South Shore Regional Board, a position he still holds today. Dangers to the existence of the program still appear regularly under the subtle pressure of various administrators and Board members. Popular support is mounting, however, throughout the region, on the basis of the results of the evaluation program and the changing conditions of Quebec society.

After leaving the Board the parent member was asked to serve on an Education Committee of the new Regional Board, and shortly after headed one of its subcommittees on the teaching of French. She invited the two Study Group members, with whom she had worked the most since 1963, to join the committee. Other members included French consultants, teachers, parents, and several administrators in an ex officio capacity. The French Subcommittee, later to become the French Committee, became an additional way the parents could keep an eye on the bilingual experiment and recommend its continuation and expansion. It was also an opportunity to show that they were interested in the whole problem of second-language teaching on the South Shore. They never did want to write off the children who did not choose the bilingual option or those who had missed it because of age. Several reports were written by the French Committee from this perspective. These reports and pressure from the communities themselves were instrumental in having the bilingual program extended to other areas of the South Shore. A few innovations in the general French program, such as the employment of French-teaching aides, also resulted from the committee's recommendations.

The favorable results of the McGill testing program were well publicized in the press, and increasing numbers of parents wanted to get on the bilingual bandwagon. In other areas a backlash developed; in one area an administrator was suspected of stirring up an unfavorable reaction, with the result that parents were petitioning the Board not to extend the experiment to their school. Later he resigned and moved to another province. Shortly after, the program was successfully introduced there at the request of the parents, the petition apparently forgotten, or the protestors outnumbered.

It is interesting to note that by 1967, several Board members were struggling with French language courses sponsored by their employers (e.g., Northern Electric, Bell Telephone, etc.). Those involved became more receptive to "easier" ways of learning French. This was a fortunate coincidence as far as the Study Group was concerned.

At no time would the Board undertake to accept the experiment for more than a year at a time, claiming annual authorization from Quebec was needed. This authorization usually came after the fact, as it happened. However, it meant that every spring was a time of tension for the parents. Since 1970, it has become inconceivable that the program would be withdrawn in the early years. The outcry would be too great. Nevertheless, the fate of the Pilot Class continues to hang in balance. Would the parents' desire to maintain bilingualism through high school be respected? Pressures for French unilingualism now rampant in the Province mitigate against the full endorsement and development of the program because this endorsement might appear to constitute support for a loss of English-schooling rights. Also English-speaking teachers feel their positions threatened by the program, and this threat must be acknowledged and solutions sought.

Study Group as Proselytes and "Animateurs"

Members of the Study Group unwittingly became proselytes of bilingual education away from their home environment. Not only were they asked to speak to parents in various communities on the South Shore, but they were invited as guests of Home and School Associations in Montreal and outlying areas, between the years 1967 and 1970. Generally they were received very favorably, though sometimes they felt they were being used simply as object lessons for boards who were not moving fast enough in the area of French language instruction.

In St. Lambert, the Study Group continued to walk a tightrope between parents, administration, the Community, and McGill. The role of mediator, "animateur," and watchdog, kept the Study Group "ungainfully employed" an hour or two a day for a number of years, and more at certain critical periods. For example, they prepared for the parents a pamphlet entitled "Bilingualism without Tears", a list of do's and don'ts to cover such novel situations as not understanding the children's homework, or to explain the French reading methods, or the use of cursive writing in grade I. They also made an effort to keep up with research on language teaching and bilingualism by attending meetings such as the one held by the American Association for the Advancement of Science and by taking further university training in education, psychology, and linguistics.

When school restructuration and language issues came into political prominence, they felt called upon to express their views. In 1968 they sent a letter to Education Minister Guy Cardinal suggesting that the bilingual option should not be overlooked in any restructuring of the schools along language lines in the Province of Quebec. It was felt that division by language might polarize each sector and make the cooperation desirable for bilingual education more difficult to attain.

In 1970, a Study Group member assisted in the preparation of a submission to the Gendron Commission, a provincial commission on the status of the French language in Quebec. The brief was sponsored by the South Shore University Women's Club and emphasized the desirability of bilingual education. The member defended the submission before the Commission and later was invited to a colloquy of the Commission, to which were invited educators and linguists from McGill, Montreal, and Laval Universities, and the Ontario Institute for Studies in Education, etc.

At times the Study Group attained a certain respectability with the South Shore administration. The nucleus of three members was routinely included in any meetings with Dr. Lambert, or on curriculum. In turn, they did not hesitate to call the administrators to meet with the McGill team or with the teachers, if they thought a critical issue was developing. This abnormal situation was tolerated, probably because it was recognized that the Study Group had creative approaches to what was, after all, their brainchild.

Extension of Experiment

Today the experiment involves more than 700 children in six communities of the South Shore Region. It can therefore be said that the experiment has been successfully institutionalized for the early grades. The leadership of the project by joint committee, based on a recognition of the interdependence of the parents' group, the Board, and McGill, and which marked the early years of the experiment, is now shifting to a new formula. The prominent role of the parents has of necessity been reduced, and the brunt of the leadership appears to be passing into the hands of the evaluators. Whether this is the best solution or not is subject to question. The excellent evaluation program and support did not to date include the area of pedagogy, and whether a university Department of Psycholinguistics is the best source of pedagogical leadership remains to be seen. The Study Group has always advocated local leadership in the form of the appointment of a special consultant for the project. This person would be in touch with a wide assortment of "specialists" on both the French and English sides, as well as with the parents and teachers. So far this principle has not been accepted by the South Shore Board.

An Unexpected Outcome of Project

By one of the ironies of history, what was always intended and fought for as a freely chosen educational option is in danger of becoming a blueprint for English education in the province of Quebec as a result of the recent passage of a bill requiring compulsory French instruction in grade I. If English parents are voluntarily submitting their children to the French language and French culture, one wonders if there is any need or even if it is desirable to tamper with this goodwill by legislating a policy of bilingual education on English schools. Political expediency in this case may well have a negative rather than a positive effect on what is a natural and free choice of a growing number of Anglophone parents.

The St. Lambert Formula "Abroad"

The St. Lambert formula has been adopted and adapted by a number of school boards outside the South Shore area. In Quebec, these include several Protestant and a few Catholic boards in the Greater Montreal area. Outside of Quebec, almost entirely as a result of the publicity on the evaluation program and contacts of the McGill team, programs modeled on St. Lambert have been started in Ontario, New Brunswick, various communities in the United States, and even in countries on the other side of the globe. In the city of Ottawa, 90 per cent of English Catholic children offered the program are in a French immersion kindergarten which they attend in addition to the regular English program. Next year many more will be involved.

Visitors from as far afield as the Philippines have come to inspect the bilingual classes in St. Lambert. One of the reasons for St. Lambert's importance as an educational experiment is that it is the first experiment in bilingual education to be submitted to longitudinal testing. The Pilot Class is now finishing grade V, and it is the parents' wish that the bilingual program continue to be evaluated and developed as scientifically as possible to the conclusion of the children's school careers.

Conclusion

With the expansion of the bilingual program and its rise to prominence in educational circles both nationally and internationally, the role of the parents as change agents has largely come to an end. However, it may be said with certainty that a small group of parents, by virtue of developing certain persuasive and intellectual skills, as well as by expending considerable energy, was able to effectuate a radical change in the curriculum of a conservative public school system. The times they were living in and the environment in which they were operating were on their side. The change they affected may well have more far-reaching results than were ever anticipated.

Many problems remain to be solved in the future development of the program, but the basic pattern has been established. This pattern will undoubtedly influence educational thinking for some years to come as an increasing number of children come in contact with this form of education. It is hoped and believed that these children are not the pawns of an educational experiment but the beneficiaries of an education that will be rewarding to them personally and to the society in which they live.

Olga Melikoff
June 1971

APPENDIX B

DESCRIPTIONS OF THE CLASSES IN ACTION[1]

Kindergarten

First impression is of a well-organized, very disciplined class, where "disciplined" is used with a European meaning. That is, the class seems more French, or European, than a typical kindergarten in North America. The teacher speaks a great deal; actually she speaks all of the time and accompanies her speech with gestures, mimics.

There is less free play and individual activities than one usually finds in North American kindergartens. For instance, I did not see a dolls' corner, or building blocks' corner which could have been used by a child alone. All activities were group ones, some involving the whole class, others smaller numbers of children, but all teacher-directed. Even when the children were given their choice of cutting or gluing or coloring, they sat in groups of four or five at different tables prepared with materials in advance by the teacher who told them what to cut out (e.g., a big fish or a small fish) or how to paste on colored paper.

The teacher circulates all the time, keeping up a steady flow of conversation, commenting, approving, asking questions. The children speak English to her. She repeats their sentences in French, answers them, and tries to have the child repeat the answer in French after her. However, she never puts pressure on the children to do so.

---

[1] Observations made in early October 1971 by Mme. Benoite Noble, an experienced teacher from France who has taught in France, England, and Canada. This was her first introduction to the school. The observations are based on visits of two hours in each class. Certain subject matters, such as mathematics and science, did not happen to be in progress during her visits.

Every day the teacher goes through routines, using the same sentences or words; the weather is an example. These routine sentences are very easily understood, and in this respect there is a sort of ritualistic use of French.

There are more group activities involving all the children when the teacher turns to storytelling with picture books, or singing. For other activities the children sit on the floor in a big circle, and take turns doing what the teacher wants them to do. For example, I saw a fishpond game. Three children at a time went to "fish" with a rod with a string and a magnet attached. As each cutout was fished up, the teacher asked questions about it: What is it? Is it big? Who caught it? and so forth, and then another child was asked by the teacher to take a turn.

The teacher waits for the children to answer a question. If no answer is given, or if the answer is given in English, the teacher provides one in French. The children then repeat it together.

The "effort" is almost all the teacher's. The children are very passive towards speaking French. They speak English together and to the teacher.

The children pay great attention and seem more quiet than in an ordinary kindergarten.

Grade I

Very much like a European (or traditional) class. The children sit at desks, are not allowed to move freely in the class, and have to raise their hand before talking. Everything is directed and controlled by the teacher, and most activities are group ones. Again the teacher talks a great deal and gives explanations accompanied by more gestures than would be the case if the children were French-speaking.

Reading is also a group activity at the start. The teacher reads the text slowly and gives many explanations. All the children follow in their books, putting their finger or a ruler under the line being read aloud. Then the children read one after the other. Some reading is mimeographed, and in that case difficult words are depicted pictorially and not written.

For dictations, the teacher prepares stencils with all the words in the text, but in a random order. The children cut out each of the words, and paste them one by one on a sheet of paper as the teacher dictates slowly. Everything is done following directions and suggestions of the teacher: close your books, put them in your drawer, take a pair of scissors, cut the word "le," and so forth.

The children speak mostly English to the teacher and always English to each other. When they speak French, at the urging of the teacher, it is done haltingly and hesitantly, and the teacher has to fill in. However, when they read a text already studied in the group, they read very well and with hardly any English accent. The reading book is one used by French-speaking children in grade I. The workbook that accompanies the text is not used, because it is too difficult. The teacher prefers to prepare stencils to accommodate the limited vocabulary of the children.

There is less "free time" than in a conventional first grade. The emphasis is on understanding French and on acquiring structures and vocabulary, and many activities are directed towards that goal. The class is more "regimented" and "disciplined," but the children do not seem disturbed, nor do they show signs of tension. They seem happy and proud of their work. There is no noise or chatter. The main impression is that the teacher is completely in control of her class, and that everything comes from her. At all times, the children do what she wants them to do.

The incentive and effort come from the teacher.

Grade II

Very similar to a European French class. The children sit at individual desks, raise their hands to speak, and do not move around. The teacher stands and circulates. She hardly sits down.

The teacher feels that there are too many children in the class—thirty-three, eleven of whom are French-speaking.[2] The children are very disciplined, sit at their desks, obey the teacher. The number of French-speaking children is a handicap, as they answer rapidly and the teacher has to tell them not to speak first in order to give a chance to the slower-reacting English-speaking children. In grade II the children make an effort to answer or speak French to the teacher. They have a noticeable English accent when they speak spontaneously but little accent when they read or recite. When they have made a mistake, they willingly repeat the correct sentence after the teacher.

The teacher speaks less than in grade I, since the written work takes more time.

The subject matter is the same as that taught to French-speaking public-school children in grade II. However, the lessons on language and vocabulary and the "récitations" are taught with reference to the special needs of the pupils involved. The teaching centers around the reading lesson, which provides the core from which the dictation, the vocabulary, and the grammar are taken. A great deal of thought and preparation is evident because the lessons are well planned. The workbooks provided with the reading book are not used for the same reason as in grade I. The teacher prepares stencils according to the children's needs and her own plans.

---

[2] As mentioned in the text, the French Protestant children are now integrated with the new Experimental classes. This was not the case in the Pilot and Follow-up Classes, however.

The text of the dictation is taken from the reading lesson. It is written on the blackboard in the morning, read aloud, spelled, and explained by the teacher. Then it is erased and the dictation is given only in the afternoon. It also serves as an exercise in penmanship.

The short poems learned by heart at school are recited in unison or individually. They become a good exercise for correct pronunciation and function as a model for the acquisition of the rhythm and intonation of the French sentence. The children like them very much.

Every day the children watch a TV program for elementary school children called "les Oraliens."

The books are from France, or adaptations for Quebec, apart from the mathematics text, which is a translation of an American one.

The "effort" emanates mostly from the teacher.

Grade III

More like a conventional class in public school. The children's tables are grouped together. The teacher is French-Canadian.

The children speak more spontaneously in French. They still use English when they do not know the French equivalent, and the teacher provides the fill-ins. The teacher speaks less and there is more individual, silent work done. The reading is silent first, then the teacher reads aloud and explains or asks questions to determine if the children understand. Then the children read one at a time, sentence by sentence. When everyone has had a turn at reading, the children are tested. They answer, in writing and in their own words, questions prepared by the teacher; the questions are on stencils which are placed in each child's "cahier de questions." This serves also as a "rédaction" exercise.

Each child also has a "cahier-dictionnaire," which is very popular. In this they write the definitions of words they do not understand after looking them up in a Larousse dictionary.

The children understand their teacher very well. They appear not to express themselves so well as they understand since they make many grammatical mistakes, spelling errors, use strange constructions, Anglicisms, etc. However they speak willingly and are not self-conscious or shy.

Grade IV

The class is very quiet and organized. The children's desks are placed in rows, two by two. The children raise their hands and wait until the teacher asks them what they want. The teacher gives many explanations, asks many questions, and generally speaks more than she would with French-speaking children. The children willingly speak French to her and English to each other. In French, they still make mistakes such as: j'ai tombé, je suis faim. The teacher keeps a record of such errors and prepares exercises to improve defective structures.

The dictation is written in advance on the board with spelling mistakes made on purpose. The children have to determine whether the words are written correctly or not. They seem to like this type of exercise very much and consider it to be a game. After the text is corrected, it is erased and dictated.

The written work is very neat. The children are obviously proud of the high standards which are expected of them.

Geography is taught for the first time in grade IV. They use a book for French-speaking children in grade IV. The children are given numerous explanations by their teacher.

The class is very teacher-controlled and disciplined. The teacher does not raise her voice and speaks calmly, the children are quiet and very relaxed. The teacher mentioned that she cannot work with a noisy group and must be able to hear perfectly at all times in order to correct the slightest mistakes.

The children have homework every day.

Grade V

The teacher, a French Canadian, is bilingual and teaches also in English in another class, but not with the same children. There is a problem: six Anglophone children who have not had any French instruction previously were put into this class in September.[3] They are unable to follow the program and the teacher must help them a great deal. She objects to this situation and says that it slows the program down. There are also two or three Francophone children who do not speak English. As a good deal of the program is in English at grade V, their inclusion hampers the progress of the class as a whole. The program is the same as in a fifth-grade French-Canadian school. The reading book is Canadian *(l'Invitation au voyage: Education nouvelle)*. The children read very well, with practically no accent. When they speak, an English accent is apparent and they make grammatical mistakes that a French-speaking child would not. They answer orally questions asked about the reading, and then answer other questions in writing in their exercise books.

There is more talking between children (sometimes in French), moving in the room, getting up to sharpen pencils, and so forth. When the planned work is finished, they are allowed to begin something else of their own choice. The class is not noisy, but seems less organized.

History is taught for the first time in this grade and is taught in French. There is no adequate book for the children (so the teacher told me) and she has to prepare the lessons on her own.

The children have homework to do at night.

---

[3] As of September 1971, parents in the region were allowed to request schooling in French for their children of any age, and the school authorities had to provide it.

Summary

These general impressions remain: the teachers speak French all the time; they like, are even enthusiastic about, their work; they are competent, experienced elementary school teachers, not second-language specialists; the teachers have a great deal of team spirit in that they often get together to talk about their program, exchange ideas, give each other advice and encouragement; the lessons are well prepared in advance and one has the impression of very well-organized work, where nothing is left to spur-of-the-moment improvisation; on the whole the atmosphere is very French, or traditional; the teachers control their classes, expect good work, provide the incentive; the teachers speak *more* than they would for French-speaking children, use *routine* sentences more often, circulate more to give each child individual attention and encouragement. They keep up a steady flow of commentary without checking to see if the children understand everything; they find that the more contact between teacher and child there is, the more progress the children make in their ability to verbalize; the children seem to pay more attention than usual; they also seem to be proud of their work and to enjoy the program very much.

Benoite Noble
October 1971

References

d'Anglejan, A. "Sociolinguistic Correlates of Language Register in Three French Canadian Settings." Unpublished master's thesis. McGill University, 1971.

Association of Catholic Principals of Montreal. *A Brief to The Commission of Inquiry on The Position of the French Language and on Language Rights in Quebec*. Montreal: June 1969.

L'Association des Principaux de Montréal, Inc. *Communiqué*, Montréal: September 1969.

Bloom, B. S. *Stability and Change in Human Characteristics*. New York: Wiley, 1964.

Campbell, R. N., G. R. Tucker, and D. M. Taylor. "Teachers' Views of Immersion-type Bilingual Programs: A Quebec Example." Montreal: McGill University, September 1971. (Mimeo)

Cheeseman, H. R. In A. Isidro, *Ang wikang pambasa at ang paaralan*. Manila: Bureau of Printing, 1949.

Cole, M., and J. S. Bruner. "Cultural Differences and Inferences about Psychological Processes." *American Psychologist*, 26 (1971), 867-76.

Cronbach, L. J. *Essentials of Psychological Testing*. New York: Harper & Row, 1970.

Davé, R. H. "The Identification and Measurement of Environmental Process Variables That Are Related to Educational Achievement." Unpublished doctoral dissertation. University of Chicago, 1963.

Davine, M., G. R. Tucker, and W. E. Lambert. "The Perception of Phoneme Sequences by Monolingual and Bilingual Elementary School Children." *Canadian Journal of Behavioural Science*, 3 (1971), 72-76.

Davis, F. B., ed. *Philippine Language-Teaching Experiments*. Quezon City, Philippines: Alemar-Phoenix, 1967.

Dunn, L. M. *Peabody Picture Vocabulary Test*. Nashville, Tenn.: American Guidance Service, 1959.

Elashoff, J. D. "Analysis of Covariance: A Delicate Instrument." *American Education Research Journal*, 6 (1969), 383-401.

Entwisle, D. "Form Class and Children's Word Associations." *Journal of Verbal Learning and Verbal Behavior*, 5 (1966), 558-65.

Ervin, S. "Changes with Age in the Verbal Determinants of Word Association." *American Journal of Psychology*, 74 (1961), 361-72.

Feenstra, H. J. "Aptitude, Attitude and Motivation in Second Language Acquisition." Unpublished doctoral dissertation. University of Western Ontario, 1968.

———, and R. C. Gardner. "Aptitude, Attitude and Motivation in Second-Language Acquisition." University of Western Ontario, 1968. (Mimeo)

Fennessey, J. "The General Linear Model: A New Perspective on Some Familiar Topics." *The American Journal of Sociology*, 74 (1968), 1-27.

Fishman, J. A., R. L. Cooper, and R. Ma. *Bilingualism in the Barrio*. Final Report to U.S. Department of Health, Education, and Welfare. New York: Yeshiva University, 1968.

Gardner, R. C. "Motivational Variables in Second-Language Acquisition." Unpublished doctoral dissertation. McGill University, 1960.

———, and W. E. Lambert. "Motivational Variables in Second-Language Acquisition." *Canadian Journal of Psychology*, 13 (1959), 266-72.

Getzels, J. W., and P. W. Jackson. *Creativity and Intelligence*. New York: Wiley, 1962.

Guilford, J. P. "Creativity." *American Psychologist*, 5 (1950), 444-54.

Hayes, A. S., W. E. Lambert, and G. R. Tucker. "Evaluation of Foreign Language Teaching." *Foreign Language Annals*, 1 (1967), 22-44.

Heyerdahl, T. "The voyage of Ra II." *National Geographic*, 139 (1971), 44-71.

Jones, F. E., and W. E. Lambert. "Attitudes toward Immigrants in a Canadian Community." *Public Opinion Quarterly*, 23 (1959) 537-46.

———, and W. E. Lambert. "Occupational Rank and Attitudes toward Immigrants." *Public Opinion Quarterly*, 29 (1965), 137-44.

———, and ———. "Some Situational Influences on Attitudes toward Immigrants." *The British Journal of Sociology*, 18 (1967), 408-24.

Kittell, J. E. "Bilingualism and Language." *Journal of Educational Research*, 52 (1959), 263-68.

———. "I. Q. Performance of Children from Bilingual Environments." *Elementary School Journal*, 64 (1963), 76-83.

Lambert, W. E. "A Social Psychology of Bilingualism." *Journal of Social Issues*, 23 (1967), 91-109.

———. "What Are They Like, These Canadians? A Social Psychological Analysis." *Canadian Psychologist*, 11 (1970), 303-33.

———, and E. Anisfeld. "A Note on the Relationship of Bilingualism and Intelligence." *Canadian Journal of Behavioural Science*, 1 (1969), 123-28.

———, H. Frankel, and G. R. Tucker. "Judging Personality through Speech: A French-Canadian Example." *Journal of Communication*, 16 (1966), 305-21.

———, and R. C. Gardner. *Attitudes and Motivation in Second-Language Learning*. Rowley, Mass.: Newbury House Publishers, 1972.

———, R. C. Gardner, R. Olton, and K. Tunstall. "A Study of the Roles of Attitudes and Motivation in Second-Language Learning." McGill University 1962. (Mimeo)

———, M. Just, and N. Segalowitz. "Some Cognitive Consequences of Following the Curricula of Grades One and Two in a Foreign Language." *Georgetown Monograph Series on Languages and Linguistics*, 23 (1970), 229-279.

———, and O. Klineberg. *Children's Views of Foreign People: A Cross-national Study*. New York: Appleton-Century-Crofts, 1967.

———, and J. Macnamara. "Some Cognitive Consequences of Following a First-Grade Curriculum in a Second Language." *Journal of Educational Psychology*, 60 (1969), 86-96.

———, G. R. Tucker, A. d'Anglejan, and S. Segalowitz. "Cognitive and Attitudinal Consequences of Following the Curricula of the First Three Grades in a Foreign Language." McGill University, 1971. (Mimeo)

———, G. R. Tucker, A. d'Anglejan, and F. Silny. "Cognitive and Attitudinal Consequences of Bilingual Schooling: The St. Lambert Project through Grade Five." McGill University, 1972. (Mimeo)

Macnamara, J. *Bilingualism and Primary Education.* Edinburgh Univ. Press, 1966.

Malherbe, E. G. *The Bilingual School.* London: Longmans, 1946.

Metropolitan Achievement Tests, Primary I Battery. New York: Harcourt, Brace & World, 1959.

Osgood, C. E. "On the Nature of Meaning." *Psychological Bulletin*, 49 (1952), 197-237.

Peal, E. "A Comparison of the Cognitive Functioning of Monolinguals and Bilinguals." Unpublished doctoral dissertation. McGill University, 1964.

———, and W. E. Lambert. "The Relation of Bilingualism to Intelligence." *Psychological Monographs,* 76 (1962), 1-23.

Prator, C. H., Jr. *Language Teaching in the Philippines*. Manila: U.S. Educational Foundation in the Philippines, 1950.

Prince, V. "L'avenir du français au Canada et au Québec." *Le Devoir*, 30 décembre 1970, p. A-15.

Rabinovitch, M. S., and L. M. Parver. "Auditory Discrimination in Monolinguals and Polyglots." Paper presented at meeting of Canadian Psychological Association, Montreal, 1966.

Raven, J. C. *Coloured Progressive Matrices: Sets A, Ab, B*. London: Lewis, 1956.

———, *Standard Progressive Matrices: Sets A, B, C, D, and E*. London: Lewis, 1958.

Reynolds, A., N. Wargny, and W. E. Lambert. "The Development of Ethnic Attitudes among Children Schooled in a Second Language." Paper presented at meeting of Canadian Psychological Association, Winnipeg, June 1970.

Richardson, M. W. "An Evaluation of Certain Aspects of the Academic Achievement of Elementary Pupils in a Bilingual Program." Unpublished doctorate of education dissertation. University of Miami, 1968.

Samuels, M., A. G. Reynolds, and W. E. Lambert. "Communicational Efficiency of Children Schooled in a Foreign Language." *Journal of Educational Psychology*, 60 (1969), 389-93.

Santos, E. H. "A Study of the Roles of Aptitude, Attitude and Motivation in Second Language Acquisition." Unpublished master's thesis. Philippine Normal College, 1969.

Snedecor, J. W. *Statistical methods.* Ames, Iowa: Iowa State College Press, 1956.

Torrance, E. P., J. C. Gowan, Jing-Jyi Wu, and N. C. Aliotti. "Creative Functioning of Monolingual and Bilingual Children in Singapore." *Journal of Educational Psychology*, 61 (1970), 72-75.

Tucker, G. R., W. E. Lambert, A. d'Anglejan, and F. Silny. "Cognitive and Attitudinal Consequences of Following the Curricula of the First Four Grades in a Second Language." McGill University, 1971 (Mimeo)

———, ———, A Rigault, and N. Segalowitz. "A Psychological Investigation of French Speakers' Skill with Grammatical Gender."

———, ———, and ———. "Students' Acquisition of French Gender Distinctions: A Pilot Investigation." *International Review of Applied Linguistics in Language Teaching*, 7 (1969), 51-55.

———, F. T. Otanes, and B. P. Sibayan. "An Alternate Days Approach to Bilingual Education." *Monograph Series of Language and Linguistics.* Ed. J. E. Alatis. Washington. D.C.: Georgetown University Press, 1970, 23, 281-99.

Vygotsky, L. S. *Thought and Language.* Cambridge, Mass.: M.I.T., 1962.

West, M. *Bilingualism (With Special Reference to Bengal).* Calcutta, 1926.

Winer, B. J. *Statistical Principles in Experimental Design.* New York: McGraw-Hill, 1962.

Wolf, R. M. "The Identification and Measurement of Environmental Process Variables Related to Intelligence." Unpublished doctoral dissertation. University of Chicago, 1963.

Yeni-Komshian, G. H. "Some Training Procedures Applicable to Teaching the Sound Systems and Vocabularies of Foreign Languages." Unpublished doctoral dissertation. McGill University, 1965.

Index